Third-Party Matters

Third-Party Matters

Politics, Presidents, and Third Parties in American History

Donald J. Green

 PRAEGER

AN IMPRINT OF ABC-CLIO, LLC
Santa Barbara, California • Denver, Colorado • Oxford, England

Library of Congress Cataloging-in-Publication Data

Green, Donald J.
  Third-party matters : politics, presidents, and third parties in American history / Donald J. Green.
      p. cm.
  Includes bibliographical references and index.
  ISBN 978-0-313-36591-1 (hardcopy : alk. paper)—ISBN 978-0-313-36592-8 (ebook) 1. Third parties (United States politics)—History. 2. United States—Politics and government. I. Title.
  JK2261.G77   2010
  324.273—dc22   2010004231

ISBN: 978-0-313-36591-1
EISBN: 978-0-313-36592-8

14 13 12 11 10   1 2 3 4 5

This book is also available on the World Wide Web as an eBook.
Visit www.abc-clio.com for details.

Praeger
An Imprint of ABC-CLIO, LLC

ABC-CLIO, LLC
130 Cremona Drive, P.O. Box 1911
Santa Barbara, California 93116-1911

This book is printed on acid-free paper (∞)

Manufactured in the United States of America

To Nell, Maggie, and Ann

Contents

Acknowledgment

I deeply appreciate the advice, suggestions and encouragement of Dr. John M. Belohlavek, professor of history, University of South Florida.

Introduction

The presidential election of 1860 roused my interest in third-party politics. In the most critical political contest in American history, the underlying issue was the future of slavery, but the candidates' more immediate concern was whether slavery should remain legal in the western territories, which had not been organized for statehood. The four nominees adopted different positions on the question. Abraham Lincoln, the Republican, opposed slavery's extension westward. The Democrats split into northern and southern factions. Illinois senator Stephen Douglas, the candidate of the northern wing, favored a policy called popular sovereignty, which would allow residents of a territory to decide for themselves, whereas Vice President John Breckinridge of Kentucky, representing southern interests, insisted that slavery remain legal in the West. Tennessee slave owner John Bell stood for the newly formed third party, the Constitutional Unionists. Bell was concerned about the future of the Union, so he took a moderate position that he hoped would tamp down sectional passions, urging his countrymen to follow the Constitution and the law.

Of course, the winner was Abraham Lincoln. His popular vote was an unimpressive 39.9 percent, but he swept the northern states and overwhelmed the Electoral College, with 180 votes out of 303 or 59 percent. Within three months of election day, by February 1, 1861, seven southern states seceded from the Union and two months later, in April, the war was on. This realized Bell's worst fears. His neglected candidacy caught my eye because so little has been written about him and his party. I wondered just who was this man? What did his party want to achieve, and how many votes did he actually get? It turned out that he did not do so badly after all. His defeat does not mean the Constitutional Unionists did not matter. After all, he won 40 percent of the vote in the South and carried several important states in the Electoral College. His relative popularity revealed that many southerners opposed the headlong rush into secession.

I turned my attention to the impact of other third parties. By their very definition, third parties need the two established parties as electoral foils. By 1840, the modern two-party system coalesced around the Whigs and Democrats. When the Whigs imploded in the 1850s over slavery, the Republicans took their place, and so for 169 years the United States has had an unbroken tradition of two-party rule. Each offered a philosophy of governance, a large competitive following, and an organization to support nominees at the local, state, and national levels. This very stability gave third parties their opportunities. In catering to an established constituency and their dearly beloved beliefs, main parties are less likely to stray into unknown territory unless forced to by a compelling third-party insurgency.

In the stream of American political history, the Constitutional Union Party of 1860 has been only one of more than 100 third parties representing almost 300 individual candidacies. In 2008, the most recent election, 21 third-party candidates ran against Democrat Barack Obama and Republican John McCain. None had an impact on the race. The leader of the "thirds" was Ralph Nader, making his fourth run at the White House. He won less than 1 percent of the vote (739,051) but beat out second-placed former Georgia congressman Bob Barr of the Libertarian Party (523,717), to say nothing of Charles Jay of the Boston Tea Party, who picked up only 2,473 votes. The 20th position fell to Bradford Lyttle, the U.S. Pacifist Party nominee, who garnered 111 votes out of more than 100 million cast. With 12 U.S. wars since the Revolution, Bradford should have known better.

Of all the third-party candidacies the 11 deemed significant are the focus of this book. They were selected on the basis of meeting at least one of three criteria: (1) Their presence changed the outcome of an election. In other words, they were spoilers for one of the two main parties; (2) Their major platform proposals proved so compelling that they eventually became the law of the land, or they had an important influence on the future course of politics; and (3) They attracted mass support, defined here as 10 percent or more of the popular vote. The stories are organized chronologically, so it's easy to see how the concerns of Americans at a particular time in history prompted the formation of one or more third parties. When African bondage became an issue, antislavery parties emerged in the 1840s. With the first mass migration of non-Protestants into the United States in the 1840s and 1850s, an anti-immigrant, anti-Catholic party was formed. In 1860, when the Union was threatened with dissolution, the Constitutional Unionists emerged. During the industrial expansion that followed the Civil War, farmers and workers organized parties to protest the dominance and exploitive practices of the new capitalist class.

Issues still mattered in the 20th century, but third parties came to be personality driven. In 1912, former President Teddy Roosevelt's personal pique and policy and political differences with his hand-picked successor, President William Howard Taft, led TR to form the Bull Moose Progressives. In 1924, Sen. Robert M. La Follette of Wisconsin took up the progressive cause in the post–World War I era. Because charisma played an important role with 20th century candidates, later chapters will reveal the fascinating personal stories behind the ascent of these independent and third-party dynamos. After La Follette's run, a 40-year dry spell ensued before a significant third party would stir. However, for sheer political theater, if clearly not for the reasons behind its popularity, the wait may have been worth it. In 1968, a feisty southern governor named George Corley Wallace Jr. would rouse and channel white resentments into a political realignment that lasted a generation. With a bankroll big enough to match the high level of discontent with politics-as-usual by the early 1990s, Ross Perot became the only third-party candidate who actually might have won the White House, but for reasons discussed in Chapter 5 it was not to be. Finally, in 2000, Ralph Nader, consumer advocate extraordinaire, won enough votes where it mattered and altered the outcome of a presidential contest and thus of history.

To provide a broader view of the variety of causes that prompted men—and women—to organize independent or third-party candidacies, brief sketches of also-rans are presented that include the first-ever third party, the longest-running third party, and parties organized by and about women and racial and ethnic minorities, as well as by early-20th-century socialists and by John Anderson in 1980.

1

Antebellum Third Parties: Liberty, Free Soil, American (Know-Nothings), Constitutional Union

Thank God Lincoln is chosen. What a growth since 1840.
—Joshua Leavitt, antislavery crusader

In 1776, when Thomas Jefferson declared the great moral truth that "all men are created equal," one of five Americans was owned by other Americans. In the spirit of the Revolution, the northern states took Jefferson's words to heart. Between 1777 and 1804, they either freed their slaves outright or instituted programs of gradual emancipation. Not everybody needed a poke from Jefferson or the war for liberty to see the immorality and injustice in human bondage. Well before the American Revolution, Quakers were at the forefront of the antislavery movement. Quaker shopkeeper John Woolman, born in New Jersey in 1720, gave up business at age 36 to devote his life to an antislavery crusade. One hundred years before the Civil War he warned of God's wrath if slavery were not abolished: "The seeds of great calamity and despoliation are sown and growing fast on this continent."[1] English-born Quakers Ralph Sandiford, a Pennsylvania farmer, and Benjamin Lay, a four-foot hunchback and philanthropist, believed that the New World had been defiled by slavery. At first, fellow Quakers ignored the threesome, but a crisis of confidence and reexamination of their attachment to the material world made them devoted to the poor and downtrodden. By the

Revolution, Quakers had ended their involvement in the slave trade and required fellow Quakers to free their slaves.[2]

At the end of the Revolutionary era abolitionists anticipated a future without bondage. Even in Virginia, the largest slave-holding state, a brief period opened for legal manumission. In 1787, under the Articles of Confederation, the national government banned slavery from the future states of Illinois, Indiana, Ohio, Michigan, and Wisconsin, and in 1808 the slave trade was banned by Congress. However, other developments worked against the end of slavery. The U.S. Constitution, ratified in 1788, recognized slavery by requiring the return of runaways and, in the three-fifths clause, gave states extra representation in Congress based on their slave population. With the invention of the cotton gin in 1793 cotton became a highly profitable commodity. Mills in Massachusetts and northern England clamored for Southern cotton, and the demand for land and slaves soared. Mississippi and Alabama, barely populated when the gin was invented, achieved statehood by 1820, with a combined population of 220,000, 36 percent of whom (80,000) were slaves. As the wealth of southerners increased, so did their power and influence in Washington. They were not about to relinquish millions of dollars in human assets to fulfill the moral demands of the antislavery crusaders. Yankees dependent on the South for shipping, insurance, and financial services revenue did not dare alienate a lucrative source of income.[3]

The belief in black inferiority worked against the willingness of most whites to agitate the end of slavery. Americans believed that the United States was a white man's country, and many questioned the mental fitness of blacks to become citizens even if they were freed. For some, the solution lay in colonization—sending freed slaves back to Africa, leading a group of reformers to found the American Colonization Society in 1817. The colonizers viewed slavery as a great evil but were reluctant to force Americans to confront their racist attitudes. Practical problems such as funding and logistics, plus the refusal of African Americans to return to their ancestral homelands, limited the success of the voluntary plan. Only 6,000 former slaves returned to Africa.[4]

Despite the efforts of the antislavery movement, the South's peculiar institution continued to grow. Morality was no match for the "pickings" of the South's wealthy white whales and the pilot fish up north. In 1820, abolitionists were shocked when Congress voted to admit Missouri as a slave state, while other territories south of 36°30′ (southern border of Missouri) could be organized with slavery. Despite early successes in the North, the abolitionists were confronted with a growing slave society in the South. From a bonded population of 654,121 in the census of 1790, slave numbers grew threefold to 1,983,833 by 1830. Clearly, a new approach was needed.[5]

On January 1, 1831, 26-year-old journalist William Lloyd Garrison founded *The Liberato*r, a weekly newspaper devoted to the moral case for abolition. Garrison demanded immediate uncompensated freedom for all slaves, rejecting colonization in favor of freedom and political rights for all. He declared in the opening issue, "I am in earnest. I will not equivocate. I will not excuse. I will not retreat a single inch. I will be heard."[6] Garrison understood that the racial attitudes of northerners helped underpin slavery. With the help of wealthy whites and free blacks, including escaped-slave Frederick Douglass, Garrison set about changing hearts and minds. In 1831, he founded the New England Antislavery Society. Two years later, with the help of New York abolitionist Arthur Tappan, the New England Antislavery Society merged into the broader-based American Anti-slavery Society. By 1838, with headquarters in New York, the American Antislavery Society grew to 1,500 chapters with 250,000 members. Most Americans opposed the Society's antislavery activities, concerned that alienating southerners would endanger the Union.[7]

While fending off violence from outside the tent, disagreements emerged within the movement from abolitionists who favored political action. Garrison opposed founding a political party, fearing that too few voters had undergone the spiritual transformation necessary for a favorable political outcome and that the desire for victory and political spoils would compromise the antislavery cause. By the late 1830s, a split developed over the proper role for abolitionists. Political abolitionists favored direct political action through an independent third party. Moral abolitionists, led by Garrison, rejected "all human politics," called voting a sin, and continued to favor moral suasion. Meanwhile, political activists instituted a system of interrogation. Whig and Democratic candidates would be questioned about slave-related issues such as the annexation of Texas as a slave state, ending slavery in the District of Columbia, and the gag rule, which prevented antislavery petitions from being debated in Congress. The candidates, however, were cagier than the naive, inexperienced interrogators. After elections politicians rarely kept their promises. Adding to the frustration was the simple truth that Americans were not sufficiently roused to make slavery a priority on election day.[8]

On February 7, 1839, Kentucky Whig Henry Clay delivered a Senate speech that caused a sensation in abolitionist circles. Clay, a slave owner who was theoretically opposed to slavery, lashed out at the abolitionists, calling them "reckless,. . . arraying one portion against another portion of the Union . . . and stimulating the rage of the people in the free states against the people in the slave states." He declared, "the liberty of the descendants of Africa in the United States is incompatible with the safety and liberty of the European descendants. . . ."[9] Clay, planning a third try for the presidency, needed southern support. Printed in its entirety in *The Emancipator*, an abolitionist newspaper, the speech galvanized the abolitionist movement toward the formation of a third political party. Political abolitionists realized that neither of the two major parties could be counted on in the fight to end slavery.[10]

THE LIBERTY PARTY

Voices in support of an independent party, such as New York lawyer Alvan Stewart, were now taken seriously. On a trip through the South he observed slavery firsthand, and in 1835 he organized the New York Antislavery Society. Stewart believed that slave insurrections were justified and slaveholders would not give up their human property through moral suasion. He helped organize a national abolitionist conference in Albany in July 1839 to discuss the case for a third party and to nominate presidential and vice presidential candidates. However, with Garrison still opposed to political action and others tentative the enterprise went nowhere.[11]

Gradually, support for a third party increased. Especially influential were Joshua Leavitt, editor of *The Emancipator* and a member of the Executive Committee of the American Antislavery Society, and Myron Halley, who oversaw construction of the Erie Canal and who believed that neither of the two existing parties would ever choose candidates acceptable to the abolitionists. Together they organized a convention of more than 500 antislavery men in Warsaw, New York, for November 13, 1839, to nominate candidates to head an abolitionist ticket in 1840. James K. Birney was offered the presidential nomination, with Francis J. Lemoyne of Pennsylvania as his running mate. Initially, both declined: Birney, because too many abolitionists opposed direct political action through a third party. Finally, in April 1840, the politicians got their way at an Albany meeting. Although lightly attended with only 121 delegates (100 from New York), the National Antislavery convention nominated Birney to head the ticket, with Thomas Earle, a Pennsylvania Quaker, for vice president. Birney accepted this time because he viewed the Whig presidential nominee, William Henry Harrison, as unabashedly proslavery. Birney believed that if the abolitionists wanted to remain a political force, they would have to run their own candidate. The new party would run under several local names but with a unified platform. They would all take the name "Liberty Party" in 1841.[12]

Although a relative unknown, Birney underwent the personal transformation from slaveholder to abolitionist that antislavery crusaders hoped all slaveholders would experience. Born in 1792 into a Kentucky slave-owning family, Birney had frequent discussions about slavery with his father and grandfather, both of whom wanted Kentucky to enter the Union as a free state. After attending Princeton, he became a lawyer and married Agatha McDowell, whose family presented the newlyweds with several house slaves. In Huntsville, in 1821, Birney purchased 19 Africans and settled into life as a lawyer and planter. After financial reverses stemming from an extravagant lifestyle and a general economic downturn, Birney moved into town and accepted his wife's religious faith. He became aroused by the mistreatment of Indians and slaves, so in 1832 he accepted the position as the southwest director of the American Colonization Society, at one-fourth his previous income. Eventually he abandoned colonization and embraced abolitionism. In 1837, at the age of 45, he moved to New York City as executive secretary of the American Antislavery Society. From this high-profile position he jumped into presidential politics.[13]

The new Liberty Party did not demand the immediate uncompensated end of slavery as did the Garrisonians. The Liberty men recognized that slavery was legal under the Constitution, and as political abolitionists and realists they wanted to work through the political system, so they did not advocate interference with the institution in states where it existed. However, they wanted the federal government to ban slavery in the nation's capital and in all new territories and states and to end the interstate slave trade. The latter provision would hurt the upper South's lucrative trade of selling surplus blacks down South. Liberty men attacked the "slave power" or "slavocracy," the so-called conspiracy of the planter class to control the national government and spread slavery. The also favored ending oppression and discrimination against the free black population.[14]

Hoopla and spin characterized the election of 1840, the first modern presidential campaign in American history. Although more (white) men voted than in any previous election (80 percent), serious issues need not apply, as least as far as the two main parties were concerned. The Whigs nominated William Henry Harrison of Ohio, and the Democrats, incumbent president Martin Van Buren of New York. As the Whigs searched for a campaign angle, the Baltimore

American, a Democratic newspaper, ridiculed Harrison's frontier manner, saying: "Give him a barrel of hard cider . . .[;] he will set [sic] the remainder of his days in a log cabin." The *American* would come to regret this characterization, for the Whigs seized on the imagery and turned it into an electoral jackpot. They transformed Harrison into the reincarnation of the ever-popular, beloved (by Democrats) war hero and man of the people, President Andrew Jackson (1829–1837). To accomplish this feat and broaden their base beyond an elite commercial constituency, the Whig spinmeisters presented Harrison as a hard cider–drinking, log cabin–living, backwoods war hero. The reality was another matter. Harrison was born into the Virginia slave-owning aristocracy, and by 1840 he had taken up residence in a 22-room manor house on a farm in North Bend, Ohio. There was a bit more truth to the war hero line, but even this was dated and exaggerated. In his "great" victory, known as the Battle of Tippecanoe 29 years earlier in 1811, Harrison led a corps of 1,000 men to victory over the Shawnee chief Tecumseh, burning an Indian village in the process, and taking inordinate casualties. The campaign summed it all up in the political battle cry, "Tippecanoe and Tyler too" (John Tyler of Virginia was his running mate). President Van Buren, the underdog, was blamed for the ongoing economic depression known as the Panic of 1837 and was dubbed "Martin van Ruin."[15]

Harrison emerged from his 22-room "log cabin" victorious, with 1,275,612 popular votes (52.9 percent) and 234 electoral votes, compared with Van Buren's tally of 1,130,033 (46.8 percent). Fortunately, Birney and the Liberty men realized they had no chance of winning, but even with low expectations, the results were disappointing. Birney received only 7,053 votes of 2,412,698 cast, or less than one-third of 1 percent. Sixty-three percent of his total came from just two states: New York and Massachusetts. Even in these abolitionist strongholds he received less than 2 percent of the ballots. Considering the 250,000 members of abolitionist societies, the vote should have been substantially higher.[16]

Like all third parties, the Liberty men faced many obstacles, but made matters worse by the lack of an aggressive campaign. Birney was out of the country from May to November, the height of the campaign season, attending an antislavery convention in London. Poor organization also hurt. Before 1888, political parties printed and distributed their own ballots. Too few Liberty ballots were printed and distributed to polling places. Liberty men had to contend with loyalty to the two major parties that had solidified by 1840. Whigs saw a chance to capture the White House for the first time, so even antislavery Whigs did not want to "waste" a ballot on a third party. With slavery of no concern to most Americans, the issue was ignored by the press and by the two main parties, who had nothing to gain from publicizing the matter. Perhaps the icing on the cake—or salt on the wound—was the message from William Lloyd Garrison, who urged his followers to refrain from supporting Birney.[17]

The poor showing was a blow to the fledgling organization and to Birney personally, but in the aftermath they committed to building an organization with broader appeal in preparation for the election of 1844. Salmon P. Chase, an Ohio politician who became Lincoln's treasury secretary (1861–1864) and chief justice of the U.S. Supreme Court, joined the Liberty Party in 1841 and quickly became an influential leader. An opponent of slavery and a political opportunist, Chase would bring a new sense of realism to the Liberty Party. On August 30, 1843, 1,000 delegates from the free states gathered at Buffalo to adopt a platform proposed by Chase and to nominate a ticket headed by Birney and Thomas Morris of Ohio. Chase's document broadened the appeal of the Liberty Party. Again, it demanded an end to slavery in the District of Columbia and in new territories and states. The platform declared the Constitution's fugitive slave and the three-fifths provisions null and void. Free blacks were welcomed into the party. In an appeal to poor southern whites, aristocrats were condemned for limiting educational opportunities. For northern farmers and workers, Washington was encouraged to seek out overseas markets and to use free labor instead of slave labor for public works projects. The platform launched a general attack on the slave system, calling it "a derogation of the principles of American liberty and a deep stain on the character of the country. . . ."[18]

The election of 1844 focused on the issue of westward expansion. The election pitted former Tennessee governor and Democrat James K. Polk, a slave owner and enthusiastic territorial expansionist, against Whig senator Henry Clay. Territorial expansion in 1844 meant annexing Texas as a slave state, an issue on which Clay equivocated. Under pressure from Southern expansionists, he finally came out in favor of annexation under certain conditions, writing, ". . .I should be glad to see it without dishonor, without war and with the common consent of the Union and upon just and fair terms."[19] For the first time Liberty men responded to questions on a range of issues including the tariff, internal improvements paid for by the national government, a national bank, and the naturalization of immigrants, but they always insisted that slavery was the main issue. They expanded press coverage so lacking in 1840. Twenty-five newspapers supported Birney, including three dailies, 20 weeklies, and two semi-monthlies. Birney became an active campaigner. A biography was published, and his portrait sold for $1.[20]

With the Whig party as the home of most abolitionists, an intense rivalry developed between Whigs and Liberty men. Whigs maintained that the Liberty Party was a stalking horse for the Democrats, declaring the more Whig votes the Liberty Party could steal, the more likely the Democrat Polk would win. Clay's minions attributed to Birney the more extreme statements of the Garrisonian abolitionists, who advocated ending the union of the free and slave states. Of course Birney believed no such thing. The Liberty men countered with the claim that Clay was working for the slave power. And so it went! Polk emerged victorious with 1,337,243 votes (49.5 percent) and 170 electoral votes, 32 more than necessary. On his third try for the White House, Clay had lost again, garnering 1,299,062 popular votes (48.1 percent) but only 105 electoral votes. This time the Liberty Party had had a significant impact on the outcome of the election. Not only did its popular vote increase ninefold over that of 1840—62,300 popular votes (2.3 percent), but its tally in New York,15,812, shifted the state's electoral vote into Polk's column by 5,106 votes, giving him the White House. If only a third of Birney's New York vote (5,270) had gone to Clay, he would have taken New York's 36 electoral votes and the White House. This was the first time that a third party played the spoiler![21]

The 1846 off-year election was the Liberty Party's electoral zenith, garnering 74,017 votes, but it accomplished little; many considered the movement a failure, and interest waned. Whigs accused the party of doing more harm than good by helping the expansionist proslavery Polk seize the White House (within a year Texas entered the Union as a slave state). Horace Greeley attacked the Liberty Party in the *New York Tribune*: "You third party workers forced this man [Polk] upon us instead of the only anti-Texas candidate who could possibly be elected. On your guilty heads shall rest the curse of unborn generations. Rot in your infamy and rejoice in its triumph but never ask us to unite with you in anything." In 1845 Birney suffered a paralytic stroke, ending his political career. He lived until 1857.[22]

THE FREE SOIL PARTY

Polk's expansionist war with Mexico proved a catalyst for the struggling antislavery movement. In August 1846, four months after an attack by Mexico on American soldiers in disputed Texas territory,

Polk requested a $2 million appropriation from Congress to negotiate a speedy settlement of territorial issues with Mexican authorities. David Wilmot, a 34-year-old congressman from Pennsylvania, inserted a proviso in the bill that would ban slavery from any territory bought or won from Mexico, so Polk's request never passed Congress. The war continued until an American victory in 1848. Mexico ceded more than 500,000 square miles of territory to the United States in the Southwest and the Far West.

The Wilmot Proviso became a rallying cry for a new antislavery organization called the Free Soil Party. These were not abolitionists like the Liberty men. The Free Soilers sought no interference with slavery where it existed, even in the District of Columbia. What they demanded was no extension of slavery in new territories or states. The Free Soilers attracted former Liberty men, antislavery Whigs called Conscience Whigs, and antiextension Democrats, mostly from the New York faction called Barnburners. The motivation of the Conscience Whigs and Barnburners was not always pure, however. Local intraparty rivalries played a role in their conversion to the Free Soil. The Barnburners, led by former president Martin Van Buren, sought revenge against the rival New York Hunkers and the national Democrats. Not only was Van Buren denied the 1844 presidential nomination, but after going all out to elect his rival, Polk, the new president gave the Hunkers control over patronage that determined who ran the state's Democratic organization. The Barnburners agreed with antiextension, but revenge had as much or more to do with their sudden conversion to Free Soil. In Massachusetts, the Conscience Whigs walked out of the state's 1848 Whig convention when the Cotton Whigs (mill owners sympathetic to the South) sided with Whig presidential nominee and slave owner General Zachary Taylor. The Conscience men were indignant but were truly committed to antiextension.[23]

On August 9, 1848, thousands of sweating delegates of differing political backgrounds, prejudices, and colors, lured with discount fares and the promise of celebrity speakers, met under a gargantuan tent on Court House Square in Buffalo to nominate a president and vice president on the Free Soil ticket. For the first time in American history a full-fledged third party emerged based on a range of issues, the most important being antislavery. Because of the spoiler role played by the Liberty Party in the election of 1844 and the furor over the Wilmot Proviso two years later, slavery could no longer be ignored by the two main parties.[24]

Former Liberty men, Barnburners, and Whigs had their own preferences for the presidential nomination. Liberty men had already nominated John Parker Hale of New Hampshire at a gathering in 1847, so Hale was considered the frontrunner. Barnburners, the most influential of the three factions, insisted on 64-year-old Van Buren. The Whigs preferred Judge John McLean of Ohio.

To stave off a rush to Hale and make the nominating process "more manageable," Chase and Ben Butler, Van Buren's law partner, maneuvered a select committee into presenting the mass assemblage with the nomination of Van Buren. Chase recognized the enormous prestige of a former president at the head of the ticket. The Whigs had doubts about Van Buren because he had supported slavery and as president had promised to veto a bill to abolish slavery in the District of Columbia. Nonetheless, when Butler presented Van Buren's name under the tent, he thought a personal touch might paper over any lingering doubts. Butler described his recent visit to Van Buren's estate in Kinderhook, New York, noting the pride the former chief executive took in his fields of grain, cabbage, and turnips. A delegate rose to his feet and screamed out "damn his cabbage and turnips, what does he say about the abolition of slavery in the District of Columbia." Butler improvised, promising that Van Buren would support a bill to abolish slavery in D.C. That won over the delegates. Charles Francis Adams, the son of former president John Quincy Adams and the grandson of President John Adams, received the vice presidential nomination.[25]

Chase designed the platform to appeal to everyone but the abolitionists. Its main plank called for noninterference with slavery where it existed but for a ban in the new territories, which would be preserved for whites to start new lives away from oppressive eastern factories, European tyrants, and degrading competition from slave labor and even from free blacks. The platform concluded with the phrase, "Free Soil, Free Speech, Free Labor, and Free Men." The new party was clearly racist in its appeal to the white working class. Black abolitionists such as Frederick Douglass were in a quandary over whether to endorse the party. Because the Free Soilers wanted to limit the geographic extension of slavery, Douglass reluctantly endorsed the movement, while making it clear that his heart and soul were with a higher authority, Garrison's abolitionists! Other planks were designed to placate various constituencies. For the Whigs, the platform called for internal infrastructure improvements in roads, canals, and harbors paid for by the national government. For the antiprotective-tariff Democrats it offered a tariff for revenue purposes only. To fulfill its "free soil" ideology, it promised a homestead bill that would set aside land for small farms in the new western territories.[26]

Free Soilers denounced the Democratic and Whig nominees as be-
holden to the slave power. Of course, neither of the two main parties
could afford to alienate southerners or Yankees on the slavery issue.
Michigan's Lewis Cass, the Democratic presidential nominee, a former secretary of war and minister to France, took the middle road
by supporting popular sovereignty in the new territories: letting the
settlers decide whether a new state would be slave or free. Whig
candidate Gen. Zachary Taylor, a hero of the Mexican War, managed to slither down both sides of the slavery issue. Southerners
could never imagine that Taylor, as a resident of Louisiana with
extensive land and with slave holdings in Mississippi, would turn
against their interests. To win votes up north, the Taylor campaign
promised that he would never veto antiextension legislation.[27]

With a former president at the head of the ticket and a vice presidential nominee who was the son and grandson of presidents, the
Whigs and Democrats could not ignore the Free Soilers. They
focused much of their campaigns on personal attacks against Van
Buren and Adams, including an eight-page encapsulation of all the
nasty comments that Adams had made about his running mate. The
Boston *Atlas*, a Whig journal, called Adams a huckster who lives
off the reputation and wealth of his family. Van Buren was called a
traitor and hypocrite, the Judas Iscariot of the 19th century who
put revenge and ambition above patriotism. Perhaps most damaging
the Free Soilers were called abolitionists, almost akin to being called
a Communist in the 1950s. The Free Soilers countered by repeating
Taylor's brag that he had "little time or inclination to investigate
the great issues or subjects of discussion." His lack of education
and political experience were duly noted. Cass was accused of selling out to the South to win the presidency. The Free Soilers were
lucky to have John Van Buren, Martin's son, as his chief surrogate.
"Prince John" (he hobnobbed with British royalty) gave 30 major
speeches in two months throughout the North, tearing into the
malevolent designs of the slave power to control and corrupt
the national government, adding that the Whigs or Democrats were
going to help the planter class do just that. He claimed that only the
Free Soilers could save America from this unrepublican fate. Press
support for the ticket came from newly founded Free Soil newspapers, along with some Whig and Democratic journals that endorsed
Van Buren.[28]

The Free Soilers' enthusiasm made the results that much harder
to swallow. The uneducated, uninformed, politically inexperienced
general, a man who never voted in an election, came out on top.
Gen. Taylor polled 1,360,099 popular votes (47.3 percent), winning

163 electoral votes, 19 more than necessary. Cass, with 1,220,544 popular votes (42.4 percent) landed 127 electoral votes, whereas Van Buren secured 291,263 popular votes (10.1 percent) but no electoral votes. The Free Soilers were of two minds on the outcome. Some, like Sen. Charles Sumner of Massachusetts, were encouraged. After all, they received 15 percent of the northern vote, five times the Liberty Party's total just four years earlier, and emerged second (ahead of the Democrats) in three states: Massachusetts, New York, and Vermont. Writing to Chase on November 16, 1848, Sumner commented: "Looking over the field now, I feel we have cause for high satisfaction. We have found large numbers of men through all the Free States who are willing to leave the old parties and join in a new alliance of principle. The public mind has been stirred to depths never before reached: and much information with regard to the Slave-Power has been diffused in quarters heretofore ignorant of this enormous tyranny." However, Sumner was in the minority. Most in the new party were disillusioned. Gradually, they drifted back to their old loyalties. The Barnburners made peace with the Hunkers, both realizing that without unity neither had a chance for political spoils in the Empire State.[29]

Why didn't the Free Soilers do better? Party loyalty was a big factor, but old prejudices and ingenious arguments also played a role in bolstering the tendency, especially among sympathetic Whigs, many of whom believed that Martin Van Buren was not a sincere Free Soiler. Although inaccurate, people knew that even his running mate, Charles Francis Adams, shared this view about Van Buren. The fact that Van Buren was the slave-owning Andrew Jackson's hand-picked successor colored attitudes toward him. In Massachusetts, a struggle for control of the state's Whig party confused many, thereby reducing the Free Soil vote among impassioned antislavers. Finally, Whigs made the argument that party unity was more important for the nation's future than a vote for Free Soil.[30]

The message from the public was that the Free Soil Party was too extreme. The nation needed a moderate solution to antiextension that would not disrupt the political system. The seemingly ingenious answer arrived with the Compromise of 1850. Fashioned by the Great Compromiser himself, Sen. Henry Clay, and passed as a series of individual bills, it offered each section of the country some of what it wanted. For the North, California would enter the Union as a free state, and the slave trade, but not slavery, would be abolished in the District of Columbia. The South got a tougher fugitive slave law that would force citizens to assist in recapturing runaways. The territories of New Mexico and Utah could be organized with or without slavery (i.e., popular sovereignty).[31]

The public believed that the Compromise settled the territorial issue, so slavery and free soil principles disappeared from the public debate. Some in the Free Soil movement believed the Compromise just postponed the inevitable conflict. Doggedly, they organized a convention in Pittsburgh in 1852, in preparation for the fall presidential election. John Hale of New Hampshire was given the top spot, and George Julian of Indiana was nominated for vice president. Their opponents were the Democrat Franklin Pierce of New Hampshire and the Whig Gen. Winfield Scott of Virginia. The Free Soilers condemned the Compromise of 1850 because it allowed slavery in the New Mexico and Utah territories. They faulted the Fugitive Slave Act as repugnant and unchristian and demanded its repeal. Like the Liberty party platforms in 1840 and 1844, they demanded that the national government separate itself from slavery by abolishing the institution in the District of Columbia. Against tradition, Hale and Julian actively campaigned. Julian bravely spoke before hostile audiences. The public, however, was apathetic, believing Congress had settled the slavery question. With the Barnburners back in the Democratic fold and diminished interest in antislavery, the Hale-Julian ticket received only 156,667 votes (4.9 percent)—half the number garnered in 1848. The Democrat Franklin Pierce won a landslide victory with 1,601,474 votes (50.9 percent) and 254 electoral votes. The election was a disaster for the Whigs, who gathered 1,386,580 popular votes (44.1 percent) but only 42 electoral votes, carrying just four states.[32]

Two years after the election of 1852, Congress passed the Kansas-Nebraska Act, creating two territories from the Louisiana Purchase; the bill also (1) repealed the Missouri Compromise of 1820, which had banned slavery north of 36°30', and (2) determined that citizens would decide for or against slavery (popular sovereignty) in any states formed from their lands. Now, hundreds of thousands of square miles that had been off-limits to slavery might have it. The North felt betrayed and angered, reinforcing the suspicion that the slave power really controlled the national government. The Democrats managed to stay unified because they held power, but the Whigs split along sectional lines, ceasing to exist as a national party. Now, the former Free Soilers, with some northern Democrats and Whigs, were determined to found a new northern party dedicated to antiextension and free soil. By the election of 1856, the Republican Party would replace the Whigs, but another issue—immigration—would take center stage and momentarily divert attention from slavery.

THE AMERICAN PARTY (KNOW-NOTHINGS)

The immigrant population grew rapidly in the decades before the Civil War. In 1830, only 1 percent of the white population was foreign born; by 1860 this slice of America grew to 15 percent. Economic hardships, the potato famine in Ireland, and political unrest in Germany prompted a mass migration across the Atlantic. Most unsettling to native Protestants was the large Irish and German Catholic component. They reminded Americans of their ancestors' enemies in England, France, and Spain. The Germans tended to scatter to the cities and farms in the Midwest where they were less visible. The deepest and most widespread antipathy was reserved for the Irish, whose symbol was "Paddy." Whether man, woman, or child, Paddy was synonymous with the three Ps: popery, poverty, and political corruption. Paddy was seen as dirty, unruly, and mercurial and as being from a separate race of people, incapable of assimilating into American life. The unskilled Irish concentrated in the big cities, mainly along the eastern seaboard, where they competed for jobs and political influence with native Protestants. Democratic party bosses successfully wooed the Irish, whose numbers often influenced the outcome of elections, much to the chagrin of natives. Worse still, Americans were taxed to provide relief for the poverty-stricken newcomers.[33]

Propagandists portrayed the immigrants as a radical criminal class and a menace to American republicanism. The Reverend Lyman Beecher and Samuel Morse (inventor of the Morse Code) claimed that they possessed evidence of a plot directed by the Pope to engage in an epic struggle in which the Catholic Church would use unknowing immigrants to dominate church and state in America. With their national reputations and the originality of their message, Beecher and Morse were able to exploit anti-Catholic prejudices and make their claims believable. Control of school systems emerged as a sore point between natives and newcomers. Catholics demanded that public funding for New York schools, long controlled by the (Protestant) Public School Society, be shared. When a proposal backed by Catholic bishop Hughes and New York governor William Seward to divide school funding was rejected by the state legislature, Hughes retaliated by instructing Catholics whom to vote for in the next election. The tactic worked, and in a turnaround the legislature banned all religious instruction from the public schools; however, Protestant suspicion of the Church's "undemocratic" nature was now confirmed. A similar dispute erupted in Philadelphia, leading to bloody riots and the torching and destruction of two Catholic churches.[34]

Perhaps no incident revealed the depths of native anger and resentment more than the events surrounding the murder of Bill Poole, known to the locals as "Butcher Bill." Poole was shot by Lewis Baker, an immigrant, in a barroom brawl at Stanwix Hall, a bar in the Bowery, a working-class district in Lower Manhattan. The Butcher died of his wounds 11 days later. The outpouring of public grief was unprecedented. The *New York Times* reported that 250,000 people crowded Lower Manhattan to pay homage to the dead "hero." A funeral procession of 6,000 mourners, led by a grand marshall, a 52-piece band, local politicians, and the instantly formed Poole Associations from New York, Baltimore, and Philadelphia, marched for six hours, ending at the cemetery. The outpouring might suggest that Poole was a respected member of the community, perhaps a minister, a respected politician, or a charitable family man. Although he had a wife and children, most of his free time was devoted to drinking and womanizing at local bars and brothels and hanging out with fellow gang members who spent election days intimidating voters at the polls. The Butcher even had a case pending against him for assault with intent to kill. Why the outpouring? His murder was seen as a parable for the victimization of natives by Irish Catholics. Just as Poole, the native, had been murdered by Baker, the immigrant, the native workers felt they were being killed economically and politically by the influx of foreigners. Butcher Bill's last words were reported to be: "Good-bye boys, I die a true American."[35]

Emerging out of the conflict, disorder, and resentment were anti-immigrant secret societies with names like Order of United Mechanics, Order of Sons of America, and the most notorious, New York's Order of the Star Spangled Banner. With an array of special handshakes, signals, and secret communication and thriving on hysteria, the nativists carried out anti-immigrant agitation. Of course, it didn't help matters when Bishop Hughes claimed that the Pope planned to convert all Americans to Catholicism. In 1852, James W. Baker, a dry goods merchant and organizational genius, decided to convert the Order of the Star Spangled Banner into a political organization that would spread rapidly through the Northeast. Members took an oath of secrecy, learning special signs, hand grips, and signals of distress and pledging to oppose public office for Catholics and immigrants. At first, they supported sympathetic politicians from the existing parties. By 1853, when they adopted the name American Party, they were referred to as Know-Nothings, a name bestowed by *New York Tribune* editor Horace Greeley because, when asked about their secret workings, members would claim "I know nothing." In 1854 and 1855 they won elections in New York, Pennsylvania, Massachusetts,

Delaware, Rhode Island, Kentucky, New Hampshire, and California. Eight states had heavily Know-Nothing legislatures. The Thirty-fourth Congress claimed 48 members of the American Party. Know-Nothings support skyrocketed because the anti-Catholic message resonated. Nativist former Whigs were comfortable with the party's principal message, but many Whigs, overlooking the anti-immigrant rhetoric, joined because of the party's strong pro-Union stance. Now a political force, the Americans were confident of replacing the Whigs as the second major party and capturing the White House in 1856.[36]

The true believers (and not-so-true believers) gathered in Philadelphia on February 22, 1856, to select a presidential nominee and running mate. Two hundred delegates from 27 of the 31 states attended the convention, but that nagging slavery issue would not go away, even for a few days, in the City of Brotherly Love. When the convention refused the demand of northerners to include a plank in the platform calling for a ban on slavery north of 36°30', many northerners bolted the convention, leaving southerners in control. The final platform combined a call for noninterference in the affairs of the states (states' rights) and honest government. Know-Nothing demands focused on a 21-year waiting period for citizenship and voting rights, the requirement of citizenship to hold public office, and opposition to the union of church and state.[37]

Former Whig president Millard Fillmore (1850–1853), who ascended to the White House when Zachary Taylor died in office, and Andrew Jackson Donelson, President Jackson's nephew, were nominated for the top slots. Although a prestigious ticket, Fillmore may not have been the best choice to head the campaign. Many northerners came to view him as too sympathetic to the South when he signed the Fugitive Slave Act in 1850. Oddly, Fillmore was no nativist. He joined the Americans because of its pro-Union credentials. He and others like him thought they could take over the party and make it nonsectional. At the moment of his nomination he happened to be in Europe where he obtained an audience with the Pope. Luckily for him (and the Pope) there was no satellite news. During the campaign he hardly mentioned nativism, focusing instead on the message of preserving the Union. Fillmore's Democratic opponent was 65-year-old Pennsylvanian James "Old Buck" Buchanan, a man of southern sympathies. A former senator and secretary of state under Polk, Old Buck had the good fortune of being out of the country as minister to Great Britain (1853–1856) during the Kansas-Nebraska Act controversy. Appearing above the fray, he managed to wrestle the presidential nomination from Sen. Stephen Douglas. In their first presidential campaign, the Republicans selected

John Fremont of California. The 43-year-old antislavery champion and veteran of the Mexican War was nicknamed "Pathfinder of the West" because of his extensive explorations of the region.[38]

In a heated, polarizing campaign, the slavery issue was front and center. Southerners were concerned about the growing popularity of the Republicans who adamantly opposed slavery in the territories. Republicans took up the cry: "Free Speech, Free Press, Free Soil, Free Men, Fremont, and Victory." The Democrats claimed a Republican majority would not be tolerated in the South. Old Buck's boys spread rumors of southern secession should Fremont come out on top. They dubbed Fremont a Black Republican because of the party's alleged sympathies for the slaves. He was also accused of being a secret Catholic, having married in the Church and sending his adopted daughter to a Catholic school, but Fremont himself was an Episcopalian. Fremont countered by calling Democrats reactionaries who wanted to reverse the principles of liberty embodied in the Declaration of Independence.[39]

Buchanan carried the day, winning 1,838,169 popular votes (45.3 percent) and 174 electoral votes, 25 more than needed for victory. Fremont came in second with 1,341,264 popular votes (33.6 percent) and 114 electoral votes, all from the North. Thus, the Republicans emerged as the second major party replacing the defunct Whigs. With 874,534 popular votes (21.5 percent) the Americans garnered the most votes yet for a third party, but only eight electoral votes, all from Maryland. Their hopes dashed, they went into a rapid decline. Despite the secret handshakes and many state victories, they accomplished few of their nativist goals and so were seen as ineffective. Republicans and Democrats had refused to cooperate with the Know-Nothings because they competed for the immigrant vote. Native resentment cooled as immigration leveled off and the economy improved. Perhaps most significant were the increasing tensions over slavery that took over the spotlight during the second half of the 1850s. Many northern Know-Nothings deserted to the Republican Party, but the pro-Union southern wing, concerned about the growing threat to the Union, would seek out another political alternative to preserve the Union.[40]

THE CONSTITUTIONAL UNION PARTY

Sen. John Crittenden of Kentucky was one of the pro-Union Whigs who followed Millard Fillmore into the American Party. With the demise of the Know-Nothings after the election of 1856, Crittenden looked for a new political home. Through his southern connections he became convinced that if Republicans captured the White House in 1860, Southern Democrats would urge secession, so the 73-year-old follower of Henry Clay decided to found a new national party dedicated to the preservation of the Union.[41]

Crittenden began a round of speechmaking, attacking the two major parties for their incessant agitation over slavery. In a New York appearance in November 1858, he claimed that people were fed up with the issue: "I am sick and tired over this Negro question in all its forms in which it can be presented and I would to God we can get back to those days when our fathers lived in harmony and peace together and there was not a word on that subject between them. . . . What have we gained by this enormous agitation? Anything but dissention . . . a united people divided, a sectional line between us." He was prescient about the future of the United States: "We have a great country worthy to occupy the affections and gratify the ambitions of everyone and each of us can help it on its career of prosperity and happiness. The child is living this day who will see you number a hundred millions of people. . . . Just think of that great future it is worth living for, dying for."[42] Crittenden's predictions were more accurate than he could have imagined. In a Senate speech two months later, in February 1859, he argued that politicians had lost sight of the fact that the Constitution and not party platforms were supreme. He demanded "no more platforms instead of the Constitution or of conventions that are masters of the people."[43]

During that year, a movement emerged for a union of the "opposition" (to Democrats and Republicans). In December 1859, Crittenden called a conference of 50 "opposition" members of Congress, and by January 1860, plans were launched for a new national Constitutional Union Party. On February 22, Washington's birthday, in an address to the American people, printed in its entirety in the *National Intelligencer*, the party's mouthpiece, the editors commented on the nation's state of mind and issued a dire warning: "The political aspect of the country fills the public's mind with painful apprehension. The people everywhere are disturbed with the fear of some disaster. Many are alarmed for the safety of the country." The paper condemned both political parties and warned of "a sectional struggle far exceeding in violence any that has yet occurred, the result of which may be disastrous for the country." A nominating convention was scheduled for May 9, 1860, in Baltimore.[44]

The old First Presbyterian Church at the corner of Fayette and Fourth Streets housed the gathering. Red, white, and blue bunting decorated the galleries. Behind the dais was a full-length portrait of George Washington. Just in case somebody didn't get the patriotic hint, the father of our country was surrounded by an eagle and two giant American flags. Lapel pins just wouldn't do in 1860! Additional flags decorated the walls above and below the galleries. By 11:00 A.M. the hall was densely packed. New York sent the largest contingent headed by former governor Washington Hunt. Virginia, Tennessee, and Pennsylvania also had sizable delegations. In all, 21 of the 31 states were represented, the remainder being too far from Baltimore or too small to matter. Among the notables were Gustavus Henry, grandson of Patrick Henry; John Todd Stuart, Abraham Lincoln's law partner; and Andrew Jackson Donelson, Andrew Jackson's nephew and the American Party's vice presidential candidate in 1856.[45]

Optimism permeated the hall. Delegates considered the divisive events at the Democrats' convention in Charleston and the probable outcome to the Republican Chicago gathering one week later. In Charleston, Southern Democrats walked out when northerners refused to agree to a slave code for the western territories, opening the possibility of two weakened sectional Democratic tickets, neither able to capture the White House in November. The Republicans, many assumed, would nominate Sen. William Seward, a perceived radical antislavery man. With the Democrats split and conservative Republicans perhaps abandoning the party, the Constitutional Unionists could attract moderates from both and sweep to victory. John Crittenden opened the proceedings with a brief speech that positioned the Constitutional Unionists as the party of the "whole country." New York's Washington Hunt followed, reiterating the aim of the convention: "We have come on a mission of peace to strengthen the chains of Union and revive the spirit of national affection." So frequent were the interruptions with applause that Murat Halstead, a Republican and reporter for the *Cincinnati Daily Commercial*, commented, "the delegates were worse than an Irish audience at an Archbishop's lecture." With the slavery issue off the table inside the convention hall, rumors flew that any delegate who mentioned slavery or the Negro would be ejected. A reporter from the *New York Herald* noted, "The delegates may sleep with the nigger, eat with the nigger, but don't allow his wooly head to come in the convention."[46]

The first order of business was the presentation of the platform. Crittenden kept it brief, recognizing no other principal than "the Constitution of the country, the union of the states, and the enforcement of the laws." Although seemingly neutral on slavery, in fact, the Constitutional Union platform was southern leaning, and when written and approved, slavery was legal in all new territories. With the Dred Scott Decision of 1857, the Supreme Court made it possible for slave owners to bring their slaves west without any restrictions.[47]

Frequently mentioned for the presidential nomination were Texas governor general Sam Houston, 1852 Whig presidential candidate Gen. Winfield Scott, former Tennessee senator John Bell, and former Massachusetts governor Edward Everett. The real favorite was John Crittenden, but he opted out in favor of a younger man. He also used his considerable prestige to oppose Houston, considering him too close to the image and style of his old enemy Andrew Jackson. Scott was pushed aside because of his disastrous showing in 1852. The convention settled on John Bell, who appealed to border state voters and northern moderates. Edward Everett was nominated as his running mate for sectional balance.[48]

Sixty-three-year-old John Bell, a principled but unexciting choice for the nomination, was born on a farm near Nashville. After studying law he entered Congress in 1827, rising to Speaker of the House in 1834 and Secretary of War in the cabinet of William Henry Harrison. Although he owned 160 slaves, he was a moderate who disliked extremists on both sides of the issue. He knew there was limited use for slaves in the West and asked why agitate and antagonize Yankees. His vote against Kansas-Nebraska (favored by his state) cost him his senate seat. When secession came, he fought to keep Tennessee in the Union.[49]

The Democrats split along sectional lines; the northerners nominated Stephen Douglas of Illinois, the author of the Kansas-Nebraska Act and a supporter of popular sovereignty in the territories. Southerners selected Buchanan's vice president, John Breckinridge of Kentucky, who favored allowing slavery in the territories. The Republicans, meeting in Chicago one week after the Constitutional Unionists, did the unexpected. Instead of nominating the favorite William Seward, they gave the nod to a moderate, former one-term Illinois congressman (1847–1849) Abraham Lincoln. Without Seward to scare conservative Republicans into the arms of Bell, many Bell supporters reassessed their chances. Perhaps now a deadlocked Electoral College could force the election into the House of Representatives. Once again slavery was the key issue in the campaign. On the surface, the question was about the future of slavery in the territories, but just below the topsoil, southerners wondered about the roots, i.e., would the Republicans attempt to abolish slavery altogether if they triumphed.

Republicans had the key campaign elements: money, speakers, newspaper support, literature, and enthusiasm. The Constitutional Unionists were not without resources of their own. Supporters marched in torchlight parades with "bell" ringers—cowbells, tea bells, dinner bells—in not so subtle allusions to the party's standard bearer. Glee clubs performed original patriotic songs. Although John

Bell stayed home, the tradition for candidates of the day, surrogates traveled the circuit speaking on his behalf. Crittenden, most in demand, traveled extensively throughout the border states. In Louisville on August 2, he received national coverage in the *New York Times* and the *National Intelligencer*, when he claimed that the dangers from sectionalism brought the new party into existence as a middle ground between the southern Democrats and northern Republicans and that Lincoln would be a disaster for the nation: "The mere fact of his election would be a calamity. . . . He is personally upright, honest, and worthy. But politically, he is the agent of a party that brought him into political existence. As a Republican president he would be a terror to the South." Breckinridge was attacked as a "southern disunionist," and Douglas was portrayed as a "nonthreat, but ultimately ineffective in restoring moderation and good government." Crittenden called for the slavery issue to be banished from the councils of government.[50]

The Constitutional Unionists could not counter the rising tide of enthusiasm for Lincoln in the North and Breckinridge in the South, nor could they ignore the danger of disunion, but Lincoln had little to gain from the issue, so he ridiculed the threat of disunion. Donn Piatt, a well-known Ohio journalist, was alarmed over Lincoln's cavalier attitude about southern intentions should he win. To the candidate it was just another southern bluff. "Lincoln cannot be made to believe that [this time] the South meant secession and war."[51]

Bell's correspondence with his campaign chairman Alexander Boteler of Virginia revealed shifting sentiments about the party's strategy and chance for victory. In July, Bell seemed optimistic about winning most of the South but saw Lincoln victorious in the North and in the Electoral College. He considered fusion—a combined ticket with Douglas—in the big industrial states that, if successful, could deny Lincoln a victory in the College. As a nonthreatening moderate he could garner enough support in the House of Representatives to enter the White House. Eventually, he became convinced that the South would secede if Lincoln won: ". . . . I have become satisfied from the information received from the South that a more widespread determined purpose exists in the South to attempt separation of the states in that in the event of the election of Lincoln than I had before thought existed. . . ." He ordered Boteler to issue an appeal to the American people to support moderation and reject sectional candidates. The missive notes how the slavery issue had always been handled with moderation and compromise and then attacked the Kansas-Nebraska Act, sponsored by Douglas and the Democrats, as the culprit behind the rise of the northern Republicans. The appeal predicted that neither Douglas nor Breckinridge would win and that the contest would come down to a choice between the inexperienced Lincoln, representing northern interests, and Bell.[52]

Lincoln was the clear favorite, needing only 38 more votes than his Republican predecessor John Fremont in 1856. If Lincoln could carry Pennsylvania's 27 electoral votes plus Indiana's 13 or Illinois' 11, he would enter the White House. Eventually, Bell got serious about forming fusion tickets with Douglas and Breckinridge in several states. However, any optimism about stopping Lincoln was dashed when state elections in September and October turned up big Republican victories in bellwether Pennsylvania, Indiana, and Illinois. Results in the Keystone State didn't lie. On November 6, Lincoln carried the electoral college with 180 votes, 28 more than necessary for victory, winning all the northern states with the exception of New Jersey, which he split with Douglas. However, his popular vote was an unimpressive 1,856,452, slightly less than 40 percent (39.9). Bell-Everett came in fourth with 588,879 popular votes (12.6 percent) and 39 electoral votes, the third highest tally in American history for a third party. Bell carried the upper South border states of Virginia, Tennessee, and Kentucky, where he won a combined 45 percent of the popular vote. He garnered a substantial minority of the popular vote in the lower South (35 percent) and a combined 40 percent in the South overall, indicating that a significant minority of southerners were in no rush to leave the Union. Breckinridge swept the lower South, winning 72 electoral votes (849,781 popular votes: 18.1 percent). Douglas came in second with 1,382,000 popular votes, but because of the winner-take-all system, he only won 12 electoral votes, from New Jersey and Missouri.[53]

Despite their noble intentions, the Constitutional Unionists were overwhelmed by determined sectionalists. By combining the Lincoln-Breckinridge vote, assuming it represented the extremes on the slavery issue and comparing it to the more moderate Douglas-Bell vote, we see that the former pair received 58.0 percent of the popular vote, whereas Douglas and Bell together obtained just 42.0 percent. This is not to suggest that Lincoln and Breckinridge loyalists wanted a war, but that the moderation that Bell advocated was doomed in 1860. Could Bell have done better? Perhaps. The historian Allan Nevins observed: ". . . only a fervent crusade for the Union could have succeeded and the whole Bell-Everett enterprise was too balanced, laodicean [lukewarm], and timid."[54] Douglas broke with tradition, traveling the states and warning about the danger to the Union of a Lincoln victory. Bell should have done the same. Perhaps a personality that made him so moderate on the issues was not one that could rouse the public to the danger posed by Lincoln.

2

The Revolt of the Farmers: Greenback, People's (Populists)

You farmers have got to stop raising corn and start raising hell.
—Mary Elizabeth Lease, Populist agitator

Industrial capitalism emerged as the driving force behind America's economic growth after the Civil War. Backed by elected officials and the courts, businessmen and bankers grabbed the lion's share of the new wealth, leaving workers and farmers with the bare minimum, if that. Farmers fought back through self-help organizations and the formation of independent political parties. They demanded their fair share of the riches and promoted a new idea, a role for government in making lives better for average Americans. For 30 years farmers struggled against an unresponsive, calcified political system rooted in Civil War loyalties. People voted as they shot. Most northerners remained loyal to the party of Lincoln and Grant, while southerners clung to the Democrats. Nonetheless, despite third-party failures in national elective politics, many of their ideas that seemed radical for the time eventually triumphed in the 20th century. In fact, if politics can be defined at its core as a clash of ideas, the third parties of the late 19th century may be regarded as ''first parties'' in the stream of American political thought.

The movement west that began before the Civil War with a trickle of miners, ranchers, and farmers accelerated with passage of the Homestead Act of 1862 and completion of the transcontinental railroad seven years later. The Act was meant to fulfill the Jeffersonian dream of a nation of yeoman farmers and the Republican Party's prewar commitment to white workers for an escape from eastern factories and European oppression to a life of independence and prosperity. According to its provisions, anyone 21 years or older could purchase 160 acres for a small fee provided they lived on the land for five years. Legislation passed during the next 15 years upped the limit to 1,280 acres.

The earliest settlers moved West by wagon train, a slow difficult journey. The opening of the transcontinental railroad in 1869 accelerated the movement. Railroad companies ran massive advertising campaigns in the United States and Europe luring settlers with cheap fares and promises of quick and easy wealth. For the railroads the program worked wonders. Between 1860 and 1910 the number of farms and total output increased dramatically. For brief periods farmers prospered, and at times, high commodity prices and cheap credit to buy more land and equipment was plentiful. Even Mother Nature might cooperate with abundant rainfall. Productivity improved with inventions like barbed wire, the McCormick reaper, and windmills that brought water to the surface.

All was not well, however, for the western farmer. Social isolation and loneliness bred discontent. Medical care and educational and cultural opportunities were nonexistent. Farmers, no longer idealized as the heroic minutemen of the revolutionary era, were called hayseeds by the new urbanites as many saw their children leave for better opportunities in the cities. Early successes encouraged them to buy more land and labor-saving devices on credit, but periodic economic downturns, rising costs, overproduction, and competition from newly opened lands in Canada, Australia, and Brazil fostered frustration and anger. The farmer was caught in a complex web of market forces over which he had no control and little understanding. Most frustrating was the farmer's dependence on the railroads that had lured him west in the first place. As output outstripped demand in local markets, farmers turned to the railroads to ship produce to eastern markets and to store excess production in privately owned elevators.

The fees charged by the owners were based on what the market would bear rather than what the farmer could afford. Farmers were aware that the rail lines charged lower rates in eastern markets where they faced competition. Caught between dependence on unforgiving impersonal market forces and the stranglehold of bankers, suppliers, and the rails, farmers sought a way out.

Oliver Hudson Kelley (1826–1913) was a big city boy from Boston who moved to a Minnesota farm at the age of 20 in 1846. In 1864, he took a position with the U.S. Department of Agriculture in Washington. When the Civil War ended, he traveled extensively, visiting farm communities in the West and the South where he saw a need for an organization to help farmers learn scientific methods and bring them out of social isolation. In 1867, Kelley helped organize a secret association called The Patrons of Husbandry, commonly known as the Grange. With women welcome to join, membership grew rapidly; by 1870 more than 10,000 local chapters were organized with more than one million members. The impetus behind the rapid growth was the call for regulation of railroad rates and cooperative purchasing of equipment and supplies direct from manufacturers at wholesale prices.[1]

The movement to control rail rates through political action came to a head in Illinois. In 1871, the Assembly enacted a series of Grange laws to prevent extortion and discrimination in setting railroad and warehouse rates. The railroads fought back by trying to unseat state legislators who supported the Grange laws, by bypassing towns that supported Grange lodges and by filing lawsuits that claimed lack of due process. At first, the Grange laws were upheld by the Supreme Court in *Munn v. Illinois* (1877), stating that property "in which the public has an interest" must submit to the common good. Eventually, in the Wabash case of 1886, the Court would rule that states could not set interstate rates. In any event the antimonopoly movement waned because railroad regulation proved too narrow a cause on which to base a political party.[2]

THE GREENBACK PARTY

In 1873, a new issue arose related to the money supply. Before the Civil War paper currency was backed by specie or hard money (gold and silver). The financial pressures of war forced Congress to authorize issuance of legal tender treasury notes—paper money that was not backed by gold or silver. Because of the green ink used on the notes they came to be known as greenbacks. When the war ended in 1865, $450 million in greenbacks was circulating. They added liquidity to the system along with inflation and higher prices. Bankers and other holders of government bonds pressured Washington to take the greenbacks out of circulation and return to hard money. They argued that gold-backed currency was orderly and civilized, even patriotic, with intrinsic value, whereas fiat or paper money not backed by metal was money only because legislators said it was, making it morally corrupt. Lurking behind all the moral homilies favoring specie were businessmen and bankers who were holding government bonds and wanted to be paid back in preinflationary money.[3]

Compounding the money issue was a depression touched off by the Panic of 1873. Real estate speculation culminating in a credit crunch and the failure of the prominent financial house, Jay Cooke and Company, led to the panic. Eventually the crisis on Wall Street ran its course, but the nation felt its effects for five years. Railroads defaulted on bonds, thousands of businesses failed, and many workers lost their jobs. In New York City the unemployment rate reached 25 percent. Farm prices collapsed. In 1874, Congress voted to print paper currency to increase the money supply, an inflationary move that would help farmers by raising prices while reducing the value of farm debt. President Grant vetoed the bill. In 1875, to compound the problem in the minds of farmers, Congress passed the Specie Resumption Act designed to take all Civil War greenbacks out of circulation and put the currency on a strict gold standard. The gold-backed dollar became the mantra of the Republican Party and most Democrats.[4]

Farmers saw greenbacks as their salvation. With both major parties favoring hard money, farmers organized the Independent Party, commonly known as the Greenback Party. On May 17, 1876, the Greenbacks held their first convention in Indianapolis to nominate national candidates and approve a platform. More than 240 men attended, including many holdovers from the antimonopoly movement. After an unsuccessful attempt to nominate Judge David Davis, an Illinois Supreme Court justice and Lincoln's chief strategist in the 1860 election, the convention turned to 85-year-old New Yorker Peter Cooper. Gen. Samuel Cary of Ohio was nominated for the vice presidency. An unlikely choice because of his advanced age, Cooper could not be counted on to campaign vigorously but promised a large campaign contribution to compensate. An inventor and manufacturer of iron rails, Cooper produced the Tom Thumb, the first locomotive in the United States in 1830. Public spirited and an avowed abolitionist before the war, he endowed The Cooper Union Institute to prepare men and women for careers in business.[5]

The Greenback platform's main planks demanded the issuance of legal tender paper money and repeal of the Specie Resumption Act of 1875. Cooper's opponents were New York's Democratic governor Samuel Tilden, a conservative millionaire lawyer and reformer, and Ohio governor Rutherford B. Hayes, a Republican Harvard Law graduate and a Civil War major general. It should have been an easy year for the Democrats. People were fed up with corruption in the Grant administration and the sufferings of a severe depression. Both major candidates endorsed "hard money" but tried to play down the issue. Hayes's backers tried to maintain loyalty in the ranks by the typical post-Civil War tactic of "waving the bloody shirt," i.e., accusing the Democrats of disloyalty as the party of southern secession. Except for a small disappointing campaign contribution from Peter Cooper, the Greenbacks had few funds, making a vigorous campaign out of the question. Some newspapers promoted the party's position on the currency question. Several thousand Greenback clubs were formed, but aside from a major rally in Chicago there was little to rouse the masses to the Greenback cause.[6]

Tilden won the popular vote by a margin of 242,224 of 8,411,019 votes cast (4,285,992 Tilden; 4,033,768 Hayes). Needing 185 electoral votes to win, Tilden came up one vote shy. With the electoral votes of three southern states up for grabs—Florida, South Carolina, and Louisiana—Hayes agreed to end Reconstruction by pulling all remaining federal troops out of the South. Thus he gained the 20 electoral votes of the three states, giving him the votes needed to capture the White House. The Greenback Party garnered only 81,737 votes, slightly less than 1 percent of votes cast, but outperformed that figure in five Midwestern farm states: Iowa (3.3 percent), Kansas (6.2 percent), Indiana (3.9 percent), Illinois (1.8 percent), and Michigan (2.9 percent).[7]

The depression continued as labor disturbances, notably the national railroad strike of 1877, brought additional support to the Greenback Party from industrial workers. On February 22, 1878, delegates from 28 states convened in Toledo where a series of prolabor planks were added to the Greenback platform, including the demand for reduced working hours and regulation of working conditions. State conventions demanded suffrage for women, direct election of the president and U.S. senators, railroad regulation, a graduated income tax, and antimonopoly legislation. In the off-year election of 1878, the Greenbackers nominated candidates in every state and polled more than one million votes, electing 15 congressmen and many state legislators. In Iowa, where they fused with the Democrats, Greenbackers won 48 percent of the popular vote. In Texas and Mississippi, with Republican support, they pulled in more than 20 percent of the vote. Even in the urban industrial East they did well, winning 34.4 percent in Maine and 42.7 percent in Massachusetts, in fusion with the Democrats. However, the alliance between western farmers and eastern workers was an uneasy one. Easterners resented western dominance of the party leadership, and conflicting economic interests—farmers wanted higher prices for their crops just as eastern consumers demanded lower retail prices—were also a source of friction.[8]

In 1880, at their Chicago convention the Greenbackers nominated James B. Weaver, an Iowa congressman, for president and Alison B. West of Mississippi for vice president. Weaver, a lawyer, a prewar abolitionist, and a Civil War brevet general, became disenchanted with Republicans' postwar big business orientation, so he joined the Greenback Party and won a congressional seat in 1878. The Party's 1880 platform combined earlier demands with new planks, many of which have eventually become law: paper money as legal tender for all debt, an eight-hour workday, sanitary conditions in industrial plants, inspection of mines and factories, restrictions on child labor, regulation of interstate commerce, government control of railroads and communications, ending of monopolies, a graduated income tax, a vote for every citizen, and the unlimited coinage of gold and silver.[9]

Weaver's Republican opponent was log cabin–born James Garfield, a 49-year-old Ohio congressman, who was known as amiable and a good-natured hugger of men and women. When caught in an affair with a Mrs. Calhoun of New York City, he apologized to his wife, who forgave him for this "lawless passion." Maj. Gen. Winfield Hancock, a Civil War hero who blunted Pickett's Charge at the battle of Gettysburg, won the Democratic nomination. The campaign was lackluster and typical of most post-Civil War elections. Little separated the two main parties on the issues, with the exception of the tariff; the Republicans favored a protective tariff for business interests, whereas the Democrats called for a lower, revenue-producing tariff. The Democrats accused Garfield of taking bribes in a major financial scandal, and Gen. Hancock showed his ignorance of the issues by calling the tariff a "local matter." Weaver was dismissed as a crackpot because the provisions in the Greenback platform were so radical for the time. Typical for the period, neither of the two main parties was willing to address the plight of the workers and farmers that produced these so-called radical demands.

Just two years after polling more than one million votes in the off-year election, Weaver's tally fell to only 308,578 or 3.3 percent of the total votes cast. Garfield won the White House with a slim 9,464 vote margin out of more than nine million popular votes (4,454,416 to 4,444,952). The electoral count was 214 for Garfield and 155 for Hancock. However, Weaver polled more than 10 percent in four states: Iowa, Michigan, Missouri, and Kansas. Despite a vigorous national campaign Weaver was hampered by dissension between workers and farmers and hostility in the South because of the party's support for equal rights. Also, prosperity had returned by 1880, and the Republicans claimed the credit because of their backing for hard money.[10]

After the election many supporters returned to the major parties. The Greenbacks ran one final campaign in 1884, nominating Ben Butler of Massachusetts to head the ticket. Once again neither of the two major-party candidates, New York governor Grover Cleveland for the Democrats or Maine Republican James G. Blaine, had anything new to say about the plight of the workers and farmers. Cleveland defeated Blaine in another close election. The Greenback Party drew only 175,370 votes (1.7 percent).[11]

Despite its defeat at the polls, the legacy of the Greenback Party was profound. It was the first third party to achieve national significance by combining the forces of farmers and workers and to insist that the national government play a part to make lives better for working Americans. It passed on many of its ideas to the more influential Populists, the Progressive Movement of the early 20th century, and even to the New Deal. Many of its members went into hibernation, only to reemerge with the formation of the broader-based People's Party or Populists.

THE PEOPLE'S PARTY (POPULISTS)

Just as the Greenback Party folded, a new wave of agrarian unrest swept through the West and the South fueled by a new economic downturn in the late 1880s, falling prices, low rainfall, and a more conservative Supreme Court that made it nearly impossible for states to regulate interstate rail rates. In the South, the effects of the crop lien system resulted in even more hard times as farmers lost their homesteads to foreclosures, threatening a whole generation with the reduced status of landless peasants.

Southerners got an added dose of personal humiliation. When the Civil War ended Dixie's capital base was destroyed. Banks were so rare that small farmers turned to local merchants to carry them over until the cotton crop was harvested. These merchants came to be known as the "furnishing man" or "the man" to the local African American community. In the "crop lien" system the furnishing man advanced the local farmer food and equipment during the growing season in exchange for a lien against his crop. Every week or two the farmer would arrive at the general store with a list of needs. The furnishing man pulled from his shelves all or some of what the farmer wanted, based on an assessment of what he already was owed and what he thought the crop would eventually bring for the year. He entered each item in the account book. For a can of beans that might cost 10 cents for a cash customer, the farmer was charged 14 cents plus interest, so by the end of the season the cost of the beans amounted to 19 or 20 cents or double that to a cash customer. The farmer could not grow his own food or trade with another merchant. He was locked in to his crop lien with the one merchant who governed his economic life in a state of near bondage. The arrangement was repeated in millions of similar transactions throughout the South. It is safe to say that more than three-quarters of all farmers, white and black, were locked-in to the crop lien system. When the cotton was picked, the farmer and merchant would meet at the local gin and settle the account for the year. With the decline in commodity prices, the crop did not always "pay out," so the farmer's debt might be carried over to the next season. Eventually the farmer might have to turn over the deed to the farm to make a final settlement. He could become a sharecropper or tenant or pack up and move west to Texas for a new start. Each year more than 100,000 southern farmers moved across the Mississippi to the Lone Star State.[12]

When the southern farmer moved west, he faced a set of problems similar to those of the wheat and corn farmers of the Great Plains. He needed a social outlet, knowledge of scientific farming, and a way to confront the capitalists who controlled the railroads and supply houses. Reduced prices for his crops and lower rainfall compounded his problems. In 1883, A. O. Davis, a former Mississippian raised under the crop lien system organized a farmers' alliance in Texas. Davis, a great speaker whom the farmers could relate to because of his background, attracted large crowds with his denunciations of the railroads, credit merchants, and the "money power." Other speakers joined Davis with a message of self-help and self-respect, instilling in the farmers the idea of uniting and transforming the dynamics of their relationships with the powers that kept them in a state of near peonage.[13]

The Alliance organized cooperatives for buying supplies and equipment and selling cotton in bulk without middlemen. Eventually, the Southern Farmers' Alliance had three million members. When opposition arose from merchants and bankers, the Alliance concluded that political activity was the only way out. A similar movement known as the Northern Alliance was founded in Kansas with a membership of more than two million. Delegates from the Northern and Southern Alliances met in 1889 to agree on a common program. Foremost was the solution proposed by the Greenbackers, an expansion of the money supply. Only now they demanded free coinage of silver as the solution, along with a graduated income tax and government ownership of railroads. Local parties put Alliance candidates on the ballot in 1890. Speakers included "Pitchfork" Ben Tillman of South Carolina, "Sockless" Jerry Simpson of Kansas, James Weaver of Iowa, and the inimitable "Queen Mary" Elizabeth Lease of Kansas, whose famous line, "you farmers have got to stop raising corn and start raising hell,"[14] became a rallying cry. With so much enthusiasm 53 congressmen were sent to Washington. Encouraged by their success, the Alliances met in Cincinnati in May 1891, to form an independent political party called the People's Party, commonly known as the Populists. A nominating convention was called for Omaha on July 4, 1892. The 1,400 delegates nominated former Greenbacker James B. Weaver for president and James G. Field an ex-Confederate from Virginia for vice president. The platform protested the corruption of the political system, control of the media, and impoverishment of labor by the capitalist class. Specific planks called for unlimited coinage of gold and silver at the ratio of 16 to 1 and expansion of the money supply to $50 per capita, a graduated income tax, a government-run postal savings bank, and government ownership of the railroads and telephone and telegraph systems. The Populists wanted the government to reclaim all corporate land and natural resources in excess of their actual need.[15]

Weaver's opponents were former president Grover Cleveland (1885–1889) and the Republican incumbent President Benjamin Harrison. The tariff was the dominant issue in an otherwise unexciting campaign. Once again the two main parties failed to address any of the issues of concern to farmers and workers. James Weaver campaigned actively, even visiting the South, where he faced hostile audiences because of the platform's demand for equal rights. Cleveland came out on top again with 47.1 percent of the popular vote (5,556,543) and 277 electoral votes compared with Harrison's 43.8 percent (5,175,582) and 145 electoral votes. The People's Party topped one million popular votes (1,040,886) or 8.8 percent and captured 22 electoral votes from six farm and silver-producing states: Colorado (4), Idaho (3), Kansas (10), Nevada (3), North Dakota (1), and Oregon (1). This was the highest number of popular votes for any third party to date and second in electoral votes to the Constitutional Union Party in the election of 1860, but Weaver could not break the Democrats' hold on the South, where Civil War loyalties and race held sway. Even most farmers in the Midwest stayed with the two major parties. Weaver's votes came from the more isolated rural areas from farmers who were out of the mainstream and looked to the People's Party to act on their behalf. The better integrated farmers hoped to achieve their objectives through the Democratic Party.[16]

One year after the election of 1892 another depression struck the nation. Known as the Panic of 1893, the downturn started in Europe and spread to the United States as foreigners cut back on the purchase of American products. Concern about the stability of American currency prompted Europeans to demand gold for U.S. securities, resulting in a decline in the money supply. Falling prices hurt farmers whose costs were now higher than their incomes, forcing many into foreclosure. Wages for industrial workers fell, making it increasingly difficult for them to pay the rent and feed their families. By the end of 1893 more than 15,000 firms were in bankruptcy. Three million Americans, or 20 percent of the workforce, was out of work. Meanwhile, the rich partied on, sharing none of the pain, prompting populist agitator Sockless Jerry Simpson to describe "a struggle between the robbers and the robbed."[17] Democratic president Cleveland and many political leaders were reluctant to respond, believing the Federal government had no role to play in such a crisis.

Farmers were convinced that tight money policies pursued by Cleveland and the eastern bankers were responsible for the decrease in demand. Like the Greenbackers after the Panic of 1873, they believed that their problems would be alleviated by increasing the money supply, only this time through the unlimited coinage of silver. Cleveland stood steadfast behind the gold standard, but the starving and the desperate, including many in his own party, were not interested in Cleveland's principles. So the Democrats dropped Cleveland as their 1896 nominee and decided between silverites Richard Bland, known as "Silver Dick," and former Nebraska congressman William Jennings Bryan. Bland was dropped because many believed his name was all too descriptive of the man, nor was he helped when a rumor spread that Bland's wife was Catholic. A pamphlet warned: "If you want to see a confessional box in the White House, vote for Bland." At age 36 Bryan became the youngest man in history to receive his party's nomination. He said Democrats should have the same feeling for Cleveland as "toward the trainman [sic] who has opened a switch and precipitated a wreck." Bryan favored the unlimited coinage of silver, whereas Ohio governor William McKinley, heading the GOP ticket, stood behind the gold standard.[18]

The Populists scheduled their convention after the Democrats and Republicans, assuming that the two main parties would back the gold standard, giving them a clear difference and a decided advantage. When the Democrats turned to silverite Bryan, the Populists faced a dilemma. Should they throw their support behind the Democrats and lose their own identity or run a Populist candidate and risk splitting the pro-silver vote, practically guaranteeing the election of McKinley. Most delegates decided to support Bryan, but they would not endorse Arthur Sewell, the Democrats' vice presidential nominee. Sewell was a silverite but surprisingly he was also a banker and industrialist, making him unacceptable to the Populists. So they ran their own ticket with Bryan at the top and Tom Watson of Georgia as their vice presidential nominee.[19]

For the first time since the Civil War, Democrats and Republicans differed on issues and substance. To Democrats, the most important issue was free coinage of silver at a ratio of 16 to 1 with gold. They also supported a tariff for revenue only, immigration restriction to protect American workers, more powers to the Interstate Commerce

Commission to control the railroads, the protection of states' rights, and a two-term limit for the presidency. Among key provisions in the Republican platform were support for a protective tariff, retention of the gold standard, restrictions on immigration, voting rights for all citizens, condemnation of lynching, and equal pay for women. The Populists' platform repeated many of the key provisions from 1892, including free coinage at the gold-to-silver ratio of 16 to 1, an increase in the volume of currency, a graduated income tax, and government ownership of railroads and telegraph. They added new planks designed to promote democracy, including the right to citizen initiative and referendum, direct election of senators and the president, and the right to public employment during a depression.[20]

Bryan ran a vigorous campaign, traveling more than 18,000 miles and giving more than 600 speeches to more than five million voters. He attacked the "money power," repeating the famous line from his nomination speech: "You shall not crucify mankind upon a cross of gold." McKinley ran a stay-at-home campaign, refusing to compete against his energetic opponent, commenting, "I might just as well put up a trapeze on my front lawn and compete with some professional athlete as go out speaking against Bryan." However, McKinley was heard through 1,400 surrogates and 10 million pieces of literature printed in more than 30 foreign languages. He raised more than $3 million from a business community fearful of a Bryan victory, compared with Bryan's $500,000. McKinley supporters attacked Bryan as a radical and an anarchist. Bryan countered by calling McKinley a tool of Wall Street.[21]

Election returns gave McKinley the White House with 50.7 percent of the popular vote (7,111,607) and 271 electoral votes compared with Bryan's 47.9 percent (6,509,052) and 176 electoral votes. The Bryan-Watson ticket on the Populist line garnered 222,581 votes or 1.5 percent of the popular vote but no electoral votes. Even combining Bryan's popular votes on the Democratic and Populist lines (6,731,697), he underperformed McKinley. Bryan carried 24 southern and western states including silver-producing states where most of his campaign funding originated. McKinley carried 23 states in the East and the Midwest. It was the first election in which a Democratic candidate failed to carry an eastern state. The Populists did best in Texas and Kansas, the two states accounting for more than 60 percent of their total vote.[22]

The Republicans were able to convince most Americans that the gold standard was the key to a prosperous and stable future. The depression had eased by 1896 as gold production skyrocketed and currency became plentiful. The Populists faded away, but much of their program would be enacted during the 20th century.

3

The Progressives: Bull Moose Progressives, Progressives of 1924

> We propose boldly to face the real and great questions of the day
> and not skillfully to evade them as do the old parties.
> —Theodore Roosevelt

In 1900, just as the laissez-faire Republican administration of William McKinley won a second term to the White House, three states in the heartland sent a very different message about the future of the relationship between corporate America and government of the people. Robert La Follette of Wisconsin, Samuel Van Zant of Minnesota, and Albert Cummins of Iowa were elected as anticorporate, radical, trust-busting governors, signaling the rise of the Progressive Era, which would last until the "return to normalcy" under President Warren Harding in 1920. The so-called money question—whether the United States should remain on the gold standard—had been settled for now with the election of McKinley and the defeat of silverite Democrat William Jennings Bryan. However, a host of other issues championed by worker and farmer groups regarding the relationship between government, big business, and the people remained to be settled. The insurgency of the Populists was over. Now, largely Protestant middle- and upper-class urbanites, called Progressives, would lead a new fight for reform in a great social reaction against the abuses of the preceding age.

By the turn of the 20th century, the top 1 percent of the population held 50 percent of the nation's wealth, and the top 12 percent owned 90 percent. The wealthy monopolized the political system through contributions to national parties and state legislators that appointed U.S. senators who, in turn, represented special interests. In effect, a small minority of the population that reaped all the benefits of the new industrial age used its wealth to control the system. The masses created much and earned little. Now, reform elements in both political parties questioned whether industrialization in the United States of America should result in permanent farmer peasantry and worker poverty.[1]

Most progressives did not call for an end to capitalism, but knew that corporations would not regulate themselves; government needed to step in and direct a solution to the problems created by industrialization. Before they could reform business, however, they needed to bring change to a government system that seemed incapable of functioning in the new civilization. Reform began at the local level in the cities where the problems were most obvious. Progressives tried to improve municipal governance by wiping out corruption, eliminating bossism, and installing city managers and commissioners with a better understanding of the underlying problems of poverty and good government. Schools and parks were built. Some cities cut streetcar fares and gas rates and provided work relief for the unemployed. Middle-class women moved into settlement houses, living among the urban poor to provide social services not available through government agencies.

At the state level, broader reforms were instituted. By 1912, most states passed laws regulating child labor, requiring workman's compensation for on-the-job injuries, and establishing maximum working hours for women. Some states used their taxing power to limit profits on corporations and redistribute wealth through income and inheritance taxes. At first, conservative courts overturned many of the new laws, citing the Fourteenth Amendment, which forbade the taking of life, liberty, or property without due process, but under pressure from progressives the Supreme Court liberalized its views, now taking into account the social as well as the economic costs.

Nationally, progressives sought to expand the franchise by pushing for direct election of senators and the right of women to vote. By 1912, 30 states began choosing senators by direct primary. One year later the 17th Amendment was ratified, providing for the popular election of U.S. senators. By 1914, 11 western states had given women the vote; six years later in 1920 the 19th Amendment was ratified, giving all women the right to vote.

Progressives had been at odds with the intensely conservative administration of William McKinley (1896–1901), but on September 5, 1901, President McKinley was shot by an assassin while attending the Pan American Exposition in Buffalo. He died eight days later. Vice President Theodore Roosevelt was sworn in as the 26th president, the youngest man ever to hold the job. TR was born on October 27, 1858, in New York City, the son of Theodore Roosevelt Sr., a high-born New York philanthropist and humanitarian, and Martha Bulloch Roosevelt, a Georgia-born plantation belle who secretly aided the Confederacy during the Civil War from her upper-class perch on East 20th Street. Reputed to be Margaret Mitchell's model for Scarlett O'Hara in *Gone With The Wind*, Momma Martha, known as Mittie, remained an unreconstructed southerner until the day she died on February 14, 1884.[2]

Teddy Roosevelt began his political career as a Republican in the New York State Assembly in 1882 where he crossed party lines to support Democratic governor Grover Cleveland's successful push for civil service reform. A proponent of the vigorous life, he moved to North Dakota in 1884 to work as a cattle rancher and as deputy sheriff of Billings County. After losing the race for mayor of New York City to his Democratic rival Abram Hewett in 1886, he campaigned for Benjamin Harrison, the Republican victor in the 1888 presidential election, who rewarded him with an appointment to the U.S. Civil Service Commission (1889–1895). To the extreme irritation of party professionals, who preferred the old patronage system, the number of jobs that came under civil service classification doubled during his tenure. In 1895, he returned to New York City and was appointed police commissioner, routing out corruption and appointing the first women and Jews to the department. Always, like his father, with a strain of sympathy for the underprivileged, TR struck up a friendship with Jacob Riis, a Danish immigrant whose photographs captured the squalid living conditions in New York's slums. Riis took Roosevelt on forays into immigrant districts where, seeing first-hand the filth and hopelessness, his sympathy for human misery grew.

In 1897, McKinley appointed TR under secretary of the navy under John Long, whose frequent and extended absences made TR virtual head of the department, resulting in a whirlwind of naval activity, including preparation and support for war against Spain. When the Spanish-American War erupted in 1898, TR left the Navy Department to organize a regiment known as the Rough Riders, whose exploits in the battle of San Juan Hill made him a national hero. With his fame in place, he won the support of New York Republican boss Thomas C. Platt for a run as governor. Once in office, to the frustration of Platt and conservative Republicans in New York, Roosevelt championed progressive causes such as limits on working hours for women and children, curbing of sweatshop abuses, and a corporate income tax.

So concerned was Platt with the loss of contributions from corporate executives that he pushed President McKinley to put Roosevelt on the Republican ticket as vice president in 1900. McKinley obliged, well aware of Roosevelt's reputation for honesty and reform, but calculated that TR could help with the progressive wing of the party. When TR entered the White House after McKinley's assassination in 1901, Ohio Republican senator Mark Hanna was reported to have commented, "Now that damn cowboy is President of the United States."[3]

Despite his liberal leanings, TR was a devout Republican who despised Democrats and Socialists. He believed in the capitalist system and had no objections to bigness through corporate consolidation, suggesting, "we draw the line against misconduct, not wealth."[4] But in his first address to Congress he horrified Republican conservatives when he asked for an attack on "serious social problems": regulation of business combinations and railroads and the conservation of natural resources. House Speaker Joseph Cannon and Senate leader Mark Hanna refused to cooperate, but on May 1, 1902, when the United Mine Workers went out on strike for a shorter workday, better wages, and union recognition, the power relationship would shift in TR's favor. The strike lingered for five months. The owners rejected negotiations despite the threat to the public welfare as winter approached. In October, Roosevelt offered to intervene as an honest broker, the first time that a president did not automatically back big business. The union was willing to submit to arbitration, but the owners denied TR's right to intervene in any way. Finally, the president threatened to call out troops to operate the mines. The owners had a sudden change of heart; they willingly submitted the issues to a presidential arbitration board that granted the workers a 10 percent pay increase and a nine-hour day (down from 12), but no recognition of the union as bargaining agency. The indifference of the mine owners influenced public opinion, giving TR leverage with Congress.

With his popularity soaring, Roosevelt was a shoo-in for the Republican presidential nomination in 1904. Although the Democrats were considered the more liberal of the two main parties, they nominated Judge Alton B. Parker, a conservative New York lawyer. The charismatic Roosevelt claimed the day, winning 56 percent of the popular vote and 336 electoral votes to Parker's 140.[5]

Some say that TR talked a bigger progressive game than he accomplished. Perhaps he did, but he wanted to keep the progressive and conservative wings of his party united. Nonetheless, under his administration much progressive legislation was enacted. Congress established the Department of Labor and Commerce and the Bureau of Corporations to investigate mergers and warn against harmful practices. The Elkins Act of 1903 made secret railroad rebates illegal; the Hepburn Act of 1906 empowered the Interstate Commerce Commission (established in 1887) to set reasonable railroad rates. More than 150 million acres of timberlands were transformed into national forests under the administration of Chief Forester Gifford Pinchot. States were encouraged to form conservation commissions, and in 1906 Congress enacted the Pure Food and Drug Act, which banned the use of harmful drugs, chemicals, and preservatives.

When TR was elected in his own right in 1904, he promised, to his later regret, that he would not seek a third term: "The wise custom which limits the President to two terms regards the substance and not the form and under no circumstances will I be a candidate for or accept the nomination for another." Because of his popularity he was able to handpick his own successor, William Howard Taft of Ohio. TR expected Taft to carry on his own work while maintaining unity within Republican ranks, but Taft was no TR. Lacking Roosevelt's political skills, a rift soon developed between the conservative and progressive wings of the party, and between the two men, that would lead to the third-party candidacy by Roosevelt in 1912. The estrangement resulted from matters of policy, politics, and ego.

Taft was an amiable, good-natured supporter of TR—some said, errand boy, but Taft was conservative by nature. He served as governor of the Philippines under McKinley and as secretary of war under Roosevelt. He would rather carry out someone else's policy than make it himself, and he never really wanted to be president, but was pushed by his ambitious wife Nellie, who suffered a stroke three months after becoming First Lady in 1909. In some ways Taft appeared to be more progressive than Roosevelt. He instituted more antitrust suits in one term that TR did in two. He supported the eight-hour workday, legislation to promote safe mining practices, strengthening the Interstate Commerce Commission, and the process that led to an income tax (Sixteenth Amendment). However, there was some mistreatment of TR's family by Nellie Taft during the presidential transition and the dismissal of Roosevelt's cabinet members. Progressives were enraged over Taft's support for a higher tariff, which played into the hands of eastern industrialists and the reversal of TR's conservation policies, including the firing of Chief Forester Pinchot.

There were also matters of style and personality. Taft's ponderous, uninspiring speeches paled in comparison to TR's dynamic rants. Taft's equally ponderous weight—all 350 pounds of it—combined with rumors that he needed to be pried out of the White House bathtub and to have a new olympic-size tub installed, made him the butt of jokes among D.C.'s tittle-tattle tongues.

In the 1910 midterm congressional elections, Taft ill-advisedly campaigned against the progressives, just as voters turned on his conservative allies. The Democrats picked up 13 Senate seats and enough House seats to give them a majority for the first time in 16 years. Meanwhile, Roosevelt, now The Great White Hunter, was off in Africa after big game with his son, Kermit, naturalists from the Smithsonian, and 200 African porters. Nevertheless, he kept in touch with supporters back home and was increasingly concerned about the Grand Old Party's (GOP) weakened state with Taft at the helm. After two years out of office Roosevelt had become even more progressive in his political views. Therefore on August 31, 1910, five months after his return from Africa, he agreed to make a speech at Osawatomie, Kansas, to celebrate the legacy of abolitionist John Brown.

TR introduced the theme New Nationalism, which called for government supervision of corporations and natural resources ("a moral issue") and other progressive measures. He said, "The American people are right in demanding New Nationalism without which we cannot hope to deal with new problems. The New Nationalism puts the national need before sectional or personal advantage. . . . The New Nationalism regards the executive power as the steward of the public welfare. It demands of the judiciary that it shall be interested primarily in human welfare rather than in property. . . . The prime problem of our nation is to get the right type of good citizenship and, to get it we must have progress and our public men must be genuinely progressive."[6]

Although not optimistic about Republican chances to keep the White House in 1912 with Taft heading the ticket, his yearning to get back into the game started him thinking about 1916, but a decision by Taft changed his timetable for a new run at the White House. Ironically, it was a decision applauded by many progressives, but not by TR. As president in 1907, Roosevelt allowed U.S. Steel to acquire a competitor, Tennessee Coal and Iron, despite the risk of greater concentration in the steel industry. He was told by U.S. Steel executives that bank failures might follow the collapse of Tennessee Coal and Iron. Four years later in 1911, President Taft decided to prosecute U.S. Steel under the Sherman Antitrust Act, infuriating TR, who took Taft's action as a personal affront, prompting the former president to enter the race for the Republican nomination.

Roosevelt competed in 10 state primaries against Taft winning nine, but primaries were not binding. The Republican National Committee held the real power, and disqualified scores of Roosevelt's delegates, thereby handing the nomination to Taft. Roosevelt felt robbed of the nomination and considered a third-party run, provided he could get financing. Publishing tycoon Frank Munsey, who pioneered the use of high-speed presses to produce cheap pulp fiction magazines aimed at working-class audiences, and George Perkins, an insurance executive and partner in the House of Morgan, promised financing, so TR took the plunge into third-party politics declaring, "My hat is in the ring."[7]

THE BULL MOOSE PROGRESSIVES

The new party convened in Chicago on August 5, 1912, to nominate Roosevelt. There were few party bosses and their assorted hangers on. Instead, scores of well dressed, respectable middle-class citizens attended, more like Garrisonian abolitionists of the 1830s than the practical political operators expected at a typical party convention. They were militant and intense and were dedicated to the progressive cause. There were suffragettes, social workers, urban planners, conservationists, political reformers, and idealists. African Americans came because of their interest in solving the social problems that afflicted their race. When TR appeared on the platform to accept the nomination and present his "Confession of Faith" acceptance speech, he was greeted by a 52-minute standing ovation. He had no need to placate the conservatives in his old party—they belonged to Taft now—so he was free to launch an attack on the old parties, calling them "husks" with "no real soul," "boss-ridden," and controlled by professional politicians in the interests of Wall Street and the privileged classes. He promised that the new Progressive Party would "put at the service of all the people the collective power of the people through government agencies." He elaborated on many of the platform's (32) planks, which fell into six categories: (1) more democracy; (2) social and industrial justice for farmers and workers; (3) control of trusts, large corporations, and holding companies; (4) promotion of general prosperity; (5) conservation; and (6) foreign affairs. To promote more democracy, TR demanded election of senators by popular vote, use of the initiative (people propose laws), referendum (people approve laws), and recall (people fire elected officials), simplifying amending the Constitution, women's suffrage, limitations and disclosure of campaign contributions and party expenditures, direct primaries for state and national office, and recording of all congressional committee votes. Regarding justice for farmers and workers, the platform promised the following: prohibition of injunctions during strikes, on-the-job safety and health standards, workman's compensation, old age and unemployment insurance, prohibition of child labor, an eight-hour day and one day of rest, minimum pay for women, and an end to tenant farming. Trusts would be controlled by a federal commission to supervise industrial corporations, by strengthening the Sherman Antitrust Act and the Interstate Commerce Commission and by government supervision over investment vehicles (e.g., prospectuses).[8]

To promote the general prosperity, TR proposed teaching agricultural science at schools; designing a tariff by special commission to balance the needs of industry and consumers; a national currency system controlled by the federal government; internal infrastructure improvements (including Mississippi River flood control); promotion of assimilation, education, and advancement of immigrants; pensions for soldiers and sailors (including Confederate widows); a parcel post system; enforcement and expansion of civil service reform; and graduated income and inheritance taxes. TR said there was no greater issue than conservation. "Just as we must preserve our women and children we must conserve the resources of the land on which we live." He wanted forests and lands to be useful but also to preserve them for all the people. He viewed Alaska as a great natural resource that should be developed at once.[9]

He wanted to use government to maintain a balance between workers and industry and between conservation and exploitation. He ended with an attack on the Republican party that, he claimed, was not dominated by honest men but rather by individuals "with a sneering indifference to every principle of right, so acted as to bring a shameful end to a party which had been founded over half a century ago by men whose souls burned the fire of lofty endeavor [anti-slavery]. . . . Now to you men, who, in your turn, have come together to spend and be spent in the endless crusade against wrong, to you who face the future resolute and confident, to you who strive in a spirit of brotherhood for the betterment of our nation, to you who grid yourselves for this great new fight in the never ending warfare for the good of humankind, I say in closing: We stand at Armageddon, and we battle for the Lord." Brought to an emotional frenzy by their great hero, the crowd erupted into the Civil War's fighting anthem, "The Battle Hymn of the Republic."[10]

The rapture was not total, however; there was also rupture over two points: race and antitrust. Taft Republicans had won the loyalty of the South's anti-Democratic black leadership, but TR's radical reform message attracted southern blacks to the convention who then contested the all-white southern delegations. So TR came up with a feeble solution that recognized the reality of race in early 20th century America but fell far short of a progressive agenda. He would seat lily-white delegations from the South and mixed delegations from the border states of Maryland and West Virginia and expressed the hope that the future would welcome mixed-race delegations from the deep South. To many a more important issue was antitrust. Roosevelt believed that economic necessity often resulted in behemoth corporations or trusts. The way to control them for the public good was through government regulation. Many eastern progressives, including TR's money men Perkins and Munsey backed TR's stance. The western progressives favored dissolution of large corporations into smaller entities. The disagreement between the two factions was never really resolved. Both proposals—TR's regulation and Sherman Antitrust enforcement through breakups—were adapted by the resolution committee. Roosevelt and Perkins ordered the Sherman plank deleted, but it was reinstated behind their backs, and most often the platform was printed with the Sherman plank included.

Roosevelt's opponents in 1912 were President Taft, Democrat Woodrow Wilson, and Socialist Eugene Debs. Voters seem to grasp the basic issue of 1912: which class of citizens should control the government and to which ends. Woodrow Wilson, the Democratic nominee and moderate reformer, was born on December 28, 1856, in Staunton, Virginia, to Joseph Ruggles Wilson, a Presbyterian minister and staunch Confederate, and English-born Janet Woodrow, an educated, loving mother of four. Wilson claimed that his earliest recollection was of standing outside the family home in Augusta, Georgia, in November 1860, when a passerby yelled, Lincoln is elected, and there's going to be war! Although he left the South for a northern education, he remained a white supremacist who believed that secession was justified. He graduated from Princeton, and with a political career in mind entered the North Carolina Bar. A change of heart steered him to academia, winning a PhD in Political Science from Johns Hopkins University in 1886. He taught at Bryn Mawr, Wesleyan, and Princeton, where he became president from 1902 to 1910 and instituted modernizing reforms in the curriculum. He attempted a similar feat in the social order at Princeton long-dominated by the traditional eating-club system. He wanted to reorganize the university around four quadrangles where all students regardless of class could sleep and eat under one roof. The plan ran into violent opposition and was dropped.

In 1911, he accepted an offer from the New Jersey Democratic machine to run for governor. Once elected, in his inaugural address he declared his independence from the bosses and proceeded to push successfully for various reforms including party primaries for all elected officials, limits on campaign contributions, establishment of a public utility commission to set rates, and workman's compensation. Wilson supported ratification of the Sixteenth Amendment for the income tax (rejected by the state) and supported antitrust legislation that passed the legislature, but was repealed after he left office.

Wilson was mentioned as a presidential contender from the minute he became governor. At the party's convention in Baltimore in June 1912, he won the nomination on the 29th ballot, when William Jennings Bryan decided to withdraw his support from Speaker of the House Champ Clark of Missouri because of Clark's close ties to the unsavory crowd at New York's Tammany Hall. Although the Democratic platform echoed many Bull Moose reforms, the Democrats were considered more moderate. For example, the Bull Moose platform contained planks about direct democracy: the citizens' initiative, the referendum and recall, easier ways to amend the Constitution, and women's suffrage. Another key difference was the matter of reigning in big business. As noted, Roosevelt favored regulation, while the Democrats favored breakups. In terms of campaign rhetoric, TR was the more radical, whereas Wilson tended to play down many of the reform planks in his own platform. The Democrats, ever mindful of their southern base, favored states' rights under the theme of New Freedom, whereas the Progressives favored the use of national power—New Nationalism—to solve social and economic problems. A fourth entry in the 1912 race was the Socialist Party candidate, Eugene Debs, the most extreme of the reformers, who called for government ownership of industry.

The campaign was a relatively tame affair. Taft and Wilson refrained from personal attacks, depriving Roosevelt of one of his strong suits, the give-and-take of sarcasm and personal invective. TR's radicalism unleashed great enthusiasm among his supporters. He made extensive visits to the Pacific Coast and the South. On a trip to Milwaukee in October, he was shot by a madman; luckily his eyeglass case deflected the bullet, which inflicted only minor injury. He would not be stopped, delivering his speech in full, claiming the Democrats were chained to an unjust past and conservative doctrines—no doubt referring to their southern racist tinge and states' rights doctrines.

Although TR was disappointed that progressive Republican governors who urged him to run did not follow him into the Progressive Party, their reluctance allowed him to pursue a more extreme agenda. On the other hand, he was vulnerable to charges of insincerity because of his association with George Perkins. TR was espousing government control and regulation of the trusts and at the same time being bankrolled by an associate of an organization—the House of Morgan—that controlled U.S. Steel, America's first billion dollar corporation.

Wilson's campaign style combined the dual personas of the articulate but distant professor and the high moral tone of a devout Presbyterian. It was all dignified and intellectual. His theme of New Freedom, to counter TR's New Nationalism, emphasized ending monopoly, free competition, and the right of collective bargaining. Wilson opposed a paternalistic society while pointing out that Roosevelt's radical proposals were "well intentioned but unrealistic."

Taft and his supporters knew that his chances for victory were slim. Campaign finance became a problem because nobody wanted to contribute to a loser, so he raised less than half the usual Republican kitty of $2 million. He avoided all personal acrimony in public, but in private he described the Roosevelt Progressives as a "religious cult with a fakir as the head of it." Taft didn't venture far from home during the campaign but was content to write letters with his views to newspaper editors, including the claim that the Republican's high-tariff policy was the cause of general good times.

The election outcome surprised no one. Wilson carried 40 states with 435 electoral votes compared with Roosevelt's five states and 88 electoral votes, the highest ever for a third-party candidate. Taft won only two states—Vermont and Utah—with eight electoral votes. Because of the GOP split, the Democrats won a majority in the House of Representatives and Senate for the first time since the Civil War. Ironically, one of TR's biggest complaints about President Taft was his inability to maintain unity within Republican ranks, but now with TR's entry into the race, the Republicans faced an even bigger disaster with the loss of the White House and Congress. Wilson's popular vote was less impressive. He won only 42 percent (6,293,019) compared with Roosevelt's 28 percent (4,119,507) and Taft's 23 percent (3,484,956). Socialist Debs's tally (5.9 percent) of the popular vote was a high-water mark for the party (901,873) Wilson won absolute majorities in only 11 states of the Confederacy, where old-time loyalties played a bigger role than a desire for reform.

However, even deducting the 126 electoral votes of the South, Wilson still would have won the election with the remaining 309 electoral votes.[11]

Wilson and Roosevelt appealed to different constituencies. TR's six state victories were in the upper Midwest (Michigan, Minnesota, and South Dakota) and the Pacific Coast (Washington and California) as well as Pennsylvania. He did best in the cities where voters favored his vision of a social democracy. Independent-minded farmers tended to be less supportive of his promise of a paternalistic society. Wilson did well in small towns and the countryside. All in all, the three candidates promising reform (TR, Wilson, and Debs) garnered 76 percent of the popular vote, indicating that Americans were in the mood for change.[12]

The 1912 election was the first and only time in American political history when a third party outran one of the two major parties in a presidential election. It was also the first of many elections in the 20th century when the candidate *was* the party, compared with the 19th century when ideas and the party came first for third parties. The election of 1912 was testament to Roosevelt's personal popularity, his prestige as a former president, his ability to win financial backing, and his success in luring local Republican organizations to the Bull Moose cause.

Unfortunately, the party's showing in local races was less impressive. The Progressives carried only one governorship and won no Senate seats and only a handful of House races. TR understood that so few local victories meant the death knell for the Progressives because they could not reward local supporters, who were the lifeblood of living parties. As so often happens in national politics, the party that wins the White House loses the midterm elections, and 1914 was no different. Wilson lost support, but the Republicans, not the Progressives, picked up seats. The final Progressive collapse came about from lack of money—Munsey withdrew his support—and infighting over Perkins and his views about trust busting. Because of his opposition to the Sherman Antitrust Act many Progressives wanted Perkins drummed out of the party, but TR refused. A further split developed over the American entry into World War I. Many Progressives opposed American involvement, whereas Roosevelt favored it. TR had hopes of capturing the 1916 Republican nomination in an alliance with Progressives, but the GOP refused, selecting New York's Charles Evans Hughes instead. When Progressives offered to nominate TR in 1916 on a separate ticket, he declined, unwilling to face another defeat. The party disbanded. Roosevelt died three years later on January 16, 1919, at the age of 61.

THE PROGRESSIVES OF 1924

Woodrow Wilson could spot a trend. Although he won as a moderate progressive in 1912, he recognized voters' desire for change. So between his victory and American entry into World War I in 1917, he supported a mass of progressive legislation unequaled by any administration up until that time. He lowered the tariff on more than 100 items. The Federal Reserve Act established the Federal Reserve Bank and Board of Governors to provide for a more elastic currency and to prevent financial crises. A Farm Loan Bank was established to lend farmers money on up to 70 percent of the value of their holdings. The Federal Trade Commission Act of 1914 empowered the government to issue cease-and-desist orders to firms guilty of unfair competition. The Clayton Act defined unfair trade methods by corporations, exempted unions from antitrust, and forbade the use of labor injunctions in most instances.

When the United States entered World War I on April 17, 1917, the era of progressive reform ended. Although, as noted, many progressives opposed American entry into the war, they were pleased with the government's shift to central planning brought on by the needs of a wartime economy. The War Industries Board took control of scarce materials needed for war production and shipbuilding. The United Railway Administration organized the railroads into a single national system for shipping goods and moving soldiers. The Council of National Defense assumed dictatorial powers over the national economy, mobilizing manpower, factories, and farms. To ensure tranquility on the labor front, the National War Labor Board established wage scales, reduced hours, and prevented exploitation of women and children. Strikers were threatened with the draft. Wilson favored the conservative American Federation of Labor (AFL) to represent workers over the more radical IWW (International Workers of the World). As such, AFL membership grew from 2.7 million members when the war started to 4 million by 1920. The mission of the Food Administration, under future president Herbert Hoover, was to stimulate grain production, reduce domestic competition, and increase exports to European allies.

Farmers responded enthusiastically, buying more land and equipment on easy credit in a wartime boom that implied perpetual prosperity. However, by 1920, two years after the war's end, the stimulative effects of the war years evaporated. The price of corn, wheat, and hogs were down between 30 and 50 percent from diminished domestic and international demand. Europeans no longer had the ability to pay for American products, just as their own production revived and non-European sources came on the world market. Domestically, population growth slowed, dietary habits changed, and new slimmer fashions reduced the demand for staples. During 1921–1922 farm incomes fell by 50 percent, whereas bankruptcies increased 15-fold compared with the rate in 1914. For farms the problems were structural; in 1900, 40 percent of the population lived on farms; by the 1930s only 20 percent farmed. For labor, the end of the war meant the end of many gains as unemployment rose and wages fell.[13]

With the election of Republican Warren Harding in 1920 under the slogan, "return to normalcy," government once again belonged to big business. The National Association of Manufacturers instituted a campaign for the nonunion open shop, called the American Plan, associating unions with Europeanism and nonunionization as all-American free enterprise. Only the railroad union emerged more powerful politically and economically. However, during the 1921 downturn railroad management cut wages, prompting a strike as the scandal ridden Harding administration obtained a court-ordered injunction against the strikers, who were forced to return to work. When Harding died of a stroke on June 20, 1923, Vice President Calvin Coolidge took charge. Under the influence of Treasury Secretary Andrew Mellon, Coolidge pushed the Mellon Plan, consisting of tax reductions for the wealthy and the lifting of restraints on business.[14]

Farmers and workers felt rejected by Republicans and ignored by Democrats. Once again, as in the late 19th century, they had a common enemy in an alliance between big business and politicians. Aside from their immediate woes of falling prices, loss of purchasing power, and foreclosures, farmers were concerned about the growth of an industrialized urbanized America that they felt was overwhelming their way of life. They had not forgotten their Populist roots of the late 19th century and wondered whether a third party might redress the balance.

Farmers had once organized through the Non-Partisan League, a farmer interest group originally founded in the Northwest in 1915 by Arthur C. Townley. By 1923, the League came on hard times, so they joined with three other reform organizations to create the Conference of Progressive Political Action (CPPA): The Railroad Brotherhoods, the Socialist Party, and the Committee of 48, an off shoot of the Bull Moose Progressives that held legal title to the name Progressive.[15]

If the Socialists were the left wing of the CPPA, then the Committee of 48 (a reference to the 48 states) was the right wing. Founded by J. A. H. Hopkins, a prominent supporter of Teddy Roosevelt in

1912, with close ties to New York bankers, the Committee had the authority to bestow the name Progressive on the new party. They opposed elite control of the national economy, acted as the brain trust for the new movement and advocated the intellectual middle ground between the extreme pragmatism of labor and the radicalism of the Socialists.[16]

The CPPA met for the first time in Chicago on February 21, 1922. The invitation sent by the leaders of the Railroad Brotherhood stated that the purpose of the meeting was not to form a political party but "to make use of those constructive forces already in existence and by cooperation to attract the widest political unity to resist the economic and social classes who controlled American political authority." The invitation was purposely vague in its content in order to attract the widest possible attendance by liberals and reformers. Three hundred attended from labor and farmer groups, political and economic organizations, and the unaffiliated. Among the speakers were Socialists Morris Hilquist, the secretary of the Farmer-Labor Party; Joy G. Brown; and Herbert Bigelow of the People's Church of Cincinnati. Offices were established in Washington, and it was agreed that active campaigns would be conducted in support of liberal candidates in the 1922 midterm election. Between February and December 32 state CPPA organizations were established in the northeast, midwest, and Pacific regions. Press support was provided in *Labor*, the official organ of the railroad unions with a circulation of more than 400,000.

The CPPA was overjoyed with the results of the 1922 election, when 140 elected members of the House of Representatives who were classified as reform minded and 93 members who were called undesirable, lost. Although the Republicans managed to retain control of the House and Senate, prominent Republican conservatives were defeated, including Rep. Joseph Cannon of Illinois, Rep. Simeon Fess of Ohio, Rep. Joseph Fordney of Michigan, Sen. Joseph Freylinghuysen of New Jersey, and Sen. Porter McCumber of North Dakota. In Wisconsin, the victory of Robert La Follette, as a Progressive, raised his profile as a presidential contender in 1924.[17]

At a second CPPA conference in Cleveland in December 1922, following the midterm election, the Socialists and intellectuals advocated a third party, but labor and farmers were hesitant. The Railroad Brotherhoods did not want to break from the established party system and were considering backing William McAdoo for the Democratic nomination; the farmers, however, wanted to follow the strategy of the Nonpartisan League, which supported sympathetic candidates regardless of party affiliation. In a final vote, the third-party course was rejected, but a platform was adopted that all factions agreed to: (1) operation of the railroads for the benefit of the people and public control of coal mines, water, and hydroelectric power; (2) direct election of president and vice president and direct primaries in all states; (3) barring courts from declaring laws unconstitutional; (4) higher prices to farmers; (5) high income and inheritance taxes and excess-profit taxes; and (6) standards for women in the workplace.[18]

Despite the seeming unity on the platform, an alliance between farmers and workers did not look promising, but events in the United States and overseas would change many minds. In Britain, the trade unions and Socialists under the Labor Party banner replaced the Liberals as one of the two major political parties. In Canada, farmers organized the National Progressive Party, winning 37 seats in Parliament. Closer to home, the unfolding Teapot Dome Scandal of the Harding administration managed to snag William McAdoo. His association with the "interests" turned the unions against him for the Democratic presidential nomination, renewing their interest in a third party.[19]

In February 1924, a third CPPA conference was held in St. Louis, Missouri. Now delegates were optimistic about a third-party run, and a nominating convention was called for Cleveland for July 4, 1924. Invitations were sent to labor organizations, farmers' cooperative societies, and progressive political parties. About 1,000 delegates attended the convention, nearly all representing one of the four component bodies of the CPPA or some other liberal group. The credentials committee screened all delegates, while 100 bouncers kept out Communist infiltrators. It was a young gathering, the majority being under 40, according to an observer. Many undergraduates were in attendance from the Ivy League: Columbia, Yale, Harvard, and Dartmouth. Perhaps the diversity can best be revealed by noting individuals such as Elizabeth Goldstein from Greenwich Village, who the St. Paul *Pioneer Press* noted, "looks like it"; James Francis Murphy, who claimed to represent The Migratory Workers of America; Robert Springer, who witnessed the nomination of Abraham Lincoln in 1860; and Rep. Fiorello La Guardia, who came to let people know "there are other streets in New York besides Wall Street. . . . I speak for Ave A and 116th Street instead of Broad and Wall." (John W. Davis, the eventual Democratic nominee's law offices were at Broad and Wall.) There was less religious fervor than at the Bull Moose Progressive convention in 1912, although a hearty rendition of "Onward Christian Soldiers" lead by a choir of 50 men and women was not neglected. Peter Witt of Cleveland brought cheers from the throng with his "red-meat" denunciation of "babbity" Republicans. Unlike the TR Progressives of 1912, there were no feeble attempts at racial inclusion. Black Yale graduate William Pinkens, representing the NAACP, aroused the crowd when he read a prepared message.[20]

By acclamation, the convention endorsed for president Sen. Robert La Follette, known for his Wisconsin Plan and for being the only candidate who could unite the disparate groups of farmers and workers. La Follette, desiring a progressive Democrat as his running mate, offered Supreme Court liberal justice Louis Brandeis the slot, but he turned it down. Democratic Rep. Burton Wheeler, who resented his party's nominee's (John Davis) connections to Wall Street, accepted.[21]

The platform reflected La Follette's belief that control by industrial monopolies was the great issue of the day. The preamble noted how monopolies "crushed competition," "stifled private initiative," and "exacted exorbitant profits from the public and endangered the peoples' [sic] fundamental rights by the influence of big business in the courts, in congress and in the executive departments." Singled out for special sympathy were farmers who were forced into bankruptcy in record numbers by giant corporations and speculators. The platform promised a "covenant with the people . . . to take back control of the government and destroy the economic and political power of monopoly."[22]

Specific planks included (1) using government to crush private monopoly, (2) public ownership of railroads and delivery of light and power at cost, (3) conservation and use of all natural resources including iron, coal, and timber in the public interest, (4) tax reduction on moderate incomes, repeal of the Mellon tax cuts on the wealthy, and a progressive inheritance tax on the wealthy; (5) congressional override of court decisions; (6) elimination of injunctions against striking workers and the right of collective bargaining; (7) reduction of the tariff; and (8) direct nomination of the president, the right of initiative and referendum, and referendum for or against war.

La Follette was a descendant of John La Follette, a French Huguenot, who fled persecution by Catholics. His grandfather, Jesse, owned a farm in Hardin County, Kentucky, adjacent to Abraham Lincoln's father, Thomas. Both men were defendants in a land dispute, common at the time because of faulty surveys. Both families had something else in common, a hatred of slavery, so they each fled the state.[23]

Like Abraham Lincoln, Robert La Follette was born in a log cabin on June 14, 1855, in Primrose, Dane County, Wisconsin. An intelligent and dedicated youth, he worked his way through the University of Wisconsin where he met Belle Chase, his future wife, who would become a key political advisor. In fact, La Follette had good relations with all women in his life and became a lifelong advocate for women's rights. In 1880, he was admitted to the Bar and ran for district attorney of Dane County in opposition to the candidate supported by the local party boss. After a narrow victory his political career took off. Four years later, in 1884, he was elected to the House of Representatives, serving three terms before being ousted in a Democratic sweep. He resumed his law practice in Madison, breaking with the local bosses and launching a program of reform against "the interests." With the support of liberals and other populists he captured the Wisconsin executive mansion in 1900 and pushed through a reform program labeled the Wisconsin Plan that put him in the national spotlight. The Plan called for legally binding direct primaries; equalization of the tax on corporate property with other property; regulation of railroads in the public interest, including freight charges; and a railroad commission. After five years as governor he took a seat in the U.S. Senate, where he won reelection to three terms. In 1912, as the leading progressive in the country he was the first choice of many progressives for the presidential nomination, but lost out to Teddy Roosevelt.[24]

In the 1924 election, La Follette's opponents were 62-year-old Vermont Republican president Calvin Coolidge and Democrat John W. Davis, a West Virginia–born lawyer who won nomination on the 103rd ballot. The country was emerging from the postwar depression, and prosperity reigned for most of the country. Coolidge skillfully eased out officials who had been tainted by the Harding scandals, as special prosecutors took years to investigate the alleged crimes. Coolidge was able to escape the taint of the Harding years and ran on the slogan "Keep Cool with Coolidge."

The Progressives' campaign opened on a wave of ebullience and idealism. Hiram Johnson noted that in California "all the enthusiasm and fervor in the campaign is in the La Follette camp." For the first time in a presidential election, the candidate kicked off his campaign via a national radio hookup that proved both troublesome and costly. In a swing through several eastern and midwestern states large crowds gathered to hear "Fighting Bob" stump for a better America that would smash the monopolies and restore power to the average American. Large audiences gathered in Buffalo, Cincinnati, Baltimore, and Cleveland, the latter estimated at 20,000. Several well-known public figures supported La Follette, including Sen. Hiram Walker of California and Sen. Smith Brookhart of Iowa,

Justice Brandeis, future justice Frankfurter, black leader W. E. B. Dubois, liberal intellectuals Herbert Croly and John Dewey, Helen Keller, Socialist Norman Thomas, and birth control advocate Margaret Sanger.[25]

Democrats and Republicans focused their fire on La Follette because many believed his candidacy would force the election into the House of Representatives. They called him a dangerous radical who took Soviet money, a threat to the judiciary because he wanted Congress to be able to overturn court rulings, and a danger to political stability because his bid could end up in an electoral deadlock. With the economy improving, the Republicans claimed that his policies would result in a return to hard times. The expression "Coolidge or Chaos" was powerful when workers were more interested in having a job than how much they earned or the conditions of employment. Business men, frightened of a Progressive victory, stepped up contributions to the two major parties, especially to the Republicans, who were able to outspend La Follette 20 to1. Republicans raised $4,400,000 to the Democrats' $900,000 and the Progressives' $220,000.[26]

Attacked by opponents, his friends in the CPPA did not come through with the cash and political support promised. When the Canadian wheat crop failed and demand rose for American wheat, resulting in rising prices, he lost farm support. Although he received the endorsement of the AFL, others in the labor movement never followed through with the promised contributions. They promised $3 million but only came through with 1 percent of that. Labor was concerned about his chances for victory, so they were reluctant to go all out and alienate the major parties they might need when the election was over.

There were also organizational problems. Time was short from the convention in July to the election in November, and it took too long to mobilize. Resources were used up getting on state ballots. La Follette leaned heavily on his Wisconsin supporters who had little experience running a national campaign. By late August, 11 states had no chairman to direct the local efforts. Even where state organizations existed, there was little direction from the national headquarters. A problem emerged between workers and farmers, who had different interests and who competed for influence. One positive note was that publisher E. W. Scripps, an old friend of La Follette, ordered the 25 editors in his newspaper chain to endorse La Follette. The candidate stood on principle, rejecting support from the racist, anti-Semitic, anti-Catholic Ku Klux Klan. The issue of the Klan tore apart the Democrats, leaving it the party of the old South.[27]

The nation decided to "Keep Cool with Coolidge." Cal swept the field, winning 54.3 percent of the popular vote (15,725,003), 382 of the 531 electoral votes, and 35 states out of 48. Democrat John Davis garnered 28.9 percent of the popular vote (8,385,586) and 136 electoral votes, all from all 11 states of the old Confederacy plus Oklahoma. Despite winning 16.6 percent of the popular vote (4,826,471, the third highest tally for any third-party candidacy in the 20th century), La Follette won only 13 electoral votes, all from his home state, Wisconsin. He came in second in 11 upper midwestern and western states behind Coolidge, ranging from Minnesota (41 percent), North Dakota (45 percent), Washington (36 percent), Oregon (25 percent), and California (33 percent). His 11 "silver medals" suggested strong rural support, but in fact, he did even better in many cities with populations in excess of 250,000. He carried Milwaukee with 56 percent, San Francisco with 45 percent, and Cleveland with 42 percent.[28]

Much of La Follette's support came from the Socialist component of the CPPA. In several important states where he ran on the Socialist line (California, Missouri, New York, and Pennsylvania), he gained the support of urban workers. He was strong in New York's heavily Jewish assembly districts, winning between 40 and 50 percent of the vote, and in working-class areas of New Jersey and Pittsburgh. In general, where La Follette had Socialists's support he made a good showing. Socialists were good campaigners who knew how to fend off the major parties, and they put their local organizations to good use, getting his name on the ballot in almost all states. At the same time Socialists scared off many Americans who continued to have faith in the capitalist system and its promise of upward mobility. Another group that stood behind La Follette were the railroad unions, one of the four organizations that made up the CPPA. However, La Follette did not win the support of most workers, suggesting that the lines "Keep Cool with Coolidge" and "Coolidge or Chaos" did their job well. Where he had support from the Scripps press he ran well, but most of the press got behind the Republican slogans.

Despite La Follette's defeat and relatively weaker showing than the 1912 Bull Moose Progressives, the persistent appeal of progressivism in the early 20th century cannot be denied. However, winning elections is not only about ideas, it's also about organizational prowess and financial support. This is where La Follette came up short compared with TR, who also had the prestige of being a former president, which invariably helps third parties. TR was able to attract some of the Republicans' local organizations and, of course, the financial backing of Munsey and Perkins. La Follette had to start from scratch in July 1924, only four months before the election. His organizational problems were compounded by inexperienced personnel choices and chaotic communications between the national organizations and the state and local level. La Follette's original intent was to build a regular party structure after the election of 1924. The Socialists, farmers, and committed progressives met to craft an organization, but with La Follette's death on June 18, 1925, at the age of 69, all hopes for a new party were dashed.

4

George Wallace and His American Independent Party

He knows where to find an itch and he scratches it.
—Joe Azbell, Wallace advisor

In his biography, *George Wallace American Populist*, Stephan Lesher calls his subject the most influential loser in modern American politics. It is hard to disagree with this assessment. Wallace's American Independent Party (AIP) may have been nothing more than a personal vehicle for an audacious run at the White House, but the issues he raised and reveled in—race, law and order, and big government—became integral to the American political scene long after he left national politics. In the tradition of major parties co-opting the issues of politically threatening third parties, the Republicans stole Wallace's thunder in 1968 when it unfurled its southern strategy. Grand Old Party (GOP) presidential candidate Richard Nixon promised white southerners—and northerners—that he would restore law and order, go slow on school integration, and appoint only strict constructionists to the Supreme Court.

Even without pressure from Wallace, who was back in state politics by 1980, Ronald Reagan fashioned his appeal to white southerners in less than subtle racial terms. At the suggestion of Mississippi congressman Trent Lott, Reagan sent a clear message to the white South by kicking off his presidential campaign for the White House with an appearance in Philadelphia, Mississippi, the town where three civil rights workers had been murdered in 1964 by the local Klan. Perhaps Reagan's most notorious foray into Wallace-style race baiting was his description of the fictional Chicago Welfare Queen, who supposedly became a wealthy (black) grand dame with a big ole' Cadillac by gaming various government assistance programs. Here, Reagan ever so efficiently combined two of Wallace's favorite themes: race and the evils of big government bureaucracy. In 1988, George H.W. Bush's campaign unleashed the not-so-subtle Willie Horton commercial, concerning an incident in which a menacing black convict released on a weekend furlough in Massachusetts (Democratic candidate Gov. Michael Dukakis's home state) raped a white woman.

Even Democrats had a hand in Wallace-style politics, if only tangentially. In 1976, Jimmy Carter, endorsed by Wallace, took up his anti-Washington mantra. In 1992, Bill Clinton, while no racist, felt the need to distance himself publicly from the demands of black activists. With the winds from Watergate at his back, Carter carried the entire South with the exception of Virginia, and Clinton was able to peel off four southern states: Georgia, Arkansas, Louisiana, and Tennessee.

Who could have guessed that a short, greasy-haired governor from a poor southern state could have so shaken the national political establishment that the winning presidential candidate for decades after 1968 would keep an eye on his rearview mirror for the shadow of George Wallace. As with so many defining moments in history, the man and the moment converged. The era of George Wallace was one of those moments, so it is essential to look at both the man and the events that shaped him and the era in American political history when this bad good ole' boy made so much political hay.

Relatives of Wallace trace their family roots to Scots Presbyterians who crossed the Irish Sea to settle in Antrim County in Northern Ireland after the Battle of the Boyne in 1690. Under William III, Protestant England defeated Catholic Ireland and encouraged people like Wallace's forbearers to establish farms on Irish land to maintain Protestant control. The first in the family to settle in the American colonies was 17-year-old James Huey, a cabinet maker who arrived in Charleston just before the start of the American Revolution. He enlisted in Washington's army, and when the war ended married Jane Walker another Scots-Irish from Antrim County. The Hueys together with other members of Jane's family moved to Harris County, Georgia, on the Alabama border.[1]

In 1836, 44-year-old gunsmith James Huey, Robert and Jane's son, accidentally shot himself to death while repairing a rifle. His wife, Eleanor McCain Huey, and her 10 children moved to Alabama, where other family members had settled. Eleanor's slave-owning South Carolina relatives assisted her in establishing a homestead in Barbour

County, just after President Andrew Jackson (another Scots-Irish son of Antrim County) forced the remaining Creek Indians to move west. As Lesher observed, in the 300 years after the Battle of the Boyne generations of Wallace's ancestors would prosper largely at the expense of subjugated peoples: Irish Catholics, Native Americans, and African Americans.[2]

George Wallace's grandfather, George Oscar Wallace, born in 1868, lost his father, a sergeant in the Confederate army, only 14 months into life. Baby and mother were forced off their farm, depending on relatives for a hand-to-mouth existence. Eventually, George earned a teaching certificate from the State Normal College. With his income from teaching he financed a two-year medical degree from the Alabama Medical College in Mobile. In 1891, he settled in tiny Clio, Alabama, a hamlet of 13 families founded after the Civil War without the antebellum pretensions of nearby Eufala. George's true intention was to acquire land to provide the freedom and security he craved. Dr. Wallace and his wife, Mary McEachern Wallace, prospered as Clio's population grew to 326 persons by 1900 and as sharecroppers tended cotton and pecans on hundreds of acres that the Wallace's had acquired. One year after their marriage, in 1897, Mary Wallace gave birth to George Corley Wallace Sr., the future governor's father and the first of her seven children. Despite being born into relative prosperity, George Sr. had a difficult life. As a baby, he developed pneumonia, so a lung was removed. Sinus trouble and blinding headaches led to a trip to Montgomery where doctors cut out a piece of his skull to relieve the pain. He attended Methodist Southern College for two years and at the age of 21, married Mozelle Smith, a Florida native who studied classical music at a Mobile preparatory school. George Sr. could not have been the ideal spouse for a refined young woman like Mozelle. Perhaps because of his disabilities or innate personality traits, George Sr. was an irritable feisty companion and a drinker, a habit abhorred by Mozelle. In 1930, during one of his explosive rages, he pulled a knife and threatened the chairman of the Barbour County Board of Education.[3]

In 1919, one year after their marriage, the future governor of Alabama, was born and was named George Corley Wallace Jr. Wallace's earliest recollections was going on house calls with his beloved grandfather in his Model T, when he saw the poverty and suffering of black and white sharecroppers. Dr. George Oscar treated them all for what they could afford to pay. On these outings Wallace would be grilled about religion and asked to recite biblical passages from memory.[4]

Dr. Wallace served on the school board, and in 1928 was urged by George Sr. to run for probate judge of Barbour County. Wallace recalled the night of the election when, as a nine-year-old, he was invited to the county seat courthouse in Clayton for the vote counting. He said it was the most exciting night of his life, being with the adults and seeing politics on the front line. Adding to all the excitement, his grandfather won the election. With the old man's victory, George Sr. used his new found influence to get a part-time state job. Then in 1930 George Sr. had another stroke of good fortune when he inherited $5,000, which Mozelle insisted they use to build a new brick house with running water.[5]

Although the family fortunes rose dramatically under Dr. Wallace, they declined under George Sr. as the Depression took its toll on the family and Alabamans in general. The acreage that George Sr. bought from his father and financed was foreclosed, causing bitterness. However, he retained some land and tenants and farmed much of it himself. Wallace recalled one of his earliest memories was watching his father behind a plough and mule walking down the field and back up again. Wallace described his father as a true-blue southerner and as a yellow dog Democrat—someone who would vote the Democratic line even if the candidate was a yellow dog. He even overcame his fear of a papal takeover of the White House when he voted for Al Smith, the first Catholic presidential candidate, in 1928. George Sr.'s personal discomforts and economic tribulations caused growing bitterness and resentment toward the North, which he blamed for the Great Depression and the impoverishment of the South after the Civil War. He complained about the lack of educational opportunities and the resistance to southerners in high office because northerners "look down on us." Wallace claimed in interviews that his father talked this way until the day he died. Despite their near poverty during the Depression, the Wallaces were better off than most. They always had enough to eat while both George Sr. earned cash from his state job and Mozelle from giving piano lessons at 50 cents a session. However, it became increasingly clear that George Sr. was not successful, and Wallace was determined not to be a failure like his father.[6]

Wallace's boyhood might be described as typically small-town, rural southern. He was obligated by Mozelle to attend church on Sunday and take care of chores on the family farm, but after that he was free to roam the nearby countryside—to swim, hunt, and play ball. Among his friends were whites and blacks, including Carlton McGinnis, a black man who worked for the Wallace family and took the boys rabbit hunting every fall. Perhaps typical of many white southerners, Wallace never displayed hostility toward blacks, just as he accepted segregation as the southern way and never gave it much thought. When he became governor, many of his programs helped blacks and whites economically, but political ambition was another matter. One of his closest advisors, attorney John Peter Kohn, an admitted racist who danced a jig when President Kennedy (JFK) was assassinated, said in a 1966 interview that George Wallace was not a racist. Kohn defined himself as someone who believes that blacks cannot do much more than "jump up and down and eat each other," whereas Wallace possessed far higher regard for blacks but had "enough practical political sense to know cursing Negroes was popular."[7] New Yorker Art Feiner, a crew member with Wallace on World War II bombing missions over Japan, recalled Wallace's racial attitudes but liked him and commented that it was part of his culture and that he didn't expect him to change overnight. With a bomber crew evenly divided between northerners and southerners, some felt that Wallace was testing the racial waters among the northerners.[8]

On his way to adulthood Wallace displayed the personality traits that would drive his quest for high political office. He tested the limits, was a fighter, and despite his small size liked to participate in challenging sports such as boxing and football. In 1936 and 1937, when he won the Alabama Golden Gloves bantamweight championship, his coach, Richard Burkits, called him "one of the hardest hitting little men in the South."[9] A high school teammate called the 5-foot 6-inch, 120-pound quarterback the "smartest football quarterback I can recall in Clio."[10] He was the organizer and driving force behind local athletic events. Once, in the third grade a classmate, Louise Sconyers, nominated him for class president. He won the election and never forgot Louise, as he would never forget the name of political supporters later in life.[11]

At 15 his father arranged for his nomination as a page in the Alabama state Senate in Montgomery. With pay of $2 a day during the depths of the Depression, dozens of young men were vying for four positions. George Sr. urged Wallace to meet all the senators before the vote and make his case. Watching the vote count from the gallery, he garnered the 18 votes, calling this "one of the happiest moments of my life." He tracked down several senators who promised to vote for him but had not, asking them for an explanation. Several claimed they had forgotten about the pledge, but Wallace never forgot them. When he ran for governor 27 years later, he reminded the individuals still around that they owed him, and many became his biggest supporters. As a page he had stood on the bronze star in the capital building where Jefferson Davis took the oath to lead the Confederacy in 1861, and on his first day in Montgomery, he thought, "I knew I would return to this spot. I knew I would be Governor."[12]

After graduating from high school in 1937 Wallace signed up for the two-year law program at the University of Alabama. To cover tuition, he landed a job at the registrar's office through political connections. For books and living expenses he waited tables at a local boarding house. Energy was never lacking in his daily 4:00 A.M. to 11:00 P.M. routine or later in life during numerous political campaigns. Just two months after his first semester began, George Sr. died from a type of typhus. Wallace offered to stay home to help Mozelle support the family, but she turned him down. Eventually, during World War II the fiercely independent Mozelle moved to Montgomery where she got a job with the Office of Price Administration, the wartime anti-inflationary agency. When the war ended, she transferred to the Alabama Department of Public Health, remaining there for 25 years, during her son's terms as governor and as a presidential candidate.[13]

After graduation from the University of Alabama in 1942 Wallace decided to enlist and become a flyer, but was rejected several times because his pulse rate was too high. Following one of the refusals he stopped in a Kresge's five-and-dime store for a sandwich and noticed a pretty 16 year old working behind the counter by the name of Lurleen Burns. She liked him, too. When they met Lurleen's parents, there was a lot of talk about politics and about his ambition to be governor some day. Eventually, Wallace was accepted into the Army Air Corps. On May 23, 1943, he sought out a friend, a Jewish justice of the peace named Adolph Forrester, to perform the ceremony, saying, "I wanted him to marry me and make the fee because he made a living that way." After a three-day honeymoon Wallace went into cadet training in San Antonio, Texas. In September 1944, he was ordered to Denver for training on B-29 long-range bombers. Under the command of Gen. Curtis LeMay, Wallace flew on 11 bombing missions over Japan, turning cities like Tokyo, Yokohama, and Nagoya into fiery infernos.[14]

When the war ended, he returned to Alabama and visited Gov. Chauncy Sparks through the auspices of Billy Watson, a Barbour County power broker. With a letter from Sparks promising help, Wallace was sent to Attorney General Billy McQueen, who had an opening for an assistant, which paid $175 a month. McQueen was polite but assumed that the governor was just trying to pawn a job seeker off on him, but in a call to McQueen, Sparks made it clear he was serious about a job for Wallace, who was hired on the spot. Both Wallace and Sparks knew that this was only a stepping stone to something bigger and better.[15]

In February 1946, Wallace took a leave of absence from the attorney general's office to run for the state legislature from Barbour

County. With a $1,000 inheritance from a great aunt he embarked on a three-month campaign using newspaper advertising and personal visits to homes, cotton mills, school plays, and church meetings. Running as a Populist, he pledged to help the working man, farmers, and the elderly and to advance educational opportunities. He invaded Clayton, the home turf of his principal opponent, a businessman who campaigned in his World War II major's uniform. However, Wallace's combat record, family name, and energy and enthusiasm won the day.[16] MacDowell Lee, who would replace him in the legislature, commented, "Hell, George knew every voter down to the chicken thieves."[17]

Wallace introduced so many bills that the wealthy would finance that he came to be regarded as a dangerous liberal. To improve the standard of living of the average Alabaman, he supported trade schools that young men could attend as an alternative to a university. He said, "Trade schools require just as much intelligence as going to college, and it's just as important to become a good welder as to get a degree in psychology." Wallace wanted to build eight schools, but money was found for only five: three for whites in Dothan, Mobile, and Decatur and two for blacks in Winona and Gadsden. The Dothan school was named the George C. Wallace Sr. Technical School. Demonstrating his interest in black education, he asked for an appointment to the Board of Trustees of Tuskegee University. Some believe he was covering his political bases should blacks become a large voting block in future years. Whatever his motivation he seems to have been a dedicated board member, missing only one meeting between 1950 and 1952.[18]

In 1952, when 80-year-old circuit judge J. Sterling Williams decided to retire, Wallace took one of his many political gambles by announcing his candidacy for a position that presided over family matters such as divorces and property disputes. His chances were not good. His opponent, Preston Clayton, a World War II lieutenant colonel, was so confident that he did little campaigning. He did not understand what he was up against. Now in possession of Dr. Wallace's 1938 Chevrolet, Wallace campaigned all day, reminding voters what he did for them as a legislator. He played the class card—suggesting that they should vote for him, a fellow enlisted man, and that former officers could do the same for Preston Clayton. It all came together when he collected 70 percent of the vote and an annual salary of $8,000, four times what he earned in his first state job after the war. Wallace, however, was never interested in the money. He told his children that the only things that matter are money and power and he never cared much for money.[19]

Wallace was respectful to all who came before the court, including blacks. He tended to sympathize with working men and insisted that African Americans be addressed respectfully in his courtroom, even warning white attorneys not to address black attorneys and their clients as "them" or "these people" but by their proper name and title. Commented J. J. Chestnut, an attorney who represented black cotton farmers in a case against the South's largest cotton oil–processing companies, "George Wallace was the first judge to call me mister in the courtroom."[20]

One year after the former Golden Gloves champ became Judge Wallace, the South was thunderstruck when the U.S. Supreme Court ruled in *Brown v. Board of Education* (1954) that public schools must integrate with all deliberate speed. An anti-integration movement swept the South from Texas to Virginia. Massive resistance to the Court became the order of the day. One year later, with the moral underpinnings from the Supreme Court's decision, Rosa Parks refused to give up her seat on a bus to a white man, sparking the Montgomery bus boycott and the emergence of Dr. Martin Luther King as the leader of the civil rights movement.

In 1956, when federal officials wanted to review judicial records in a Georgia county to determine whether blacks had been systematically excluded from grand juries, Wallace announced that if federal agents tried to access his jurisdiction's records, he would issue an order for their arrest. He denounced the attack on Georgia's sovereignty, claiming that the fine race relations that had existed in the segregated South without violence would now be upended. So appreciated was Wallace's stance that he was invited to address the Georgia legislature.

In 1957, he observed the situation at Central High School in Little Rock, Arkansas, which was under court order to admit nine black students. Gov. Orval Faubus, facing an uphill battle for a third term but noting that plans for integration were proceeding peacefully, declared, without evidence, that violence was about to erupt and ordered the National Guard to prevent the enrollment of the black students. A federal judge found Faubus in contempt, so he removed the Guard and replaced them with 70 Little Rock policemen who were unwilling to stop the violence that Faubus had unleashed. President Eisenhower, deciding that the issue was no longer integration but insurrection, nationalized the Arkansas National Guard and forced southerners to submit for the second time in less than 100 years. Sen. Richard Russell of Georgia accused Eisenhower of using "tactics copied from Hitler." The lessons for the probate judge back in Alabama with political aspirations of his own was that Faubus,

despite ineffectual posturing and lies, won a third term and that resistance to Federal authority was more important than actual results.

Six-foot 8-inch, 275-pound Alabama governor "Big Jim" Folsom,
a Wallace mentor and racial moderate, could not succeed himself in
1958. The state constitution banned two consecutive terms in the
Governor's Mansion, so Wallace decided to take the plunge and
announced his candidacy for governor. Jimmy Faulkner, a racial
moderate, and attorney general John Paterson emerged as Wallace's
main opponents. According to the experts, Faulkner and Wallace
were the frontrunners, but Paterson had several strengths. He was a
die-hard segregationist who had temporarily crippled the NAACP,
the prime mover behind integration. Paterson also played on voter
sympathy over the assassination of his father, who had vowed to
end gambling and corruption in Phenix City, Alabama. Hollywood
inadvertently helped Paterson by portraying his father as a hero in a
B-movie called *The Phenix City Story*. Paterson used clips from the
film in commercials to gain the sympathy and support of voters.

Wallace struggled from lack of funds for advertising and a broken-
down Ford that caused him to miss engagements. Nevertheless,
the Golden Gloves champ was, if anything, a fighter, and he had
learned a thing or two from Big Jim Folsom about how to draw a
crowd. Wallace invited Grand Ole Opry star Minnie Pearl, who
drew more than 1,000 attendees to a high school stadium rally. Wallace
decided to invite her back again, only to learn that her fee was
$3,000 plus expenses for each performance. Ordered by Wallace "to
take care of it,"[21] McDowell Lee, the finance chairman, managed to
convince Clio bankers to cover Minnie's big check. Such were the
improvisations that would characterize a Wallace campaign. He
spoke to any and all groups at crossroads, filling stations, men's
club luncheons, and Folsom-style downtown walkathons, where he
would stop any and all with his pitch.

Wallace was a classic liberal on all issues but race. He promised better schools and roads, old age pensions, and honesty in
government—not something Big Jim was known for—and programs
to attract new industry to the state. His racial stance was segregationist
but without violence. "We shall continue to maintain segregation in
Alabama completely and absolutely without violence and ill will. . . .
I advocate hatred of no man because hate will only compound the
problems facing the South. . . . We ask for patience and tolerance and
make an earnest request that we be allowed to handle state and local
affairs without outside interference."[22] Voters seemed unresponsive
to his sober style, and he soon realized he was losing to Paterson's
hard-hitting, race-baiting campaign. Wallace made the runoff against

Paterson but lost in the final round. Years later Paterson commented on the contest, noting "the primary reason I beat him was because he was considered soft on the race question at the time. That's the primary reason. It was political suicide to offer any moderate approach."[23] After the 1954 Supreme Court ruling outlawing segregation, even middle-class whites who had been mildly sympathetic to African Americans became extreme on the race question. Wallace seems to have agreed with Paterson's later assessment, commenting at the time: "Well, boys no other son of a bitch will ever out nigger me again."[24]

Between Wallace's defeat in 1958 and his next run for the governorship in 1962 racial tensions built throughout the South as blacks demonstrated for voting rights and school integration. No state was more defiant than Alabama. For Wallace, those four years were lost in the political wilderness as he waited for his next opportunity. He hung a law shingle at his brother Gerald's law firm in Montgomery but did little legal work. With no savings, he depended on donations from friends and admirers. He neglected his growing family, consisting of his wife Lurleen and four children. He used his inexhaustible energy looking for an audience and shaking hands in every corner of the state, buttonholing people on the streets of towns and cities in Alabama. He would visit the Elite Café in downtown Montgomery several times a day, shaking hands and chatting away to an endless stream of patrons. He assembled a group of advisors who would stay with him through his run at the presidency. Among them was Seymore Trammell, the son of a tenant farmer, who with the aid of the GI Bill became an attorney and a wealthy entrepreneur. Trammell managed a black gospel group called the Harmony Jubilee Quartet. Although as a district attorney he prosecuted whites for attacking blacks, he never supported black political rights, and in 1958 he had backed Paterson for governor. When he drifted into the Wallace camp, both agreed that race would be the bedrock of the 1962 governor's race. Trammell would raise one-third of a million dollars for Wallace, a huge sum in 1960s Alabama politics. Another pickup player on the Wallace team was Asa Carter, the founder of his very own Ku Klux Klan (KKK) chapter that was responsible for an attack on singer Nat King Cole during a Birmingham performance and the castration of a retarded 33-year-old black man. Not to be left off his most-hated list were Yankees and Jews or anyone who challenged the divinely mandated supremacy of the Anglo-Saxon race. Admittedly, Carter possessed a gift for the Anglo-Saxon language that would come in handy.[25]

In January 1962, Wallace announced his candidacy for governor of Alabama. His main opponent was Big Jim Folsom, trying for a record-breaking third nonconsecutive term. Folsom, always the racial moderate, did not change his stance to conform to the new racial polarization in the state. Wallace's other opponents included a gaggle of segregationists including Bull Connor, who would achieve national notoriety as Birmingham's police chief by unleashing the dogs and high-power fire hoses on Civil Rights demonstrators, and state senator Ryan De Graffenreid, a young, handsome racial moderate from a wealthy Mobile family. At the March 10 kickoff to the campaign, with an encore performance by Minnie Pearl, Wallace joined the segregationist chorus by pledging to defy the federal order to integrate Alabama's schools. One of his best applause lines was "I shall refuse to abide by any such illegal federal court order even to the point of standing in the school house door."[26] He promised not to drink in the mansion, a dig at Folsom for his well-known affinity for the bottle and made an even slyer dig at Folsom for hosting New York's flamboyant black congressman Adam Clayton Powell for cocktails at the Governor's Mansion during his previous term. During this campaign Wallace began using his punchy campaign oratory that would stir up the crowds for the next decade. He attacked federal judge Frank Johnson (a fellow Alabaman) as "an integrating, carpetbagging, scalawagging, race-mixing, bald face liar."[27] Soon crowds would wait for the familiar line and join in with glee. His Populist programs for education, roads, and pensions weren't ignored, but the crowds loved the attacks on integration and federal judges who upheld the High Court's 1954 decision. He later commented: "I started off talking about schools, highways, pensions and taxes but I couldn't make them listen. Then I started talking about niggers and they stomped the floor."[28]

On the eve of the election Wallace was declared the favorite. Despite his racial moderation, Folsom's popularity seemed sufficient to gain him a spot in the Democratic runoff, but disaster struck the Folsom camp on the eve of the election. Folsom arrived at the television studio for a live broadcast, with alcohol flowing through his veins and his wife and children in tow. Against the advice of aides, Folsom went on camera in a drunken stupor, forgetting the names of his children and saying to one, "Which one are you?" Folsom slipped from second place, just barely, allowing Ryan de Graffenreid a spot in the runoff against Wallace. The young moderate could not overcome Wallace's passionate defense of segregation and new attacks on the Supreme Court because it ruled against prayer in public schools. Wallace claimed that whites would lose their jobs and face increased crime, and for the first time he cited racial strife in northern cities caused by federal intervention in local matters. De Graffenreid attacked Wallace as a loud-mouthed demagogue asserting, "we need a man in the governor's chair not in a jail cell to aid our people."

Unfortunately for the young aristocrat he was perceived, just as Wallace was in 1958, as an unconvincing segregationist. In the end Wallace won with 56 percent of the vote. At his inaugural on January 14, 1963, on the same spot that Jefferson Davis was sworn in as president of the Confederate States of America 102 years earlier, he proclaimed in his now famous line (penned by Asa Carter), "Segregation Now, Segregation Tomorrow, Segregation Forever."

Just weeks after Wallace's inauguration, a federal court ordered the integration of the University of Alabama for the fall semester of 1963. University president Frank Rose reported to Burke Marshall, the assistant attorney general for civil rights, that several black applicants looked promising. Rose also reported that although the Board of Trustees might delay the court order, they would not defy it. The problem would be the new governor, who promised to "stand in the school house door." Rose was sympathetic to integration but was caught between the Kennedy administration and a governor who threatened to wreck the University by not asking the legislature for money to run an integrated school. At a meeting called by Wallace at the Jefferson Davis Hotel in downtown Montgomery, Wallace informed Rose he would keep his promise to stand in the school house door if black students were admitted. He also told the Board they did not have to play a role in the resistance, leaving him as the great defender of oppressed whites. Although he wanted to avoid violence, he knew he could not simply roll over to a court order. Talking to columnist Drew Pearson, he ridiculed South Carolina governor Fritz Hollings, who accepted a court order to integrate Clemson University. He said he was "not going to retreat an inch" and reminded Pearson that Alabama's state motto was We Dare Defend Our Rights. He said "I don't care what the other states do. I have announced that I would draw a line in the dust and I shall stand in the door to block the entry of federal troops or Federal marshals or anyone else. They will have to arrest me before they integrate the University of Alabama."[29] Of course Wallace, like Faubus before him, knew that resistance to the federal will was futile and that integration was coming; the question was how to resist, avoid jail, and make political hay with the public. That's all that mattered to Wallace.

The confrontation between the Kennedy administration and Wallace took place outside Foster Auditorium. Aides to the governor arranged for white stage lines to be drawn where Wallace and Deputy Attorney General Nicholas de B. Katzenbach would have their face-off.

Katzenbach was furious to learn that his white line was 20 feet from Wallace, and in the sun, on a day when the temperature was expected to hit 95. Katzenbach ignored the white line and positioned himself within four feet of Wallace, asking for his assurance that the two black students, Vivian Malone and James Hood, would be allowed to register and attend classes. In a statement composed by Asa Carter and John Peter Kohn, which would get widespread media play, Wallace defended the rights of the sovereign states against the power of the central government: "as governor, mindful of my duties and responsibilities under the Constitution of the United States, the Constitution of the State of Alabama, and seeking to preserve and maintain the peace and dignity of this state and the individual freedoms of the citizens thereof, I do hereby denounce and forbid the illegal and unwarranted action of the central government."[30] With cameras clicking, Katzenbach returned to his car. The public confrontation made it seem that Wallace had won, but the two students were registered later that day as the first African Americans at the University of Alabama. When Vivian Malone entered the cafeteria, several white students warmly greeted her and joined her for lunch.

Despite being the real loser at the school house door, Wallace was immediately propelled into the national spotlight, becoming the spokesman for the white South in the battle over integration. Southerners loved his defiance. He knew that he had touched a nerve in the American body politic that no one else had suspected was there. About JFK, he claimed the president ". . .encourages waves of mass demonstrations accompanied by sit ins, stomp downs, kneel ins, lie ins, shout and sing ins." Meanwhile, with the barriers broken at the University of Alabama, federal courts ordered the integration of public schools in the state.

Wallace believed he had the same obligation to make a stand against the integration of the state's public schools. Although most local authorities decided to comply with court orders and bow to the inevitable, Wallace had no intention of leaving well enough alone. Especially vulnerable to violence was Birmingham, where bombings and attacks on civil rights leaders had become a staple of civic existence. However, nothing prepared the nation for the bombing of the Sixteenth Street Baptist Church on the morning of September 15, 1963, when four young black girls attending bible study class were blown to pieces. Roy Wilkins of the NAACP put the blame on Wallace, stating that his actions had "encouraged" the murders. Others felt the same way.

Never losing sight of his personal objectives—a national political campaign—Wallace knew he had to confront and eradicate his image as an agent of violence. He decided to go on a national speaking tour to meet his toughest critics. Harvard was his first stop. Surprisingly, he was not shunned upon his arrival in Boston; rather, he was greeted by aides of Gov. Endicott Peabody; his police escort was openly enthusiastic, and he received numerous invitations to appear on television and radio shows. For the downhome touch, he even dined with Harvard's Alabama contingent. Wallace made a point of reminding his northern audiences that race was a national problem and that the North was hypocritical for looking down on the South for its racial problems while wanting to maintain its own unofficial segregation. Wallace asked employees at a television station how many blacks worked as executives, salesmen, or managers; the answer, none. Even the janitor was white. Wallace winked and walked out the door.[31]

At Harvard he spoke from remarks prepared by Carter and Kohn. Figuring that Harvard types would appreciate a refresher-course in History 101—with material inspired by his father—Wallace noted how the South was devastated by the Civil War and that "it endured the unique distinction of being the only territory conquered by the armies of the United States without having been rehabilitated."[32] Surprisingly, he veered off into hardcore racism, claiming that blacks without white ancestry were easy going, but incapable of much learning. Then he plunged into his real argument against the Supreme Court and the liberals who were subverting the Constitution. As always, his deft handling of hecklers was a high point of the evening. For those keeping score, he was booed six times and applauded fifteen. Dartmouth, Smith, and Brown were next on the agenda. Now he used prepared remarks less, preferring spontaneous Q & A sessions where his quick mind and wit could be put on display. A certain naïveté about the students slipped out, however, when he claimed that scientific evidence proved that black children were damaged more by integration than segregation. The folks back home in Montgomery were as pleased with his performance as mashed potatoes and gravy. Grover Hall, editor of the *Montgomery Advertiser*, credited the college audiences with being "a superior element of young American manhood and who were both knowledgeable and probably adverse to the Wallace viewpoint." Hall wrote: "Wallace disarmed them partially and wowed them entirely. . . . Wallace seems now to have perfected a technique which his friends believed he never would. And that is the deft light touch along with the tub thumping. . . . If Wallace can disarm and charm Harvard, how could he fail elsewhere? Wallace is plainly a potent symbolism on the American scene. His enemies, we predict, will make him more potent. . . . Wallace is an uncommon man, made so by his spirit. . . ."[33]

Early in 1964, Wallace accepted invitations to speak at college campuses in the West and the Midwest. Local media were invited to a news conference; television and radio interviews were arranged, and speeches were scheduled at local clubs. For now, he put aside historical and racial pronouncements and stuck to the theme of the national government's encroachments into people's everyday lives. His target was the proposed 1964 Civil Rights Act (it would become law on July 5, 1964) that would ban de facto racial segregation in schools and discrimination in public places and in employment. Rather than attack African Americans, he would attack the bill as a federal assault on individual rights that raised the specter of a Communist takeover of the United States. Like an old-time vaudevillian on the circuit, Wallace traveled to Oregon, Washington, and Colorado (and even to Canada) and back to Ohio and Chicago, where he reminded viewers that Martin Luther King had called the Windy City the most segregated city in America. In Ohio, Sen. Stephen Young called Wallace "a buffoon who defied the courts of this nation and who has abetted murder and violence and who has tarnished the image of our country throughout the world."[34] Rather than being upset by the attack, Wallace was pleased to realize he was making headway.

A speech at the University of Wisconsin marks the point where his national ambitions entered the realm of possibility. His message against big government and adept handling of hecklers won him the sympathy and support of a group of supporters who urged him to run in the state's April Democratic presidential primary. Lloyd Herbstreit, a conservative Oshkosh businessman turned political organizer, and his wife Dolores were so impressed with Wallace (they believed he could save the nation) that they offered to recruit a slate of Wallace delegates by the March 6 deadline. The Alabaman accepted their offer. Commented Dolores, "The appeal of Governor Wallace is not particularly his civil rights position. His appeal is as a conservative—and an articulate one. He upholds the Constitution, believes in states rights and limited government."[35] The Herbstreits saw Wallace as a harbinger of a conservative movement that would come to full flower with Ronald Reagan in 1980.[36]

Meanwhile, Wallace came under attack from the Wisconsin establishment: government, media, and labor. The state Democratic Party launched an attack on his candidacy, calling him a kook. Labor leaders turned the tables on him, calling him a carpetbagger, and the *Milwaukee Journal* reported that Wallace had described white ethnics as "lesser breeds" than white Anglo-Saxon Protestants. In response, Wallace called up his own ethnic brigade made up of Alabamans of Polish, Russian, Greek, Jewish, Italian, and German origins. He stayed away from direct racially charged rhetoric, but he devoted ample time to attacking the 1964 Civil Rights Act, linking it to a communist conspiracy against the American political system. He went after the Supreme Court, calling it an oligarchy that legislates rather than adjudicates. Using one of his favorite tactics, he reminded audiences that the North, too, has it own racial problems, the only difference being that the South is honest about wanting to keep the races apart to the ultimate benefit of both whites and blacks. He claimed he would have no objection if Wisconsin wanted full integration, but it should be up to a state how to run its schools and businesses and not bureaucrats in Washington. Wallace discovered that white ethnics were most concerned about the impact of the 1964 Civil Rights Act on their schools, neighborhood, and jobs. At a rally at the Serbian Memorial Hall in Milwaukee, Wallace launched an attack against the Act that was interrupted 30 times by applause. In a plea for their votes Wallace stated, "A vote for the little Governor will let people in Washington know that we want them to leave our houses, schools, jobs, businesses and farms alone—and let us run them without any help from Washington."[37]

The results of the election stunned the Democratic leadership. Of the 800,000 Democrats who voted in the primary, one of three voted for Wallace, but many saw race as the key to his appeal.[38] A black man commented: "Me, I'm glad he came up here and done what he did. He jerked the cover off the phonies up here. He says, 'All right boys, I'm for segregation today, tomorrow and forever and I know you cats are, too—but you too scared to admit.' So a quarter of a million of them admit it."[39] Wallace and his supporters believed otherwise, that there was growing support for the curtailment of federal power.

Next he headed for Indiana for the May 5 primary, believing he could do even better there because of the large southern contingent in the population that arrived in waves before the Civil War and after World War II. The state had been a hot bed of Klan activity in the 1920s. He tried to put race aside, claiming that his real goal was to energize opposition to the growing power of Washington over local matters and that it was just a coincidence that racial integration was at the heart of the national power grab. Gov. Mathew Welch, the stand-in for President Lyndon Johnson in the Democratic primary, tried but failed to have Wallace declared ineligible because of irregularities in his petition. Welch harshly criticized the Alabaman as responsible for the deaths of innocent children. He called Alabama a police state where blacks were denied the most basic rights. He mobilized state workers to prevent Wallace from holding rallies on state property and looked to the state AFL-CIO to hand out pro-Welch literature and transport Welch voters to the polls on election day. Wallace reacted to the pro-Welch juggernaut by playing down expectations. A new issue gave Wallace additional fodder for his anti-Washington rhetoric: the plan to bus school children out of neighborhood schools to achieve racial balance. He teamed up with Catholic bishop Fulton J. Sheen, a popular television personality, in calling for Congress to pass a constitutional amendment allowing school prayer. As the campaign drew to a close, Sen. Barry Goldwater, the Arizona Republican, took note of Wallace's appeal outside the South commenting: "The people in the North and West, while they are eager for the Negro to have all his rights[,] . . . don't want their property rights tampered with. The people feel they should have the right to say who lives near them." In the May 5 primary Wallace took 30 percent of the vote, even doing well in the industrialized Northwest.[40]

Wallace then moved on to Maryland 11 days before the May 19 Democratic primary. Exhausted and concerned about death threats, his public appearances were curtailed as he devoted his considerable war chest to radio, television, and newspaper advertising. With so much opposition to the Civil Rights Act, the state's Democratic establishment launched a full-fledged anti-Wallace effort featuring political stars such as Sen. Ted Kennedy and Sen. Abe Ribicoff. Maryland senator David Brewster called Wallace "a professional liar, bigot and an aspiring dictator and an enemy of the Constitution of the United States."[41] When 80-year-old former president Harry Truman, who desegregated the armed forces in 1948, was asked how he would handle Wallace, he said, "I wouldn't handle him at all because he would take care of himself. You don't have to handle a man who is always lying."[42] Right or wrong, Wallace wowed the voters with his opposition to the Civil Rights Act. On housing he said, "If you want to sell to someone with blue eyes and green teeth go ahead." On busing, he said, "[S]ome engineer in Washington shouldn't require you to send your children to a school to achieve racial balance unless you want to let it happen."[43] Voters liked what Wallace was selling. As the campaign wrapped up, Wallace's crowds were in the thousands, whereas Brewster's, even with the big names, totaled in the hundreds. On election day 500,000 voters turned out, 40 percent more than in Maryland's previous primary record. Wallace didn't win a majority but captured a highly respectable 43 percent of the Democratic primary vote, more than in Wisconsin and Indiana. Twice as many blacks turned out in Baltimore to vote against him, but he captured 60 percent of the Catholic vote and most of the white non-Catholic vote as well. When analysts reported that he won a majority of the white vote, his elation caused a momentary loss of self control. Said Wallace, "[If] it hadn't been for the nigger vote, we'd have won it all."[44]

Some observers tried to brush off the near victory, but Sen. Ribicoff took a different view: "We should be candid with one another, Governor Wallace won a big victory and we should not try to gloss over it. Gov. Wallace has proved that there are many Americans in the North as well as the South who do not believe in civil rights. The next twenty years will be years of strife and turmoil in the field of civil rights and it will not be in the South but primarily in the North."[45]

Despite his growing appeal on both sides of the Mason-Dixon line, Wallace's presidential ambitions would come to a halt with the nomination of Barry Goldwater as the Republican presidential nominee in 1964. The Arizona senator was in full agreement with many of Wallace's positions, including his vote against the 1964 Civil Rights Act. Wallace withdrew from the race officially on July 19, but his issues didn't go away. Northern voters continued to resent and resist expanding federal power as millions of blacks who had abandoned the South for northern cities in the postwar years began to encroach on neighborhoods, schools, and jobs.

Down home in Alabama, Wallace faced a new problem that had nothing to do with integration, law and order, or big government. Under Alabama state law he could not succeed himself when his four-year term expired in 1966. He could run again after skipping a term, but if he was out of office, he would lose the resources of the state—staff, bodyguards, and contributions—to mount his planned 1968 presidential campaign. He lobbied the state legislature to change the state constitution, successfully convincing the House, but the Senate refused to budge. In his search for alternatives he finally turned his full attention to his wife, Lurleen. The marriage had not gone well with all his energies and attention focused on the pursuit of political power. There was even talk of divorce, but Lurleen never went through with her threats. Now, she would run for governor as George's stand in on the slogan, "Elect me and I'll let George do it."[46] Her challenger was Ryan de Graffenreid, Wallace's runoff opponent four years earlier. After de Graffenreid died in a plane crash during the campaign, Lurleen swept into office with 68 percent of the vote. It appeared that there was no one could stop the George and Lurleen show ad infinitum![47]

Assured of his power base for the next four years, Wallace and Company turned their attention to the 1968 presidential campaign. Very early on Wallace decided to run as a third-party candidate, believing that neither of the major parties would ever give him the nomination. The advantage of a third-party candidacy is that even winning a plurality in a three-way race would give him a state's electoral votes. Wallace considered the name Free American Party, but in its abbreviated form, FAP, it seemed open to ridicule. He finally decided on the American Independent Party (AIP). As with so much else in the campaign, the name was Wallace's creation. There would be no national convention or local candidates who might distract from the principal star. A lengthy platform was concocted, perhaps the longest in American political history and the most ignored. Simply stated, this campaign would be of Wallace, by Wallace, and for Wallace![48]

The problem of getting on the ballot in 50 states was formidable. Each state had its own rules for ballot access, ranging from 300 signatures in Colorado and North Dakota to 433,000 in Ohio. Just getting accurate information from each state was a challenge. The campaign hired four full-time lawyers—three Alabamans and a South Carolinian—who achieved the remarkable accomplishment of getting Wallace's candidacy on the ballot in all 50 states. California and Ohio were the most challenging. Although the Golden State required only 66,000 names, it had the earliest deadline (December 31, 1967) and required that the signatories change their party registration, something that many Wallace supporters were reluctant to do. In Ohio, where 433,000 signatures were needed, the campaign signed up 500,000, but Ohio secretary of state Ted Brown declared the petitions null and void because they had been filed after the deadline. A federal court upheld Brown's decision, also stating that the AIP was "not a real party." Then, the husband of the Alabama governor did for himself what African Americans had learned to do when they felt they weren't being treated fairly by a local court: he appealed to the Supreme Court in big bad Washington, which ruled in his favor. The decision came so close to election day that all 88 counties had to reprint ballots with AIP included. The Wallace campaign claimed that they gathered 2,700,000 signatures in their national ballot access effort.[49]

The 1968 campaign organization began in a small suite of offices in downtown Montgomery and eventually found its way to a 30,000-square-foot building on the outskirts of the city. To call it an organization may be a misnomer. Ed Pearson, a reporter for the *Birmingham News* said, "[T]he idea of an organized Wallace campaign is ludicrous. . . . [T]he governor is a human machine of spontaneity, a non planner who habitually waits until the last minute before giving his supporting cast a clue."[50] Nonetheless, by mid-1967, four months after Lurleen's inauguration, a small cadre of paid employees—some paid state workers—were at hand. One year later there were hundreds of paid employees and thousands of volunteer true believers. The campaign attracted kooks and far-out right wingers and was never particular about their hatreds, so long as the individuals were useful. The assortment of meatheads would have given the display case of a kosher delicatessen a run for its money. There were neo-Nazis, kluckers (KKK), and Birchites. C. I. "Bill" West of Catoosa, Oklahoma, said he had no idea how many "paranoid schizophrenics" were running around loose until he ran an ad asking for Wallace volunteers. Controlling state organizations was a particular problem for Montgomery. In California, the head of the state operation was skimming off funds for his own right-wing movement. He was replaced by Alvan Mayall, a Bakersfield John Bircher, only to find out that Mayall's main interest was Jew baiting. They discovered the head of the Montana operation had been expelled from the local John Birch Society for "extremism."[51]

Wallace had no idea how much money he would need. More than $9 million was eventually raised, and the campaign ended with a small surplus. About $1 million in seed money came from businesses and individuals who did business with the state, primarily in the form of kickbacks arranged by finance director Seymore Trammell. Asphalt suppliers and consulting engineers who wanted state highway contracts were tapped, allowing Wallace to fulfill a campaign promise to expand the state highway system. State control of liquor sales provided another source of funds. When Wallace became governor in 1962 two Baltimore distributors, Montebello Liquors, Inc. and Majestic Distilling, suddenly emerged as the state's favored suppliers of gin, vodka, and bourbon. Well-known brands were banished from the shelves and unheard of names like Shooting Lodge Scotch and Old Settler Bourbon suddenly appeared at higher prices.[52] In a federal law suit alleging payoffs to Wallace administration officials, Al Bernstein of Montebello denied any illegal activity stating, "[T]hey are the most strait laced people in the world."[53]

Wallace attempted to raise money from other big donors but was not very successful. There were exceptions. The actor John "Duke" Wayne sent in three donations of $10,000 each, with a special message, "Sock it to em, George."[54] Rumors abounded that ultraconservative Texas oil man H. L. Hunt (keeper of three wives and assorted mistresses) was secretly funding Wallace. The two had met several times and kept up a correspondence, but Hunt never came through. However his son, Bunker, a 300-pound, paranoid, reactionary, anti-Semite, made a cash contribution of more than $250,000.[55]

More than 80 percent of the contributions came in small donations of less than $50 from direct mail solicitations and small change at rallies and luncheons. Especially lucrative were $25-a-plate fund raisers at church halls and motel meeting rooms. At campaign rallies, donations of $5, $10, or even $25 were encouraged. Volunteers were asked to approach friends. Pretty, young "Wallace girls" mingled with the crowds at rallies asking for small change. Seemingly inconsequential, this technique raised thousands. After a series of 20 rallies throughout the South, aides counted $35,000 in small change and bills donated by poor working-class people. An Alabama advertising agency strung together some footage of Wallace's best applause lines intermingled with a plea for money, called "The Wallace Story." Airing on small television stations throughout the South, the Midwest, and the Rocky Mountain states, Wallace's people were stunned by the response.[56] Said an aide, "The money is coming in by the sock full, it's a gold mine."[57]

Other than the candidate himself, perhaps the best pitchperson was a fiftyish flashy blonde (who claimed to be thirty-eightish) by the name of Ja Neen Welsh. A publicist from Indiana who latched on to the campaign (and Wallace) after a Hammond rally, she traveled on the candidate's plane and appeared at rallies. She seductively stroked the microphone and shouted to the audience, "I want *you* for the Wallace rebellion." As the bucket brigade made the rounds, she promised a big hug and a kiss for all $100 donations. Hands dug deep into pockets and came up with lots of cash. Eventually, campaign manager Bill Jones gave Ja Neen the hook. She proved to be a little too raunchy for most of Wallace's conservative followers.[58]

Wallace did not expect to win the presidency. He thought he could carry the Deep South and the border states, deny Nixon and Humphrey an electoral college majority, and then throw his support to the candidate who offered him the most concessions. Some speculated that 1968 was only a sparring match for the former Golden Glove champ; the real event would be in 1972. Of course, more than anything Wallace loved to run, and he would have been more than delighted at the political havoc he might create.

By mid-September Wallace was riding high in the polls with nearly 25 percent of the popular vote.[59] Although race was at the core of his message, it was not so blatant as it had been in Alabama. Riots in northern ghettos, anti-Vietnam war protests, and growing resentment at the Washington establishment caused rage and backlash among the white working class, described by Wallace as "cops, dime store clerks, hard hats, factory workers, beauticians, [and other] god fearing, tax paying law biding, good folks."[60] They feared for their jobs and neighborhoods and felt threatened by the demands of black militants and resented the pampered, unpatriotic, long-haired, college-educated war protesters. Wallace's people did not necessarily approve of the war; they just wanted the politicians in Washington to let the generals win it. Their sons fought and died in Vietnam while many protesters received deferrals and managed to avoid the draft altogether. Wallaceites saw a distant government in Washington to whom they paid taxes as not representing their interests. If anything, the bureaucrats were hostile to them and seemed to favor the troublemakers. They wanted to send a message to Washington, and the little man from Alabama would be their herald.

Although Wallace's personal roots ran deep into the South's past, his politics were not about past defeats and old heroes. Rather, his concerns and those of his followers were about more recent developments that were shared by some whites everywhere. White southerners disapproved the court's 1954 decision to integrate schools, whereas in the North the 1964 Civil Rights Act generated resentment, especially in tight-knit ethnic neighborhoods that abutted black ghettoes. As blacks, students, and women started to rebel against the existing order, and traditional beliefs about God, country, and family, the innate conservatism of Wallace's people made them react strongly to the threat posed to their position in it. Like any successful demagogue, whether it be Huey Long or Adolf Hitler, Wallace's genius was in understanding their fears, passions, and prejudices and expressing these emotions in a language and style they could understand and relate to. His attack on big government in Washington was personified by "a brief case carrying, pointy headed liberal, pseudo intellectual who can't park his bicycle straight." The indifference of the two major parties to the plight of the working man went down as ". . . . Tweedle dee and Tweedle dum. . . . [T]here's not a dime's worth of difference between the national Democrats and Republicans." Attacks on school busing to achieve racial balance came down to an abbreviated Anglo-Saxon term *busin*. Law and order became the watchword for the demand that urban riots and war protests cease. Just in case rioters didn't get the message, Wallace promised his own final solution, stating, "If any demonstrator ever lays down if front of my car, it'll be the last car he ever lays down in front of."[61]

A typical day on the campaign trail consisted of rallies at 10:00 A.M., noon, and 2:00 and 4:00 P.M., followed by a fund-raising dinner that might be $100 a head, but was more likely to be $25, and then finally, an evening rally. Country music warmed up the crowds and enlivened the events. As Wallace ascended the platform, the musicians broke into a rendition of "Dixie." His people never tired of hearing the same lines over and over again.

Nixon and Humphrey responded vigorously to the Wallace threat. At risk to Humphrey was the traditional Democratic labor vote in the North. For Nixon, Wallace was grabbing the southern white vote that would have gone Republican after Democratic sponsorship of the Civil Rights Acts of 1964 and 1965. In an effort to attract the Wallace voter, Nixon implemented what came to be known as the GOP's southern strategy. He co-opted Wallace's issues, hoping to attract Wallace's softer support. Nixon promised to put law and order at the top of his agenda, to go easy on school integration, and appoint only strict constructionists to the Supreme Court who would interpret the law, not make it. He enlisted the support of segregationist South Carolina senator Strom Thurmond and appointed Spiro Agnew, his running mate, to be his wooer-in-chief in Dixie. Nixon slyly endorsed a freedom-of-choice plan for schools, in which students could be enrolled outside their neighborhood on a voluntary basis. Nixon knew that without coercion very few whites would enroll their children in a ghetto school and most poor blacks might not have the inclination or resources to transfer their children to a white neighborhood.[62]

Humphrey called the freedom-of-choice plan a subterfuge for continued segregation. At a rally in Anaheim, California, Nixon said, "I do not believe that education is served by taking children who are two or three grades behind and busing them across to another district."[63]

The co-opting of his best issues by the opposition, his disastrous selection of a running mate, and a counterattack by northern unions led to a precipitous decline in Wallace's support in the final weeks of the campaign. Wallace never wanted a running mate, thinking that no one could add to his magic. However, ballot access in many states required a number two, so Wallace complied by appointing former Georgia governor Marvin Griffin as a temporary stand in candidate. When the time came to anoint the actual running mate, several names were considered. Discussions were held with Texas governor John Connolly, a Vietnam hawk, but to no avail. Conservative Boston mayor Louisa Day Hicks was another possible, as was FBI director J. Edgar Hoover (Mr. Law and Order), and from a border state—perhaps bordering on the inane—was Kentucky Fried Chicken founder Col. Harlan Sanders. In the end, Wallace's staff narrowed the field to two finalists: former Kentucky governor

A. B. "Happy" Chandler and retired Air Force general Curtis LeMay. The amiable, 70-year-old Chandler, who appeared to be the frontrunner, was in retirement, raising tobacco, and playing a lot of golf, perhaps too much golf thought Chandler, who longed for some action. The thinking was that Chandler could solidify the vote in the border states and in the North and frighten nobody, but there were problems with the racial moderate. He was baseball commissioner when Jackie Robinson became the first African American major leaguer, and he presided over the integration of Kentucky's public schools in 1947, seven years before the 1954 decision. Wallace and Chandler met in a motel in Louisville for a final interview, and an official announcement was set when word leaked about the impending selection. Several Kentuckians, however, threatened to leave the Wallace camp over Chandler's racial views, and Trammell asked Chandler to repudiate his record as a racial liberal. Chandler refused and was dropped from the ticket.[64]

Curtis LeMay, Wallace's World War II commander, was at first reluctant to become his running mate. He liked retirement in California and made good money as a consultant for a military supplier that he would have to give up if he ran. He also knew that getting into politics meant more 18-hour work days. Wallace, too, had his doubts about Old Ironpants (so nicknamed by his men because he demanded they fly direct to their bombing targets regardless of enemy defenses). LeMay might out shine him, and Wallace, the former enlisted man, may have been reluctant to give orders to his old commander, but the General had strengths that could help the ticket: He could be portrayed as Mr. Law and Order, he offered hope for victory in Vietnam, and he believed that Communists were behind the civil rights movement. On the other hand, he was proud of having integrated the Strategic Air Command.[65]

LeMay had some extreme views about America's defense policies that he expressed in his book, *America in Danger*. He looked back to a time when we could have destroyed Russia without breaking a sweat and brushed aside the idea of limited no-win wars. He demanded nuclear superiority over Russia and an all out bombardment of North Vietnam "until we have destroyed every work of man in North Vietnam if that what it takes to win the war." Wallace advisors were aware of LeMay's hawkish views and tried to prepare him for the inevitable question about the use of nuclear weapons in Vietnam. Wallace personally posed a question that the press might ask and advised LeMay how to answer it. In spite of this, Old Ironpants—and Wallace—experienced the ultimate meltdown on national television when a reporter named Jack Nelson asked, "General, do you think it is necessary to use nuclear weapons to win the war in Vietnam?" LeMay replied: "We can win the war without nuclear weapons, but I have to say that we have a phobia about nuclear weapons. I have to say there may be times when it would be most efficient to use nuclear weapons. However, public opinion in this country and throughout the world would throw up their hands in horror when you mention nuclear weapons just because of the propaganda that's been fed to them. I've seen film of Bikini Atoll after nuclear tests, and the fish are all back in the lagoon, the coconut trees are growing coconuts, the guava bushes have fruit on them, the birds are back." And just in case everybody wasn't yet convinced of the ultimate benevolence of nuclear weapons, LeMay added, "Its rats are bigger, fatter, and healthier than they ever were before." Wallace, stunned, pushed his former commander aside and said, "General LeMay isn't advocating the use of nuclear weapons, he's just discussing them with you." Nelson followed up with, "[I]f you found it necessary to end the war[,] would you use them, would you?" LeMay said, "If I found it necessary[,] I would use anything we could dream up." After more attempts at "clarification," the news conference ended. Wallace was as furious, as his opponents were elated. Humphrey referred to the Wallace ticket as the "bombsey twins." The LeMay fiasco hurt Wallace among the leaners, especially northern women who considered him dangerous on the nuclear issue and who were never comfortable with the threat of violence at his outdoor events.[66]

There were also problems among union members in the North and the Midwest who liked his segregationist views. A high official at a Chevrolet plant commented, "The men in the plants want to zap the Negro. It's as simple as that." Top union leaders decided to go after Wallace—and help Humphrey—when evidence emerged about the high Wallace vote. Using leaflets, meetings, and word of mouth, the unions pointed to the miserable conditions in Wallace's home state. They reported union-busting activity by a Wallace aide at a steel mill in Selma, that Mr. Law and Order's home state had the highest murder rate in the nation, and that Alabama ranked near the bottom of the 50 states in per capita annual income, per pupil expenditures in public schools, and literacy. To their credit the unions also went beyond the fears and narrow self-interest of the workers. They attacked Wallace for being a racist, an enemy of the highest ideals of the nation and of democracy: "The Wallace formula of divide and rule is a formula for national disaster. The hatreds and fears he is trying to exploit would be worsened, not cured. America should turn again, as it always has to the fundamental wisdom of the constitution which links domestic tranquility with the promotion of the general welfare. We must work together to make America whole, to build one nation united in the belief in the worth and dignity of every person."[67]

The co-opting of his issues, the LeMay disaster, and the frontal assault by the unions all served to cut Wallace's final election tally to 13.5 percent from nearly 25 percent at his zenith. However, his total vote of 9,906,000 was the highest ever to date in American history for a third-party candidate, and he denied Nixon, the victor, a popular majority. Wallace's Electoral College count was a disappointment. He only carried five Southern states—Alabama, Mississippi, Georgia, Louisiana, and Arkansas—for a total of 46 electoral votes. He emerged second in North Carolina, South Carolina, and Tennessee, and in the three remaining states of the old Confederacy—Texas, Virginia, and Florida—he came in behind both Nixon and Humphrey.[68]

Humphrey managed to turn a 15-point deficit to near victory by election day. His break with President Johnson over the bombing of North Vietnam (Humphrey came out against it) and help from the unions nearly won it for the vice president. Nevertheless Nixon triumphed with 43.4 percent and 301 electoral votes compared with Humphrey's 42.7 percent and 191 electoral votes. Nixon's southern strategy turned out to be good politics; it greased the way to victory in five states that should have been Wallace's: Virginia, North and South Carolina, Tennessee, and Florida. Of the 11 Confederate states only Texas went for Humphrey. Of Wallace's 9,906,000 popular votes, 5,508,000 or 51 percent originated in Dixie. With the votes from six other states—California (487,000) New York (359,000), Illinois (391,000), Pennsylvania (379,000), Michigan (332,000), and Ohio (467,000), he reached 7,488,000 votes or 76 percent of his total.[69]

Obviously, Wallace did not achieve his electoral goal of causing a deadlock in the Electoral College, thus throwing the election into the House of Representatives where he could negotiate the issues that meant the most to his people. Of course, Wallace's campaign was more about complaints, resentments, and anger than it was about policy, unless he proposed reversing the Supreme Court's ruling in *Brown v. Board of Education* or repealing the 1964 and 1965 Civil Rights Acts, which his platform did not advocate. However, Wallace did force Nixon to come out against school busing. Harry Dent, an associate of Strom Thurmond, was appointed a deputy White House council with the responsibility of defending the interests of the South (and Nixon's reelection). There were other accomplishments. Wallace managed the extraordinary feat of getting on the ballot in all 50 states. Perhaps most of all, he discovered a vein of electoral gold in the American body politic that would be mined for decades after the 1968 election, and for a man who was still a relatively youthful 49, 1972 was only four years away.

Gov. Lurleen Wallace died of cancer at the age of 41 in the spring of 1968. Lt. Gov. Albert Brewer took charge and never interfered with Wallace's use of state resources for his presidential campaign. However, if Wallace intended to make another run at the presidency, he needed to regain his base at the Governor's Mansion in Montgomery. Therefore, in March 1970, he broke his promise to Gov. Brewer and declared his candidacy for governor by entering the Democratic primary, where winning the primary was tantamount to election. Reporters noted an absence of the old passions among Alabamans as Wallace stumbled around the state in search of the issues that would ignite his campaign. He promised more and better state services and a woman in the cabinet (why not, one had just been governor) and defended Lt. William Calley—locked up in nearby Fort Benning, Georgia—who, as commander of a unit in Vietnam, was charged with the murder of 100 Vietnamese civilians at a village named My Lai. Gov. Brewer, never known as a spellbinder, campaigned on the slogan, Full Time for Alabama, and drew the support of the state's business and media elite. He promised honest government open to all citizens. Blacks rallied to him and, to the surprise of many, the reticent Brewer was actually generating enthusiasm.[70]

Watching this all from far-away Washington, the Nixon White House hoped that Brewer would finish off Wallace and eliminate the threat to Nixon's reelection in 1972. With the primary just two months away and polls putting Brewer in the lead 53 percent to 34 percent, his campaign was threatened by a shortage of funds. Thus Nixon decided to hand over to a Brewer representative $100,000 in hundred dollar bills from a secret bank account at a rendezvous in the lobby of the Sherry-Netherland Hotel in New York City. Meanwhile the Wallace team had commissioned a secret survey that revealed the extent of Brewer's popularity, along with some nagging doubts about his stand on integration. Wallace used this information to accuse Brewer of forming an alliance of African Americans and liberal whites, whom Wallace described as, "Sissy britches from Harvard who spend most of their time in a country club drinking tea with their fingers stuck up" (i.e., they won't fight for Alabama). Wallace's attacks were too little and too late. Brewer won the primary, defeating Wallace with 422,000 popular votes to 414,000. With 180,000 votes going to five other candidates, Brewer fell short of the majority, so a runoff was called. No first-place finisher had ever lost the runoff in 20th century Alabama politics, so Wallace's chances looked grim. Nixon, drooling, decided to make another cash contribution to Brewer, tripling his earlier donation, and once again using the lobby of the Sherry-Netherland for most of the handoff. Wallace, desperate, decided to throw away the image he cultivated in 1968 as a nonracist defender of states' rights and went all out with a new, old strategy spelled out by a close aide as, "Promise them the moon and holler nigger." Leaflets were distributed in small towns and working class districts of the state's cities showing Brewer meeting with Cassius Clay (soon to be Muhammed Ali) and Black Muslim leader Elijah Muhammed. Another flyer showed a picture of a beautiful blonde five-year-old in a bathing suit surrounded by seven grinning black boys. The caption read: "This could be Alabama four years from now. Do you want it?" When black leader John Cashin demanded that Brewer endorse the hiring of at least 50 black state troopers, Wallace people lunged at the opportunity, producing a radio commercial that went as follows: Ominous music, followed by a police siren and then the fantasy, "Suppose your wife is driving home alone at 11 at night. She is stopped by a highway patrolman. He turns out to be black. Think about it. Elect George C. Wallace." Wallace also played the class card, reminding country people and working-class whites how the Mountain Brook crowd (a wealthy white suburb of Birmingham) and by extension, Brewer, looked down on them as a bunch of rednecks. In the end the old black magic worked; Wallace overcame history by playing to it, defeating Brewer 52 to 48 percent (560,000/526,000). His victory was attributed to his willingness to go all out and fight for white Alabama.[71]

Now, looking forward to the 1972 presidential race, Wallace began attacking Nixon's freedom of choice program for school integration and latched onto the issue of busing to achieve school integration. Meanwhile, Nixon officials who had been investigating corruption in state government in Alabama put 75 special investigators on the job, hoping to build a case against Wallace and his administration. The governor's tax returns and those of his brothers and supporters who did business with state agencies were scrutinized. When the probe ended, a grand jury planned to indict Wallace's brother, Gerald, but not Wallace, and a dozen Wallace supporters who made millions off state contracts. Nothing happened for a while. Then on January 12, 1972, the Justice Department announced that it was dropping the case and dismissed the grand jury. The next day Wallace announced to the public that he was abandoning the AIP and would run for the presidential nomination as a Democrat. No one ever admitted that a deal was made between

Nixon and Wallace, but the impression of an arrangement was clear for all to see.[72]

After a strong showing in the Democratic primaries in Florida and several other states in the spring of 1972, Wallace headed to Maryland, which along with Michigan would be the last of the major state contests. He became increasingly concerned about the emotional intensity of the crowds, which, of course, he himself had stirred up. He commented to a reporter from the *Detroit News*, "I don't mind the kids. They're just young and full spit and vinegar. They ain't the ones I fear. The ones that scare me are the ones you don't notice. . . . I can just see a little guy out there that nobody's paying attention to. He reaches into his pocket and out comes a little gun, like that Sirhan guy got Kennedy." In Maryland, he felt the heat even more, saying, "Somebody is going to get killed before this primary is over." On May 11, a crowd of black protesters in Hagerstown forced him to end his speech early; in Frederick he was hit by a rock. On May 15, at a rally in Wheaton, Fred Farrar, a television newsman, noticed Arthur Bremer, who, because of his weirdness and "a smirk that was almost spine tingling" made Farrar want to get on camera. Sporting a Wallace button, Bremer asked a secret service man if he could shake the candidate's hand, but before that encounter could be choreographed, Wallace was hustled off to lunch. Later that day at the Laurel Shopping Center rally, Wallace thrilled the crowd with his usual script, attacking, among others, big government, the federal courts, and pseudointellectual college professors. When the speech ended, Wallace was moving to greet his fans, when suddenly Bremer stepped from the crowd and unloaded five shots from a .38 caliber revolver into him. Bremer was wrestled to the ground by onlookers, and an ambulance arrived minutes later, taking take the governor to an area hospital. One of the bullets had penetrated his spinal chord, causing him to lose all function from the waist down. His quest for the presidency suddenly ended.[73]

Actually, Bremer wanted to shoot Nixon, whom he described as The Big Bastard but was unable to get to him, so Wallace became the victim by default. According to Bremer, Wallace's positions on the issues had nothing to do with it. Later, as Wallace lay in a hospital bed in Birmingham, Alabama, the AIP held its 1972 convention in Louisville, Kentucky. With 2,000 delegates from 40 states in attendance, Wallace was offered, but refused, their presidential nomination. John G. Schmitz, a former congressman and member of the John Birch Society from southern California, was nominated to run with Thomas Anderson, a farm magazine publisher. The ticket garnered 1,101,000 votes, or 1.42 percent of the total cast in 1972. Nixon swept to a second term with 61 percent of the popular vote and 520 electoral votes. His opponent, George McGovern, carried only Massachusetts and the District of Columbia. Wallace stayed active in Alabama politics, finishing out his four-year term, running again, and winning in 1973 and 1983. The AIP meandered through the 1970s and 1980s, never winning more than 42,000 votes.[74]

5

Ross Perot

The only one who can defeat Ross Perot is Ross Perot.
—David Gergen, presidential advisor and journalist

The 1992 candidacy of Ross Perot was unprecedented in the annals of independent or third-party presidential politics. The Texas billionaire garnered more votes than any non-major-party candidate in American history. Before he suddenly and inexplicably left the race in July, only to return in October, he led in the polls and in the Electoral College. If he had behaved himself, instead of acting capriciously self-indulgent, this 62-year-old political virgin might have become the 42nd president of the United States. Yet, even after he lost to Bill Clinton in November, his issues and personal influence remained so potent that he and his supporters contributed mightily to the 1994 congressional realignment that gave the Republicans majorities in both houses of Congress for the first time in more than 40 years. To understand Perot's political rise and fall as well as his second coming, it is helpful to know why he came to have this special hold on so many Americans.

To devotees of the *Larry King Show*, the guest lineup for the week of February 18, 1992, looked like the usual array of the rich, the famous, or the forgettable, but in the middle of that week, on Wednesday, February 20, the appearance of a certain Texan would be anything but forgettable. Perot expressed his dismay about the state of the nation, pointing to huge budget deficits, the loss of good-paying factory jobs, and the so-called "mess in Washington," where lobbyists with too much clout worked against the interests of the average American. Several times during the interview King asked Perot if he would consider running for president. Perot ducked and parried, but the host persisted. Finally, the payoff came when Perot said he would run if volunteers registered him in all 50 states—not 48 or 49, mind you, but 50. It all seemed like a decision made on camera before millions. Perot's wife Margot was "surprised." Tom Luce, his long-time friend and lawyer, said he nearly fell off his treadmill. Son-in-law Clay Mulford and Perot's sister Bette both thought it was spontaneous, but like so much else about the man from Texarkana there's more to the story.[1]

In many ways the young Ross was unexceptional. He was not a great student or athlete, nor did he come from the kind of wealth that would give him an edge in life. Contrary to the myth he tried to create about a poor boy's rise from the depths of the depression (he was born on June 27, 1930), Perot came from a solidly middle-class background. His father Gabriel Elias Perot, a descendant of French traders who drifted to Texas from Louisiana before the Civil War, was a successful broker who bought cotton from planters and arranged for its sale and shipment overseas and up north. Together with his mother Lula May Ray, a housewife, Ross and his sister, Bette, grew up in a loving but disciplined Methodist household. Although Perot recalls a struggle through the depression, friends have a different memory. They recall a car, a brick house in a middle-class neighborhood, and the wherewithal to pay tuition for Ross and Bette to attend a private grammar school.[2]

What he lacked in athletic ability and book smarts he made up for with self-assurance and a highly competitive streak. Within 13 months of joining the Boy Scouts he achieved the rank of Eagle Scout (the average time was two to four years). Classmate Ed Overholzer recalled: "It was the competition . . . that set him apart. He went after it like nothing I had ever seen. . . . Even at twelve you could see the part of him that wanted to succeed."[3] One of his great strengths throughout life was as a debater. On the high school team, confidence and politeness won him kudos from his teachers. Classmates liked him, although some noted his "take-charge" attitude put some off. Said one, "Ross thought a lot of himself. . . . He always had a very healthy ego."[4] At 17 he was anxious to leave Texarkana for a taste of the wider world. A neighbor whom he admired attended the Naval Academy at Annapolis, so Perot applied in 1947 but did not receive the appointment. Instead, he enrolled at Texarkana Junior College where, once again, his competitiveness set him apart. He revived the class yearbook and was elected class president. Speech instructor Claude Pinkerton saw him as a leader with a fine personality, but he was an average student.[5]

Eventually he was admitted to Annapolis, class of 1953. He liked the Naval Academy because performance mattered, not family background, wealth, or political connections. Here, too, he was an average athlete and student (his class ranking was 453 of 925) but an exceptional debater. Classmate Arles Simmons commented, "He did a superb job. . . . [T]he whole class knew who he was. That's how he really got started."[6] James Chelsey, another classmate, called him Senator Perot. In evaluations by classmates and officers that combined grades and athletic achievement, where the highest ranking was six stripes, Perot earned four stripes but ranked in the top 1 percent for leadership. This was a remarkable achievement for someone with academic and athletic shortcomings. In his junior and senior years he was elected class president. When he headed the Honor Committee, the son of a VIP violated the honor code. Perot threatened to quit when everybody wanted the charges dropped. A classmate commented, "Ross was very ethical. Black was black and white was white. There were no shades of gray for him."[7]

On active duty he revealed another side of his character. On the destroyer USS *Sigourney*, Perot commanded the shore patrol because he was the only officer who didn't pursue women. He rescued drunken sailors from bawdy houses; in the Mediterranean he chased down naked men on beaches, recalling, "I hauled more men out of jail in the first two or three days than ever in my entire life." Although disgusted with the behavior of the enlisted men, he was especially dismayed with officers, including Annapolis graduates. Soon he was appointed chief engineer, a post usually reserved for more experienced officers. Toward the end of 1954 a new commander, Gerald J. Scott, took charge of the *Sigourney*. With a more relaxed style than his predecessor, Scott let the crew gamble and indulge in other activities that were not technically against the rules. In a trait that would become a pattern in his life, Perot clashed with authority. He controlled the liquor stock so that Scott had to go through this junior officer for a drink. The Texan managed the recreation fund that Scott wanted to use to redecorate his cabin. Perot refused Scott's requests on both counts. Scott couldn't believe this young engineer wouldn't let him have a drink or the cash. Years later he would deny the charges, but shipmates support Perot's version. Recalls Ed Ditzel, "He was strictly by the book, there was no deviating."[8]

Naval Academy graduates were expected to serve a minimum of four years on active duty in return for their free education, but Perot's frustration with Scott and other conditions made him want to resign early. On advice from Congressmen Wright Patman, he submitted a letter of resignation to Capt. Scott requesting that he be placed in the Naval Reserve. The tone of the letter was described as that of an indignant prude. Among his complaints were that the navy rewarded seniority over performance, that loose morality was tolerated even among married men (he resented having to hand out penicillin pills), and that most decisions seemed to be made on the basis of what was best for a career rather than for the navy. His father appealed his case to Sen. Lyndon Johnson and Sen. Price Daniels; his mother called Patman directly. Meanwhile, Commander Scott suggested that a toned-down letter be sent to the Secretary of the Navy. Perot's revised appeal cited the lower moral standards in the regular navy compared with Annapolis, but the main thrust of the missive was his change of heart about a naval career. He also gave his father's illness as a reason for the request. The case shot up through the ranks with notations that Perot ". . .was emotionally maladjusted for a regular navy career," and "too immature to be entrusted with the leadership responsibilities inherent in sea duty." A final review from Vice Adm. James L. Holloway, who knew Perot from the Naval Academy, denied his request, but ordered all the negative comments removed from his file in two years. He was ordered back on active duty to the antisubmarine carrier *Leyte*. During his presidential run in 1992, a reporter for the *Los Angeles Times* obtained a copy of the file with the unflattering evaluations. At the time, Perot offered a variety of reasons for wanting an early release, but blamed Bush officials for leaking the records in order to embarrass him.[9]

Back on active duty he renewed his commitment to the navy, receiving positive evaluations and additional responsibilities including that of assistant navigator. Something else good emerged from the resignation episode. An executive from IBM, impressed with Perot's handling of maneuvers on the *Leyte*, asked him if he would be interested in interviewing for a position with IBM. When ultimately offered the job he insisted on a position in Texas. IBM agreed, so in the summer of 1957, Perot and his wife Margot Birmingham Perot, a Pennsylvania native, drove off to their new life in Dallas.[10]

IBM was more like the Naval Academy than the active service. IBM required the uniform (dark suits, white shirts, and conservative ties), demanded moral behavior, and rewarded hard work and individual initiative. Perot's ambition stood out. He told office manager Henry Wendler, "I want your toughest accounts because I want to make some money." Soon he became the star performer, but alienated his colleagues when he claimed the only reason he did better was because he worked harder. He started to have some doubts about IBM when the commission structure was reset lower.

Meanwhile, unknown to IBM, Perot was spending more time at Texas Blue Cross, where he learned the basics of data processing from the client's perspective. He tried to interest IBM in the data-processing service business, but with 80 percent of their revenue coming from hardware there was little interest in the software end. So Perot quit in 1962 to set up a data-processing business offering automated billing, payroll, inventory, and accounting services. He saw a huge market for leasing downtime on existing equipment, commenting, "There was tremendous demand but I realized that people did not want computers[;] they wanted the results that came from computers." That was the idea behind his company, Electronic Data Systems (EDS). Perot drew an analogy with his experience in the navy. "It was the same old story. If I had stayed in the navy, I probably would have retired a captain because I would have been too controversial. I would have been too direct. If I stayed at IBM, I'd be somewhere in middle management getting in trouble and being asked to take early retirement."[11]

By 1964, EDS was a small start-up with more than a dozen employees and sales in excess of $400,000. However, events in Washington one year later would transform the operation and its founder into business superstars. In 1965, Congress passed legislation establishing Medicare for the elderly and Medicaid for the poor. With millions of recipients both programs had to be administered, and EDS became the dominant player; by 1971, EDS received 90 percent of its revenue from Medicare contracts. Hiring increased, a corporate structure was established, and the company moved into a modern tower in Dallas. In 1968, with spectacular growth in revenue and profits the decision was made to take the company public. The prospective suggested that EDS was a well-rounded operation with revenues from a variety of industries, but, in fact, 90 percent of their business came from Medicare. Nonetheless, on September 12, investors snapped up EDS shares. Perot's stake was worth $230 million; 18 months later with EDS trading at 162.50 a share, Perot's stake was valued at more than $1.5 billion. Perot commented, "Now keep in mind once you have money life changes. The media want to know the secret of your success." *Fortune* dubbed him "the fastest richest Texan ever." The *New York Times*, calling him "surprisingly modest," concluded that he had no political ambitions. Catapulted into a higher realm, he met presidential candidate Richard Nixon, who was interested in Perot's ideas about how computers could be used in presidential campaigns. With Nixon's victory in November 1968, Perot moved in on Washington as the ultimate insider.[12]

With his fortune made and trusted executives running day-to-day operations at EDS, the billionaire became involved in ventures that generated the publicity he came to crave, just as they captured the imagination of the American people. In 1969, he embarked on a project to deliver medicine and food for Christmas to American POWs in North Vietnam. It was his idea, planned with government assistance, although he later claimed the government asked him to do it. He chartered two Braniff jets that he loaded with himself and his staff, medicine, inflatable mattresses, underwear, vitamins, and more than 1,400 Christmas dinners. He also brought 50 Honda motorcycles and 500 Sears catalogues in the hope of bartering with village chiefs for information about MIAs, a Perot obsession that would last for decades. The planes landed in Vientiane, the capitol of Laos, where they waited for the North Vietnamese to decide whether to accept the food and gifts. In the event of a refusal, which Nixon officials thought might occur, the plan was to donate the supplies to South Vietnamese orphans and publicize the North's inhumanity. The North said they would only accept the goods through diplomatic channels, meaning Moscow, a move that administration officials adamantly opposed because they did not want to make the Russians look good. Perot was determined to push off for Moscow when the North added another condition, requiring that each package weigh no more than 6.6 pounds and be no more than 6 × 12 inches. Undeterred, he ordered the planes to Anchorage where Boy Scouts along with military and civilian volunteers reassembled the goods in less than 10 hours. Increasingly irritated at his unpredictability, the White House never understood that this billionaire didn't spend his money unless he had total control, making up his own rules regardless of the wishes of even the duly elected in the White House. The goods were never delivered, but the entire episode was a public relations coup for the former Eagle Scout. The North Vietnamese looked callous, but reports leaked out of North Vietnam that conditions had improved for the POWs. Ross emerged as an instant celebrity and became a favorite on the talk show circuit. He loved the limelight while continuing to focus on the plight of the POWs and MIAs.[13]

When the war ended in 1975, the government wanted an official celebration in Washington, but Perot arranged his own party in San Francisco. A parade was organized with appearances by Hollywood tough guys John Wayne and Clint Eastwood and a group of Green Berets who had helped free some POWs during the war. Perot personally paid for the event at a cost of $250,000, making him, even more than the administration, the leading advocate for POWs in the minds of many Americans.[14]

By the late 1970s, EDS had expanded beyond the domestic market. On December 28, 1978, Perot received a call informing him that two top executives in the Iranian operation had been arrested. Although no charges had been filed, it appeared that Paul Chiapparone and Bill Gaylord were being held in a corruption investigation. The bail was set at $12.75 million. These were the Shah's last days in power, and it appeared to be a way for him to curry favor with the public to shore up his regime. Immediately, the release of the two men became Perot's personal priority. He sought help from former officials Henry Kissinger and Alexander Haig and from diplomats at the American Embassy in Teheran. He soon gave up on the latter, calling staff at the embassy "incompetent." The staff said they were doing everything possible but claimed that by making the issue public Perot made their job more difficult. They were also concerned about 25,000 other Americans in Iran, but Perot only cared about his own executives.[15]

On January 2, 1979, Perot took matters into his own hands after assurances from Kissinger that the men would be set free failed to materialize. He arranged a meeting with Bill Simons, a retired 60-year-old army colonel who had once led an unsuccessful effort to free American POWs. Perot considered him a hero and wanted to enlist his help to free the two executives. Simons and a team of former military men now working for EDS met at Perot's weekend getaway at Lake Grapevine where they planned Operation Hotfoot (Help our two friends out of Teheran). The idea was to smuggle arms into Iran and storm the Ministry of Justice where Gaylord and Chiapparone were being held. Despite concerns about the efficacy of the plan and State Department reservations, they moved ahead with the operation. The Texan flew to Tehran with Simons and company with the hope of finding a legal solution. Ambassador William Sullivan, whom Perot had ridiculed earlier, intervened on his behalf when he heard that Perot was about to be arrested by Iranian authorities.[16]

On January 16, 1979, the Shah fled the country, and two days later the two EDS executives were moved to Gasr prison, a military complex with 30-foot walls. Operation Hotfoot was dead, but Perot visited the two men with Care packages. Simons told Perot that with a revolution underway all prisoners would likely be released, including the two Americans. Then Perot left the country to the relief of American government officials; said one, "He was too much of a loose canon while he was in Iran." On February 1, 1979, the Ayatollah Khomeini arrived from Paris to an enthusiastic welcome from millions of Iranians. He said, "I beg God to cut off the hands of all evil foreigners and their helpers." Simons, watching on television, commented to a companion, "The people are going to do it for us. The mob will take that jail." Eleven days later the mob stormed Gasr Prison, setting 11,000 prisoners free, including Gaylord and Chiapparone. The pair climbed over a wall and headed for the Hyatt where they met up with Simons, who took them to a safe house, and two days later they crossed into Turkey in two Range Rovers. The rescue team and Perot were now national heroes. The Perot myth ratcheted up another notch or two when comparisons were made with the Carter administration's disastrous attempt to free the American Embassy hostages.[17]

No doubt Perot took personal risks to help free the two executives, and he deserves credit for his actions, but not wanting to leave well enough alone, he wanted all the glory and then some. He even took credit for the mob attack on the prison when he claimed: "Our strategy became obvious—arrange for an Iranian to storm the prison. We arranged it, yes. I'm not going to get into details." However, of course he did get into details—his details—through a book and a television mini series about his exploits. To write the story, he wanted to hire Robin Moore, the author of *The Green Berets*, and John Wayne would star in the movie version. Moore was dropped, however, when he asked too many pointed questions. Perot's wife, Margot, had been reading Ken Follett's novel *Eye of the Needle*, and she thought he would be the right author. A deal was struck in which Follett would get a $1 million advance that he could keep even if Perot decided not to have the book published. Ultimately, *The Wings of Eagles* sold 300,000 copies and was produced for television. The Simons team was portrayed fighting their way into Gasr prison to free the hostages. Some thought the book should be listed under fiction, but Perot came off as a can-do hero. Congratulatory letters flooded into EDS headquarters, some even urging him to run for president.[18]

On a spring day in 1983, New York banker John Gutfriend of Solomon Brothers, informed Perot that General Motors (GM) wanted to buy EDS. Two weeks later Ross and his chief lieutenant Mort Meyerson flew to Detroit to meet CEO Roger Smith and take the grand tour of GM facilities. Smith told the duo that his interest in EDS was about acquiring data-processing skills to modernize automobile manufacturing. He assured them that EDS would retain considerable autonomy. Perot felt the alliance could double the size of EDS, to say nothing about the substantial additional fortune he and the top executives could earn from the sale. GM offered EDS $44 dollars a share compared with the $28 dollar trading price at the time. When the deal was presented to the EDS board, the majority opposed the plan, but Perot, with 46 percent of the shares, went ahead anyway, picking up $930 million plus 5.5 million Class E shares. Perot joined the GM board, but the honeymoon was brief. Smith was warned about Perot by Ed Pratt, a GM director who served on the board of the Vietnam Veterans Memorial Fund, who observed, "Perot is a bulldog and has very little restraint." At the first board meeting Perot asked if the pension funds were fully funded. When informed that only one of the three—executive, white collar, and blue collar—was, he said, "Need I ask which one." Meyerson said GM board members never questioned any decisions, when all of a sudden they had a guy at the end of the table with a Texas twang asking, hey, why are we doing this? For a variety of reasons, strains developed between GM and EDS. When GM's market share dropped, Perot piped up with, "Clearly we are doing something wrong." Finally GM decided to get rid of Perot, and in November 1986, they bought him out for an additional $743 million in "hush" money. In comments to the media, Perot wondered why it took GM five years to develop a new car when it only took four years to win World War II.[19]

With billions in the bank and two years to wait before he could start a competing business, he took up the POW/MIA issue once again. When the Vietnam War ended, 1,303 Americans did not return. Perot believed they were left behind, so he devoted considerable time and resources in his search for them. With his money and notoriety from the Iranian prison escapade, Perot became the target of various scam artists. He sent James "Bo" Gritz, an ex-Green Beret and right-wing Idaho-based survivalist, to Vietnam to determine whether Americans were still in captivity. Whether he was sincere or just liked being on the payroll, Gritz, too, became convinced of their existence, even claiming that one his units had come across 30 POWs. Perot said he would be willing to ransom them, but in October 1981, an expedition turned up nothing. Although government officials did not believe the POW sightings, some activists wanted Perot to head up a commission. He said he would be willing if the president and Congress agreed to the plan. Fellow Texan George H. W. Bush suggested that he talk to President Reagan directly, which he did at a White House reception. When Reagan thanked him for his efforts, Perot piped up, "Do I have your promise that if I bring hard evidence to you, you will follow up?" Reagan agreed. Soon Perot heard from two ex-Green Berets who claimed they had seen a videotape showing 39 POWs chained together, digging for gold in a mine in Southeast Asia. The tapes were for sale by Robin Gregson, a British con man, for $4.2 million. When Vice President Bush heard about the tapes, he offered his assistance. Gregson was in jail for fraud and said he would not help until he was released, so Perot agreed to pay off an Indian businessman to drop the charges against Gregson. When released from prison Gregson flew to Washington where federal agents tried to arrest him, but he managed to flee with the "tape." To many, the entire episode looked like a scam, but Perot had put his faith in Mark Smith, a Special Forces major, who said he had seen the tape. Perot was now certain there were POWs in Southeast Asia and blamed the government, and Bush in particular, for botching the operation. Bush tried to placate him, but against the wishes of administration officials Perot decided to take matters into his own hands by meeting with North Vietnam officials. Upon his return to Washington, he demanded a meeting with the president. At the conference Reagan spoke from note cards—even repeating one card twice—but nothing came of it. Perot told Bush that he couldn't get anywhere because of corrupt American officials. Later he complained to friends that Bush was "weak," and a "wimp." Much of his hostility concerning government inaction was directed at the vice president. White House council Boyden Grey had this take on Perot: "People get Potomac fever. What I think is that once Perot got inside, saw what it is like to have power, it got to his head. It goes beyond POWs and MIAs. Then it became who wields the biggest club in Texas." In the end, with no allies in the hunt for the missing, his quest ended.[20]

Perot popped up again in the national media in the early 1990s, criticizing President Bush for committing American troops to the rescue of Kuwait, for the growing budget deficit, for the Savings and Loan mess, and for signing on to a tax increase when he had promised no new taxes. Said Perot, "Whatever happened to watch my lips, no new taxes." At a speech before the National Press Club he was asked, "Isn't it time you ran for president of the United States?" He didn't say yes, but he took the opportunity to ask people to stay in touch by calling or writing to him in Dallas. He followed up with appearance on the *MacNeil-Lehrer News Hour* and *The Phil Donahue Show*, all the time sounding the alarm about the deficit, the Gulf War, and the need for ordinary Americans to retake control of their country.

His message clicked with many Americans, including Florida businessman Jack Gargan, the organizer of THRO (Throw the Hypocritical Rascals Out). Gargan spent his own and contributors' money on a series of newspaper ads calling for the defeat of congressional incumbents. Perot was so impressed that he called Gargan and asked how he could "help." Gargan invited the Texan to be a keynote speaker at THRO's fall 1991 gathering in Tampa, where he was introduced by

John Anderson. He outlined the themes of deficit reduction, reigning in lobbyists and PACs (political action committees), the line-item veto, and free airtime for all candidates. The crowd went crazy.[21]

Meanwhile, John Jay Hooker, a former congressional candidate and publisher of the Nashville *Tennessean* called Perot and urged him to run for president. Perot's talk at an anti-incumbency conference sounded like a campaign speech to some, and once again the crowd was enthusiastic. In December, Hooker enlisted the help of Richard Winger, an expert on ballot access. Winger thought he could get the Texan on the ballot in all 50 states, so Hooker pressured Perot with constant phone calls. At first he hesitated, but by Christmas Hooker had a strong feeling that Perot was considering a run. Said Hooker: "He began by asking the next question. . . . [H]e softened his no. It was like a girl, he was starting to show some leg." On February 5, 1992, Hooker and Perot met in Nashville for four hours of "intense discussion." Hooker remarked. "We stayed in our suits and ties, no alcohol, no food, just water. I used every argument I knew. It was an Eisenhower type opportunity—the American people are thirsting, a third are independents, we can carry two or three states and if it's close enough we can get to the House of Representatives and if we get there who knows what can happen. . . . [H]e listened intently . . . [and] then he said maybe if they qualify me in all fifty states. And I said immediately that can be done. . . . [H]e wanted a draft, and at the end of that four hours I knew I had him. I had him."[22] Hooker looked for a way for Perot to make a national announcement. Fellow Tennessean and journalist John Siegenthaler knew Larry King, so he called the talk show host saying that Hooker thought Perot wanted to run for president but that he wouldn't say yes after just one question. The appearance was scheduled for February 20. King would have to be persistent, asking him several times before eliciting a positive response. Said King, "That's why I kept coming back to it in the interview." Finally, after the fifth attempt Perot said he would run if he could get on the ballot in all 50 states.[23]

When the Gulf War ended in the spring of 1991, President Bush's approval rating was 90 percent, an all-time high. Because he looked like a shoo-in for reelection, prominent Democrats like New York governor Mario Cuomo, Sen. Bill Bradley, and Sen. Al Gore dropped out of the primaries, leaving the field to lesser-known candidates, among them Arkansas governor Bill Clinton. Beneath the euphoria over the defeat of Saddam Hussein, however, there was growing discontent with the state of the economy and the political leadership. Studies conducted by ANES (American National Election Studies) found that by the 1990s more than 55 percent of voters thought that public officials didn't care what people thought, more than 70 percent expressed distrust in the federal government, and in excess of 44 percent thought officials were crooks.[24]

On March 18, Perot made a speech at the National Press Club entitled, "You Own This Country." Carried on C-SPAN, it received one of the highest ratings ever for that network. Perot's Dallas office was swamped with calls. Appearances on NBC's *This Week with David Brinkley* and CBS' *60 Minutes* followed. On the Donahue show an 800 number was posted that received more than 250,000 calls within one hour. One week later on March 25, the self-proclaimed billionaire candidate announced that he would spend between $50 and $100 million dollars of his own money on his presidential run. By the end of April, a *New York Times* poll put him at 16 percent of the vote compared with 44 percent for Bush and 31 percent for Clinton. Ordinarily a successful third-party or independent candidate might be expected to peak at that level and then decline, but for Perot it was only the beginning.[25]

The enthusiasm of the volunteers and other followers was based on the assumption that Perot would ride into Washington on his white horse and clean up the mess left behind by the political class and their assorted handlers, image makers, and consultants. Perot said he would get under the hood and fix things, perhaps not realizing or wanting to admit that when he opened the hood, all he would find was Congress. Early on, Perot and his advisors decided against organizing a third party; he would make the run as an independent. They also decided to develop an unconventional campaign. In the various states, volunteers quit their regular jobs to found state organizations to get his name on the ballot. They believed in their candidate and felt he believed in them—the people, or the so-called bosses of America. Enthusiasm and spontaneity had to be maintained at the volunteer level, but multiple groups were declaring leadership within individual states, so conflicts invariably developed and had to be resolved. Legal niceties had to be maintained to achieve ballot access, but volunteers were often unfamiliar with state laws. Representatives from the Dallas headquarters—derisively called "white shirts" by the volunteers—descended on the locals, settling conflicts and demanding that they toe the line. With Perot not yet an official candidate, the first task was to get on the ballot in all 50 states. In this phase they wanted to keep a low nonthreatening profile, so the main parties would not make it more difficult for Perot to get on the ballots. His appeal could not be denied, and he soon started rising in the polls.[25]

A vice presidential candidate had to be selected because some state required a full ticket for ballot access. Dozens of possibilities were considered. Among the better-known were Sen. Paul Tsongas, Sen. Bob Dole, Sen. Warren Rudman, and Sen. Al Gore; Gen. Norman Schwarzkopf and Gen. Colin Powell; and California businessman and 1984 Olympics organizer Peter Ueberroff. Perot's preference was for Ueberroff, a can-do personality (like his own). Ueberroff was untainted by politics (as he was), and Perot liked the fact that the Los Angeles Olympic Games were so successful that *Time* designated Ueberroff 1984 Man of the Year. A bonus was that in the time of bulging deficits the Games produced a surplus of $250 million. Ueberroff was interested, but Perot and advisors opted for a temporary stand in. They selected Adm. James Stockdale, a friend of Perot and the highest ranking POW in Vietnam. A decent man who was not really ready for national politics, he eventually became the permanent running mate, whose participation in the televised debate proved disastrous.[27]

The ballot access process was seen as both a problem and an opportunity. While difficult to achieve in all 50 states, each success would generate favorable publicity and enthusiasm. Perot's own home state was problematic. Texas required 54,275 signatures by people who had not voted in the March primaries. Usually, 40 percent voted, leaving the remaining 60 percent in the pool of potential petitioners. The response was overwhelming. The volunteers collected 231,000 signatures that were presented to the attorney general during a rally at the state capital in Austin. The same pattern followed in other states: in California 38,000 volunteers collected 1,400,000 names, in Florida 260,000 signatures were gathered (versus 60,000 needed), in Massachusetts 100,000 (versus 10,000), in North Carolina 165,000 (versus 65,000), and in Oklahoma 106,000 (versus 35,000). Despite the legal hurdles and the ongoing friction between the volunteers and the "white shirts," the campaign would ultimately achieve its objective of getting on the ballot in all 50 states and the District of Columbia. In fact, Perot one-upped George Wallace, who had not made it onto the District ballot.[28]

As enthusiasm grew and Perot looked more the serious contender, the press started to focus on the billionaire candidate. Hundreds of calls came into the Dallas headquarters from media sources requesting interviews and asking about Perot's position on the issues. Jim Squires, a former *Chicago Tribune* editor who had been out of the newspaper business for three years, was hired as press secretary. However, as someone familiar with both Squires and the workings of political campaigns observed, the press-hating Squires was not the best choice. He bragged about not returning phone calls, not exactly a way to endear the media to the candidate, who, after all, wanted to run a media-driven campaign with little direct contact with the public.[29]

In an appearance on NBC's *Meet The Press*, Tim Russert persistently questioned Perot about his budget assumptions. The Texan remained calm on camera but exploded after the show, telling Squires that he wanted to quit the race. Perot could never admit that he was wrong. The Russert incident convinced his advisors that it was best to keep him away from direct confrontations with the media. Perot did not want to play where he was not in control! However, after his standoff with Russert his poll numbers improved. In Texas he took the lead as the choice of 35 percent compared with 30 percent for Bush and 25 percent for Clinton. In a *New York Times* national poll Perot was the choice of 23 percent, and the *Washington Post* poll put him at 30 percent. As the Clinton and Bush camps came to view him as a serious contender, stories started to appear painting Perot, the so-called outsider, as the ultimate insider during previous administrations. The tale about his attempt to quit the navy halfway through his tour of duty was also leaked. White House press secretary Marlin Fitzwater called him a "monster, dangerous and destructive."[30]

By the end of May, feeling overwhelmed by the pressures of the campaign, Perot and his home-grown group of advisors including Mort Meyerson, Perot's most trusted aid and the head of Perot Systems, and attorney Tom Luce decided it was time to bring in a team of political professionals to manage things. But these were just the types Perot railed against in his attacks on the Washington establishment. Their first choice was Hamilton Jordan who had not run a campaign since Jimmy Carter's failed reelection bid in 1980. They also considered Ed Rollins, a Republican, who was behind Reagan's success that same year.[31]

With Perot insisting that this campaign would be different, the idea of an effort headed jointly by a Republican and a Democrat had great appeal. In spite of this, Squires didn't think Perot and Rollins would hit it off. Rollins was well connected, loved press attention, took credit for everything, and loved to leak to the press, whereas Perot needed to be the star and in total control. Nonetheless, Rollins and Jordan were invited to Dallas for a chat with the candidate. Almost immediately Rollins got into trouble. According to Luce, Rollins leaked a story that he turned down a million dollar offer to be Perot's campaign manager. Then the morning of the meeting, a story appeared in the *Wall Street Journal* announcing the hiring of Rollins. Perot wanted to cancel the get together but was placated when Rollins admitted he planted the story and promised never to do it again.[32]

The two professionals came up with a grand plan to spend $150 million of Perot's personal fortune on the campaign. They stressed the importance of running early advertising (in June and July) to define Perot to the public before his opponents did so. Rollins and Jordan agreed that 1992 offered a special set of circumstances, combining public discontent, a popular candidate, and the resources to wage an all out effort. By outward appearances Perot seemed to like the plan, but underneath the pleasantries he was less than enthralled. A few days later Rollins appeared on a Sunday morning talk show without Perot's approval. Professionals hired by Rollins and Jordan arrived at the Dallas headquarters. The volunteers were offended, fearing being stifled and concerned that the grass roots nature of the campaign would lose its purity. Perot offered reassurance, telling them that professionals were needed to run the world-class campaign he had promised.[33]

Meanwhile, relations between the candidate and the two professionals stumbled downhill. Jordan showed Perot some rough cuts of television commercials designed to burnish his image with the public. Perot hated them and started to yell and scream at Jordan. Then Perot made himself unavailable to Jordan and Rollins, so the pair had to communicate through Meyerson and Luce, who really didn't understand modern campaign techniques. Rollins knew that stories would be written about Perot and that the best way to deal with the press was to feed them material that would put the candidate in a positive light. Perot rejected much of their advice including the earlier recommendation that advertising begin over the summer to define Perot to the public. Perot believed that people made up their minds during the final weeks of the campaign, so that was the best time to advertise.

The professionals did not give up easily. Rollins brought in Hal Riney, a San Francisco advertising executive who produced Reagan's "Morning in America" commercials. Riney's plan was to film supporters at outdoor rallies, who would reveal why they liked Perot. They were after "realistic" footage, but even that, Riney explained, would have to be carefully planned. Perot asked Riney what the commercials would cost, to which Riney answered, between $400,000 and $800,000 each. Perot thought that was ridiculous and asked Riney if he could do the job for between $80,000 and $100,000. Yes he could, Riney replied, but it depended on what you want to create and what impact you want to make. Then Perot, who intended to fire Riney before the meeting, posited, how about $5,000 each? Turning to Murphy Martin, a friend and Dallas TV anchor, Perot said, "We can get them for $1500–$1800 a day. They aren't Cecil B. DeMille but they are good."[34]

Perot refused Secret Service protection, believing it was too closely tied to the Republican White House. Some staffers even believed that Rollins was a Republican plant. So Perot hired his own security force that was dressed in the "uniform": wearing white shirts and polyester ties, with Perot-style haircuts, and toting cell phones and walkie talkies. They stood around headquarters and watched everybody, especially the professional staffers. Phones were tapped; conversations were recorded. In a hint of things to come, Perot commented that there so many desks that it looked liked the Pentagon. Undeterred for now, even while thinking they would be fired (some hoping it would be sooner than later), the professionals planned the fall campaign through the end of October.[35]

On July 10, just six weeks after they were hired, the end was near for the professionals just as it was for the first phase of the campaign itself. On a trip to Michigan where he would demand that the Japanese import more American cars, Perot assumed that the press would ask him about his position on this matter. Instead, the very first question at the airport upon his arrival was about his view on homosexuality. He refused to answer the question. The next day he flew to Nashville on his own without telling anybody, to give a speech to the NAACP. He referred to the African Americans as "you people," offending many in the audience. Perot was not a racist; he disavowed racism publicly in his campaign, but he was a southerner who grew up before the civil rights movement and may have been insensitive in his language. Rollins decided to force Perot to face reality even if it meant the end of his role in the campaign. In a memo he outlined three options: (1) run a professional campaign, (2) continue on his current course, or (3) drop out. Several days later Rollins knew that Perot had decided against option one: Meyerson and Luce informed Rollins that he was fired.[36]

That night at dinner with Meyerson and Luce, Perot let on that he was considering quitting the race. He mused that the election might be thrown into the House of Representatives if he stayed in, and he believed that the Republicans were waging a dirty tricks campaign against him. At the end of the evening he announced, "I am going to get out of this thing." In the public announcement that followed he gave different reasons for his decision. He said he didn't think he could win and that the Democratic Party had revitalized itself. It is hard to know what he was really thinking, but about not winning he could not have been more mistaken. By early June he was pushing 40 percent in the polls compared with 30 percent for Bush and 22 percent for Clinton, and based on various estimates, he could have amassed between 284 and 408 electoral votes, compared with

270 needed to win the election. His support was unprecedented for an independent or third-party candidate, but there had been some slippage as stories leaked about his quirks.[37]

He did not disband his organization, leading to some speculation that he would eventually reenter. He urged his now-furious volunteers to continue to work for him. The press had a field day, reminding readers of Perot's penchant for dropping out when developments were not to his liking, citing his experience in the navy, at IBM, and on the GM board. Within one day of his decision to withdraw he seemed to be reconsidering. He told Barbara Walters he would reenter the race if the country needed him. After yet another coffee klatch with Larry King, the talk show host said that he thought that Perot missed the limelight.[38]

He stayed out of the race for more than 70 days, rejoining Bush and Clinton on October 1, 1992. His campaign headquarters was not disbanded. Many volunteers pushed ahead with the ballot access process and on September 18, Arizona became the 50th state to put his name on the ballot. In the first phase of his campaign, before he pulled out, much of his emphasis was on identifying the problems the country faced: the deficit, the loss of factory jobs to overseas competitors, and the "mess in Washington." He was criticized in some quarters for not offering solutions to these and other problems.[39]

With Perot's withdrawal, the two main parties saw a chance to woo his constituency. The Democrats seemed to have the upper hand because they were closer on some of the issues. Bush was handicapped by Perot's belief that the Republicans were using dirty tricks against him. Perot had demanded an admission of guilt and an apology, but they refused. Clinton and Perot had a conversation about an endorsement, but nothing came of it because the Democrats believed that he wanted to get back in the race. Their instincts proved correct. Next, Perot called for a gathering in Dallas in which representatives from the Clinton and Bush camps would make their case to the volunteers, who would decide whether the country needed the Eagle Scout from Texarkana as its savior. So on September 28, representatives from the Democratic and Republican camps flew to Texas to plead for support. Among the GOPers (Grand Old Party) were Sen. Phil Gramm of Texas and advisor Mary Matalin, and for the Democrats, Sen. David Boren of Oklahoma and Sen. Lloyd Bentsen of Texas. Neither party was naive about the probable outcome, but they could not afford to alienate Perot's constituency by not showing up. Each side made a two hour presentation to the assembled who included the press and Perot's favorite talk show host Larry King. The volunteers were impressed with the Democrats, but the next day

Perot claimed his 800 line received more than 1.5 million calls urging him to get back into the race. So on October 1, Perot announced that he would accept the volunteers' call to reenter the contest that he had never officially entered even before he withdrew. Now he was on the ballot in all 50 states with billions in private wealth to indulge in a campaign strategy of his own choosing. He would need all the cash he could get, for his poll numbers had plummeted to 7 percent by the time he reentered.[40]

During his 75-day pit stop Perot spent millions to form a new organization called United We Stand America (UWSA), appointing former POW Orson Swindle as chief executive. A manifesto by the same name was published that offered answers to the nation's problems. Now he could one-up the Republicans and Democrats, who avoided offering real solutions for fear of offending key constituencies. On the key issue of the deficit, Clinton simply blamed the sluggish Bush economy, which he would turn around. Bush, who broke his "no new taxes" pledge, was ensnared by his angry antitax base. His "solution" was a constitutional amendment requiring a balanced budget. By contrast, Perot offered specifics on this and many other issues that justified his third-way candidacy. He advocated increasing the marginal tax rate on wealthy individuals from 31 percent to 33 percent, taxing employer provided health insurance, raising the tax on social security, eliminating the cap on the Medicare tax and increasing the tax on gasoline and tobacco products. He wanted to cut the defense budget by getting the allies to share the burden, limit the mortgage deduction to $250,000, cut government staffing in the White House and Congress by 30 percent and their special perks by 40 percent.[41]

The manifesto claimed that the political "nobility" had become immune to the people's will. To enable the citizenry to "take back their country" he wanted campaign contributions limited to $1,000. There would be no "soft money" donations from corporations, unions, or the wealthy. PACs and foreign lobbyists would face new restrictions. Electronic town hall meetings would encourage a two-way dialogue between the people and their representatives. All 2,000 pages of NAFTA and other foreign trade agreements would be reviewed to ensure they benefited Americans as much as foreigners. There was much more, including a call for rebuilding inner cities, education reform, weekend voting (to increase participation), and the elimination of the Electoral College. Issues relating to the liberal-conservative divide were avoided in order to skirt many of the contentious social issues. However, Perot admitted to his pro-choice sympathies—while encouraging adoption—and called for racial tolerance. The manifesto ended with a checklist of issues that voters could take to congressional candidates to learn their positions.[42]

The strategy for rebuilding his standing in the polls was an all-out advertising campaign consisting of half-hour infomercials starring himself and addressing a single topic. The first in the series, entitled "The Problems—Plain Talk and Jobs, Debt and the Washington Mess," drew 16.5 million viewers. Warmed-up to the idea of television exposure, he permitted Dallas adman Lanier Temerlin to produce image commercials. The tag line was "The Candidate is Ross Perot. The Issue is leadership. The Choice is Yours." Although Perot did not appear or speak in the commercials, Temerlin cleverly kept Perot involved in fashioning the message.[43]

Perot had reentered the race on the eve of the first of three televised presidential debates on October 11 at Washington University in St. Louis. Perot knew how important his participation would be to his revival in the polls, but it would be up to his rivals and the Presidential Debate Commission whether he was to be included. Bush and Clinton each had their own reasons for wanting him to participate, so the Commission extended the invitation. Perot was pleased but a bit surprised, commenting, "I was outside the system. I marveled that they let me in. . . ." One has to wonder whether the rival campaign staffs had done their homework, given Perot's long history as a top debater. It soon became apparent that those talents had not diminished. When he was criticized for his lack of government experience, he shot back, "I didn't have any experience running up a $4 trillion debt." Focus groups rating the outcome gave Perot's performance the highest grade, as did the general public. His poll numbers nearly double from 7 percent to 13 percent.[44]

The vice presidential debate followed two days later on October 13 in Atlanta, pitting James Stockdale against Democrat Al Gore and the GOP's Dan Quayle. Stockdale seemed lost much of the time, unable to articulate policy positions. In a debate for high national office, Stockdale's unpreparedness might have been a disaster, but two days later Perot's triumph in the second presidential debate in Richmond, viewed by 90 million, overshadowed Stockdale's shortcomings. The Texan's poll number improved once again, hitting 16 percent. In the third and final debate in Lansing, Michigan, Perot did another fine job, jabbing at Bush and Clinton while claiming to be the real agent of change. The networks gave Clinton the edge, but Perot's poll numbers continued to improve, reaching the 18–19 percent range. Another good sign was the drop in his negative ratings from 63 percent to 33 percent. It seemed that many voters were ready to forgive the billionaire for going AWOL! Momentum was once again with Perot.[45]

As elections near, third-party candidates usually see a drop-off in support because major parties warn voters that a vote for a third party means a wasted vote. Perot, however, didn't need help from the majors to harm his chances in the final days; he was perfectly capable of accomplishing this feat on his own. With no professionals around to restrain his worst instincts and paranoia, Perot accepted an invitation from Barbara Walters to reveal the "real" reason why he dropped out of the race in July. In front of millions of viewers he claimed that the Republicans were about to release a doctored photo that would disrupt his daughter Caroline's wedding plans. At the time he did not reveal why the picture was so embarrassing, but he was referring to 35 fake photos of daughters Caroline and Nancy in compromising lesbian situations. Perot had never seen the pictures but acted on information provided by his friend David Taylor, a Washington-based BBC producer. The original reports about the photos came from David Barnes, a Taylor friend, who later denied their existence. President Bush was reported to have commented, "The SOB is a psychiatric case," and the official White House characterization of Perot as "paranoid" appears to have stuck with many voters. *60 Minutes* conducted a full investigation into the matter and could find no evidence of Republican dirty tricks. The press loved the story, but the public didn't; they were concerned about Perot's tendency to draw conclusions before all the facts were revealed. The momentum he gained from the debates came to a sudden halt as his positive poll ratings (56–34) turned negative (44–46). Not even a series of public appearances could reverse the self-inflicted wound.[46]

Nonetheless, on election day, November 3, 1992, Perot garnered almost 19 percent (18.9 percent) of the vote, which was second only to third-party candidate Theodore Roosevelt in 1912, whose 27.5 percent as a Bull Moose Progressive was the highest ever in the history of third parties. Perot's popular vote total (19,741,647) exceeded that of any third-party or independent candidate. He did not win any electoral votes because he did not have a strong sectional base. Some Republicans blamed Perot for President Bush's defeat. Bush, with 168 electoral votes and 39,103,882 popular votes (37.4 percent) compared with Clinton's 370 and 44,909,326 (43.0 percent), would have needed to take 102 electoral votes from Clinton to reverse the outcome. However, careful studies have shown that Perot may have cost Bush only 20 electoral votes in three states: Georgia (13), Montana (3), and Nevada (4) but no more.[47]

There were regional variations in Perot support. He did best, garnering 25 percent or more of the vote, in eight states that have been described as culturally Protestant, individualistic, quirky and, at the time, culturally moderate on the social issues. These included Maine (30 percent) and seven western states: Alaska (28 percent), Idaho (27 percent), Kansas (27 percent), Montana (26 percent), Nevada (26 percent), Utah (27 percent), and Wyoming (25 percent). His weakest region was the culturally conservative south. With the exceptions of diverse Florida (20 percent) and Texas (his home state, 22 percent), he picked up less than 15 percent of the vote, ranging from 9 percent in Mississippi to 14 percent in Virginia and North Carolina. His weakest showing was in the District of Columbia with its large African American community, where he garnered only 4 percent of the vote. The size of the black vote throughout the South may also explain his low vote percentages in Dixie.[48]

Demographically, he did best among the young (ages 18–29), those who were worse off financially, and white men. Many of his supporters felt ignored by the Bush administration and threatened economically by the poor economy and the threat of more factory jobs going across the border to Mexico and overseas. Perot did least well among the wealthy (more than $75,000 per year), the most educated, retirees, minorities, and gays. He attracted independents (30 percent), whose main concern was the growing federal deficit (37 percent) followed by the economy and jobs. They wanted change and liked Perot's plans for the future. "Family values" and foreign affairs were lesser concerns. Only 8 percent viewed abortion as a major issue. Perot did well where third-party progressives scored earlier in the 20th century. His appeal was strong where Wallace did well outside the South. As in Wallace's time, Perot voters wanted to send a message to Washington.[49]

Although, as noted earlier, Perot did not change the outcome of the race, his candidacy deprived Clinton of a majority of the popular vote, thus weakening his hand at governing. (The only state where Clinton surpassed 50 percent was his home base in Arkansas.) Once in office the Clinton team attempted to woo the Perotistas by emphasizing their commitment to deficit reduction. Before his first State of the Union address, the new president personally spoke to Perot and won an endorsement of sorts. The Texan said, "Let's give him an A+ for raising the issue of the deficit." However, palpitations of the heart did not lead to a second date when Clinton failed to endorse the balanced budget amendment and certain congressional reforms. Clinton's support for free trade (NAFTA) was another source of friction between the two. In a tough confrontational televised debate over NAFTA between Vice President Al Gore and Perot, the vice president was judged the winner, thus ending any chance for a rapprochement.[50]

The spell of the Perot constituency soon descended on the Republicans. In February 1992, GOP pollster Frank Luntz made a presentation entitled "The Perot Vote and the GOP Future," which caught the attention of Georgia congressman Newt Gingrich. Republican leaders were encouraged to attend a gathering of UWSA in Amherst, New York, to discuss the dangers of the Clinton economic agenda. Gradually, relations strengthened as several Republican senators and representatives became dues-paying members of UWSA. Next, Gingrich developed an appeal to Perot voters called "The Contract with America." Luntz reported that Perot's constituency did not want just a platform; they wanted a clear and definite commitment—a contract. The ploy worked; in the midterm election of 1994 the Republicans swept the House and the Senate.[51]

Perot claimed much of the credit for the Republican victory, but to many in the media he seemed irrelevant. As bickering between the main parties increased, Perot saw a new opportunity to break their stranglehold on the two-party system through the formation of a third party. Sixty-two percent of the American public had the same idea, but they were thinking about someone else as their leader, perhaps Gen. Colin Powell. To recapture the limelight, Perot pulled off a repeat of an old stunt—he invited Democrats and Republicans to Dallas to discuss why the "Contract With America" had not adequately addressed term limits, a balanced budget amendment, and campaign finance reform. On *Meet The Press* Perot was asked whether he would consider making another bid for the White House. He replied "I can't say that I'm going to go away," and many Americans liked his answer. In a three-way opinion poll he was preferred by 26 percent, seven points higher than his 1992 vote, compared with 37 percent for President Clinton and 33 percent for Sen. Robert Dole, the Republican's 1996 nominee.[52]

While deciding to make another run, he focused on the question of whether to make it as an independent candidate or as the head of a third party. The advantage of the third-party route was that he personally would not have to commit to head a ticket until after the party convention. This would leave less time for the opposition and the press to attack him (and less time to sabotage himself) as they and he himself had done through the spring of 1992. He could also compress his campaign spending into the shorter period and have a greater impact on the race.[53]

Once again he turned to Larry King to make the announcement. On September 25, 1995, he said, "We're at a critical time in our country's history and tonight we're going to start the process of starting a new party." He boasted that his new party—the Reform Party—would replace one of the two main parties. In yet another replay of 1992, an 800 number was flashed on the screen, prompting hundreds of thousands of fans to call the Dallas headquarters of UWSA. Conveniently, Colin Powell announced that he would not seek the presidency in 1996, so the Texas billionaire had the field all to himself. Needless to say the Republicans were furious; they specifically targeted the Perot crowd with the "Contract" and were hoping to hold their loyalty in the 1996 presidential campaign. The Democrats, on the other hand, couldn't believe their good fortune; with Perot in the race the anti-Clinton vote would be split.[54]

Unlike his independent candidacy where Perot was the one and only attraction, the Reform Party fielded more than 30 congressional candidates. To qualify, a candidate had to obtain signatures from 10 percent or more of party members, agree to provisions of the 1992 platform, and refrain from personal attacks on other candidates. With his ego (and bank account), the assumption was that Perot would head the ticket, but he added a little suspense to the drama by trying to lure some big name politicians to run for the party's nomination. He contacted former Sen. David Boren (D-Okla.), Gov. Lowell Weicker (R-Conn.) and Sen. Sam Nunn (D-Ga.). They all declined, and though Perot didn't make the offer, former Colorado governor Richard Lamm, who lost a senate race to Ben Nighthorse Campbell in 1992, saw an opportunity to revive his political career and entered the fray. He was not a Perot favorite, so the Texan decided to jump into the race for the Reform Party nomination.[55]

The Party held two conventions, the first on August 11, in Long Beach, California, where anyone who received 10 percent or more of the members' vote would address the throng. Then, members would vote for their favorite nominee by e-mail, regular mail, or telephone. The winner would be announced at a second convention to be held one week later on August 18, in Valley Forge, Pennsylvania. The location was selected to associate the party with George Washington and the patriots who wintered there during the American Revolution, enduring many hardships. Not surprisingly, Perot won the nomination by a 2–1 margin, but the fight between Perot and Lamm weakened the party, as did Perot's decision to take matching government funds to pay for the campaign. Members saw this as a lessening of his personal commitment to change that was in conflict with his aim to reform the funding of political campaigns. After a brief acceptance speech the candidate ran off—once again—to an appearance on *The Larry King Show*.[56]

In selecting a running mate Perot decided against a noble but inexperienced candidate like Stockdale. He offered the spot to two experienced politicians, Rep. Marcy Kaptur (D-Ohio) and Sen. David Boren (D-Okla.); both turned him down. His final choice was Pat Choate, a PhD economist with whom he collaborated on "Save Our Country, Why NAFTA Must Be Stopped Now." Choate had been an economic advisor to governors, held senior positions in the Department of Commerce and at The Office of Management and Budget in the Ford and Carter administrations. He had authored numerous articles including "America in Ruins," about the decaying infrastructure and "Agents of Influence," about the role of Japanese money in American politics.[57]

Like Perot, Choate was an excellent debater but neither candidate would get the opportunity to put his skills to the test in the televised debates in 1996. Perhaps the major parties had learned their lesson four years earlier. A bipartisan commission consisting of two Democrats and two Republicans managed to agree on something—keeping Perot and Choate out of the presidential debates. The reason given was that the Reform Party had no chance of winning. Appeals to the Federal Election Commission, and the Federal Communications Commission failed to reverse the decision.[58]

The party platform was based on a series of reform principles: high ethical standards in the White House and Congress; a balanced budget; campaign reform; term limits; a new tax system; entitlement reforms of Medicare, Medicaid, and Social Security; and lobbying reform of foreign and domestic interests. The party wanted any budget surpluses to go toward reducing the accumulated national debt that totaled in the trillions by 1996. They advocated banning gifts to elected officials, including even trips and meals, and reducing fringe benefits enjoyed by Congress (health and retirement) to that of the average citizen. Term limits would be three for representatives and two for senators. They also favored shorter campaigns of no more than four months and weekend voting to encourage more people to go to the polls. All tax increases would have to be approved by the people in the next federal election.[59]

Perot did not do as well in 1996 as he had done four years earlier. He only garnered 8.4 percent of the vote (versus 18.9 percent in 1992) and no electoral votes, compared with President Clinton's 49.2 percent (379 electoral votes) and Dole's 40.7 percent (159 electoral votes). Perot fatigue may have set in; his negatives were higher than his positives, and he did not participate in the debates, which had given him a big boost in 1992. This time around the idea of a wasted vote for a third party may have taken its toll. Perhaps most of all, progress had been made on some of his issues, which was the bane of third parties' long-term viability. Also, the economy had improved over the previous four years, unemployment was lower (5.2 percent), and the gross domestic product was growing at a respectable 3 percent. Although the huge debt remained, Clinton had produced budget surpluses for the first time in decades. Perot may have gotten an unexpected boost late in the campaign when Scott Read, Dole's campaign manager, visited him in Dallas and asked him to withdraw from the race. The Texan's well-publicized refusal gave him a some extra visibility and perhaps, some extra votes. None of the Reform Party's congressional candidates won a seat in the House of Representatives, nor did any win more than 6 percent of the vote in their districts.[60]

Despite the loss in 1996, the Reform Party lived on. Professional wrestler Jesse Ventura won the governorship of Minnesota in 1998 under the Reform banner, and thanks to Perot's showing in 1996, the party qualified for $12.5 million in government matching funds for the 2000 race. However, with the loss of its centrist bearing under the leadership of right-wing extremist Pat Buchanan, the Reform Party garnered less than 1 percent of the vote. For a time Perot refrained from commenting on political matters, but in 2008, he launched a blog focusing on the economy and government spending. No doubt, he also devotes time to his numerous grandchildren.[61]

6

Ralph Nader and the Green Party

By the way, I do think Gore cost me the election, especially in Florida.
—Ralph Nader, November 8, 2000

Many Americans must wonder how different the world might be if Al Gore had defeated George W. Bush in the presidential election of 2000, instead of the other way around. Would the 9/11 hijackers have been foiled? Would Afghanistan and Iraq have been invaded? Would hurricane Katrina have been handled competently? Would different policies have prevented the financial meltdown of 2008? Wondering about an alternative outcome in 2000 is justified because the election was so close in the crucial state of Florida. Of nearly six million votes cast, Bush triumphed by only 537, giving him the Sunshine State's 25 electoral votes and the election.

Some blame President Clinton for Gore's defeat. After eight years of peace and prosperity under Clinton-Gore, the vice president should have been a shoo-in, but the Clinton sex scandals cast a pall over these accomplishments. Some blame Gore for his inability to connect with the American people. Then there was Palm Beach County's confusing butterfly ballot, followed by weeks of hanging chads, and finally, a conservative-leaning Supreme Court that voted to stop the recount, thereby giving the election to Bush. Of course, none of the above would have mattered if Ralph Nader, closer to Gore than Bush on the issues, had decided not to run or heeded the calls to pull out of the race when his likely impact on the outcome became evident.

When Nader entered the 2000 race as the candidate of the Green Party after 35 years as a national figure, he did not expect to win the election. His goals were more modest: to get 5 percent of the vote and qualify for federal matching funds. That money would be used to build a new national party to challenge what he called the duopoly, the domination of national politics and government by the Republicans and Democrats. When it became clear near that Nader could hurt Gore's chances, he was urged to withdraw from the race or at to least endorse Gore in the swing states. He refused, even enjoying his new-found notoriety as a possible spoiler after many years of being ignored by both parties. Whether his declination was based on the true belief in his cause, his personal animosity to Gore, or the personality quirks that seem to have driven his life's work is hard to figure. Perhaps they all played a roll.

For Nader and the country, the road to the election of 2000 began with his birth on February 27, 1934, in Winstead, Connecticut, in the state's northwest corner. His parents, Nathra and Rose, were Lebanese Christians who migrated to the United States early in the 20th century. The Naders had three other children: a son Shafeek, the oldest and the only one with an Arabic name, and Ralph's two younger sisters, Claire and Laura. Nathra ran a successful bakery and restaurant called the Highland Sweet Shop. Inside you entered a world of warm food and hot political debate. Nathra never worried about offending a customer's political sensibilities; the easily angered could go somewhere else and often did. At town meetings he was known for his strong views and the "enthusiasm" with which he presented them, which many thought were a bit extreme and out of keeping with the tenor of the region. Nathra, however, was an idealist who preferred to tackle injustices head on,[1] and he was not afraid to take unpopular positions that might make him the lone proponent of an issue. Joseph O'Brien, a town resident, described Nathra as someone "always interested in town governance but he became too much of a gadfly that it irritated the powers that be."[2] At home, the Nader children were expected to be informed about the issues and express their own opinions. Nathra instilled in his four children the idea that life was a serious business and that the person who took unpopular stands should be valued and should always be independent, i.e., not to join a political party.[3]

Nader attended the private progressive Gilbert School, where by the fifth grade he had become a voracious reader. He devoured *Moby Dick*, the life of Helen Keller, and books on ancient Chinese history and the early 20th-century muckrakers such as Upton Sinclair and Ida Tarbell, whose sense of mission to improve the lives of others impressed him. Most unusual for a boy of his age—or any age for that matter—was his interest in the *Congressional Record*, in which he studied political issues and personalities of members of Congress past and present. Encouraged by Shareek, he was drawn to the all-American game of baseball that he played with future writer and journalist David Halberstam and his three closest friends, John Bushnell, Saul Miller, and Fred Silverio. The four played chess together and were known for the focus and intellectual achievements that set them apart from the average student. In high school and in later life Ralph showed no apparent interest in the opposite sex.[4]

In his senior year at the Gilbert School, acceptance letters came from Princeton, Harvard, Haverford, and Swarthmore. He selected Princeton (class of 1955) because of its Department of Oriental Studies program, open-stack library, and size—not too big or too small. He qualified for a scholarship, but Nathra refused because the funds were not absolutely necessary. Even at prestigious Princeton, the 50s were the 50s. The all-male student body strove for the gentlemen "C" and looked forward to cushy careers in banking, brokerage, and real estate. Swaggering around campus was the wrestling star and two-time future secretary of defense, Donald Rumsfeld. Typically, Nader went against the grain, studying at the library till the wee hours while displaying himself near the windows like a department store manikin on Christmas eve. Second-year students sought entry into one of Princeton's exclusive eating clubs where members were served by African Americans in uniforms and white gloves. Nader joined the Prospect, a club for outsiders that would accept anyone.[5]

Besides the curriculum, Princeton's tradition of public service appealed to him. Princeton past president Woodrow Wilson (class of 1879) encouraged this tradition, as did Eisenhower's secretary of state John Foster Dulles '08 and George Kennan '25, who devised American policy during the cold war. Nader's favorite professor was H. H. Wilson, a self-described anarchist, whose specialty was the protection of civil liberties against the encroachment of government and big business. The subject became red meat for the young scholar and led to his interest in consumerism before the concept ever existed among the general public. He liked Eric Goldman, who focused on the early 20th-century muckrakers. One spring, Nader noticed a number of dead birds around campus, which seemed to coincide with the spraying of DDT to kill mosquitoes. Assuming its lethal effect on birds, he also wondered how it would affect humans. When he brought the matter to the attention of the *Daily Princetonian*, he was ignored. Nader was also impressed with Norman Thomas, a socialist and critic of the two main parties who was cofounder of the American Civil Liberties Union. He was Princeton '05 and a radical and was someone Nader could identify with. When Thomas visited his alma mater, Nader asked him to describe his greatest moment. Thomas replied, "Having the Democrats steal my agenda."[6]

When Nader was eight years old, Nathra took him to the local courthouse where he saw legal clashes between the rich and the poor, the haves and have nots, stirring in him the desire to become a lawyer and represent the disadvantaged and to redress the balance necessary for a true democracy. After graduation he decided to attend Harvard Law School. Once there, however, he quickly became frustrated by the narrow-mindedness of the curriculum. He described Harvard as a "high-priced tool factory" where students are trained for corporate careers and material success. He wasn't repelled enough to drop out, however; instead he focused on subjects that gripped him, like auto safety. He latched on to Roscoe Pound, who joined the faculty in 1910 and became Dean from 1916 to 1936. By the time Nader arrived on campus Pound was ignored by the Dean and faculty, who considered him an anachronism. What impressed Nader about Pound's approach to the law was that he considered data from the social sciences in arriving at a conclusion. Pound believed that the law must adapt to a changing society that was increasingly urban and industrial. Pound commented: "[L]aw must be stable and yet it cannot . . . stand still." Commented Nader, "The law writ large . . . [,] the province of Roscoe Pound[,] . . . was not in favor at Harvard when I was there. The law writ small was in favor . . . [,] very technical deep analysis of securities regulation X-10-B5 from the SEC and so forth." With his lax work habits and poor grades Nader was no candidate for the *Harvard Law Review*, so he joined the weekly *Harvard Law Record* as a staff writer. In his second year he became president of the *Record*, but after an unwelcome attempt to transform the publication into a muckraking journal he was replaced by Robert Oliver, who recalled, "[H]e wanted the paper to be more aggressive. . . . [I]t wasn't enough to publish an occasional article on a social issue. He wanted the general concept of the publication to be oriented that way. Essentially, he had the same personality (as today); he was never really a person who was inclined to make a practical compromise. He could rationalize issues easily to suit his own views."[7]

At Harvard, Nader owned a 1949 Studebaker but dumped it because of the upkeep. He hitchhiked, meeting all sorts of people who willingly picked him up in the more innocent 50s. From truck drivers he learned about auto accidents and which makes were more likely to be involved. He saw plenty of accidents himself, including one where a baby was practically beheaded when the glove compartment opened on impact. In 1956, an article about auto safety in the *Law Review* piqued his interest. The author, Harold Katz, suggested that automakers be held liable for injuries in instances of unsafe design. Nader took a course that explored issues related to the law and medicine. For his paper he researched the subject of auto safety liability, even searching out a study from Cornell Medical School about engineering innovations that might cut down on injuries. The paper, "Automotive Design Safety and Legal Liability," earned him an A.[8]

Following graduation from Harvard Law in 1958, and a stint in the army, he joined a one-man law firm in Hartford, Connecticut, owned by George Athanson, a future mayor of the state's capital. After his morning hitchhike to work he handled small accident claims. Evenings he lectured on government and history at the University of Hartford. He found time to write articles about Roscoe Pound ("The Grand Old Man of Law") for the *Reader's Digest* and auto safety for *The Nation* ("The Safe Car You Can't Buy").[9]

In 1961, Nader's Harvard roommate, Ed Levin, became a bill drafter for the Illinois State Assembly. One of the bills up for a vote would require all cars sold in Illinois to have a special attachment for seat belts that would give owners the option to buy and install them. When Nader heard about the provision, he wrote to Levin urging him to actively push for the bill's passage. Levin, less than enthusiastic, received a harsh letter from Nader, asking, "Do I want to be responsible for the loss of 50,000 lives?" Levin turned to his wife for sympathy, but she agreed with Ralph, stating, ". . .[H]e's right. . . . [S]omebody should be doing this."[10]

Not only were tens of thousands dying in accidents, but four million were being injured. In the 1960s, safety was seen as a question of driver education, strict enforcement of traffic laws for speeding and drunken driving, and better roads and highways. Nader did not agree with the conventional wisdom; he believed that design and engineering played a significant roll in auto safety. Although the 60s is perhaps best known for civil rights, Nader became determined to make it a fight for what he labeled, body rights.[11]

In 1964, Richard Grossman, a former vice president at Simon and Schuster Publishing who had gone independent, decided to publish a book on auto safety after seeing an article in *The New Republic* by James Ridgeway entitled "The Corvair Tragedy." Ridgeway refused Grossman's offer to author the book, but he recommended Nader, telling Grossman that Nader had been the source for much of the material in the article. Grossman managed to track Nader to a rooming house at 1719 19th Street NW in Washington, D.C., where Nader occupied a single room and shared the hall phone with other residents. He agreed to write the book and found to his delight that one of the best sources for information about the inner workings of the auto industry was disillusioned ex-employees. Nader observed that upper management was filled with ambitious individuals who get along politically, whereas the middle ranks contain people dedicated to building better cars.[12]

Meanwhile, in 1965 Sen. Abraham Ribicoff (D-Conn.), chairman of the Subcommittee on Executive Reorganization of the Committee on Government Operations was looking for an issue that would interest fellow senators. As governor of Connecticut he was well aware of the death toll on the highways. He also knew that Detroit remained virtually free of regulation, so the idea of investigating Detroit's practices appealed to him. Jerome Sonofsky, staff director and general council of Ribicoff's subcommittee, was told about Ralph Nader. At a three-hour meeting arranged in the Old Senate Office Building Nader told Sonofsky all about the auto industry practices, including his belief that the industry had no right to produce unsafe cars. Sonofsky called Ribicoff, telling him, "I just struck gold. . . . I just met somebody who knows more about auto safety than anyone I've ever come across. . . . I don't have to run around town gathering up various experts I just found him."[13] So Nader became an unpaid advisor to Ribicoff's subcommittee.

With Nader's book behind schedule, Grossman traveled to Washington, checked into the Gramercy Motor Inn, and summoned Nader who, under pressure, finished the book in just over two weeks. *Unsafe at Any Speed*, published in November 1965, revealed Nader's thinking about how auto industry executives make decisions that affect the lives of millions with no regard for lives and safety. He contended in the book, as he would in future investigations on a variety of subjects, that forces in corporate America, the press, and even in universities and the government use their power and influence to promote an agenda that is often detrimental to the interests of average Americans. He devoted one chapter to the accident-prone Chevrolet Corvair, which General Motors (GM) refused to take off the market because of ". . . bureaucratic rigidities and object worship of that bitch goddess cost reduction." He argued that in Detroit boardrooms, style trumps safety.[14]

Although sales of *Unsafe* did not exactly soar at first, it endeared him to Ribicoff, so Nader was asked to testify in public. Days before his appearance he received anonymous threatening phone calls. One caller suggested that he "change his field of interest." Another said, "[Y]ou are fighting a losing battle. You can't win. You can only lose." A 4:00 A.M. call suggested that he "go back to Connecticut, buddy boy." When the calls were made public, all the auto companies denied any involvement, with one exception: GM. Ribicoff was furious because GM had broken a law that makes it illegal to harass a congressional witness. Finally, the automaker confessed to a "routine investigation" because Nader was involved in a lawsuit against them. However, it didn't stop with phone calls. There were instances where an attractive woman approached him in supermarkets to ask for "help" in moving furniture into her apartment and where his enemies tried to get him for being anti-Semitic (because of his Arab roots) or homosexual. Nader sued GM for $25 million and eventually settled for $425,000.[15]

Nader turned out to be a star witness before the Ribicoff committee, so well informed and articulate that he aroused the public to the issue of auto safety. The House and Senate wrote bills, and President Lyndon Johnson proclaimed the week of May 15, 1966, as National Transportation Week. Nevertheless, Nader knew that public awareness was only the necessary first step in getting ground-breaking auto safety legislation. For a bill to be effective it was necessary to get the details right. This meant entering into a relentless protracted struggle with the auto industry lobby, which hoped to defang the new legislation, something Nader was willing and able to do. Finally, a bill passed on August 25, 1966. The legislation, signed by LBJ two weeks later, did not contain the criminal provision that Nader fought for, but he called it a "significant step forward." A National Highway Safety Bureau was created that would require the auto industry to adopt certain safety features, including mandatory shoulder straps for front seat passengers, limits on glare-producing chrome, shatterproof windshields, energy-absorbing steering columns, flashing hazard lights, and a dual braking system. A 1970 University of Michigan study found that the new safety features had resulted in 2,500 fewer deaths each year. As a result of the hearings and the new legislation *Unsafe at Any Speed* climbed to number five on national best seller lists as sales skyrocketed to half a million copies. Eventually, Corvair sales slumped from 304,000 in 1962 to 5,000 in 1968 and it was discontinued in 1969. Nader came out of the auto safety controversy a national celebrity. Now he had to figure out what to do next.[16]

Neal Smith, a Democratic congressman from Iowa in the 1960s, became aware of loopholes in the original Meat Inspection Act of 1906 that was prompted by Upton Sinclair's expose of the meatpacking industry in his book, *The Jungle*. The problem was that meat shipped intrastate did not come under federal jurisdiction. Smith noticed that certain buyers seemed to specialize in buying diseased cattle and hogs at industry auctions. He worked to amend the 1906 Act but was foiled by beef industry organizations like the American Meat Institute and the National Meat Packers Association. Smith's legislative assistant Ed Mezvinsky contacted Nader and was invited to Ralph's one-room television-free lair for a briefing. Nader was electrified by the subject that he had read about in *The Jungle* as a boy. He wrote two articles for *The New Republic*: "We're Still in the Jungle" and "Watch That Hamburger," noting that 15,000 meat-processing plants did not sell their output across state lines and thus were not subject to the 1906 Act and that certain intrastate operators bid for livestock known for the four Ds: dead, dying, diseased, and disabled. The articles caught the public's attention. Now an accomplished expert at media manipulation, Nader sent news releases to newspapers near the worst processing plants. Neal Smith introduced another bill designed to close the loophole, and Nader worked Congress. He learned that approaching senators and representatives directly was not the best way to go because they were more concerned with matters like meeting constituents, fund raising, and getting reelected. The key, according to Nader, was working with the congressional staff who brings the issue to the attention of the boss. Despite constant pressure from the meat-packing industry, a bill passed the House and the Senate.[17] Sen. Walter Mondale (D-Minn.), a sponsor and key player in the fight, singled out Nader for his role in pushing the legislation, commenting: "I commend those selfless private citizens who worked courageously and creatively in this field. I would name Ralph Nader as one of these. I am proud, as a lawyer, that we have some people's lawyers who seek no profit, but who[,] guided only by the motive of public service, are digging out the facts, and leading such blameless lives that they can stand up as examples of the finest of our profession."[18] The signing ceremony at the White House for the Wholesale Meat Act of 1967 was attended by 35-year-old Ralph Nader and 89-year-old Upton Sinclair. One year later, at the age of 90, Sinclair died.[19]

Nader once said, "Every time I see something terrible, it's like I see it at age nineteen. I keep a freshness that way." He followed up the meat act with the Natural Gas Pipeline Safety Act, the Wholesale Poultry Producers Act, and the Radiation Control for Health and Safety Act. As a result of the latter, X-rays were required to be taken with fast film, and the American Dental Association recommended the use of lead aprons when taking X-rays. In 1968, Nader decided to mobilize student power to investigate the Federal Trade Commission (FTC), the government's primary consumer protection agency. He organized a group of seven highly educated, clean-cut ivy leaguers who were dubbed Nader's Raiders by William Greider of the *Washington Post*. They included William Howard Taft IV, a second-year Harvard Law student and great grandson of President William Howard Taft, and Princetonian Edward F. Cox, who would marry Tricia Nixon, the president's daughter. What they discovered at the FTC was an abysmal enforcement record where fewer and fewer complaints were brought against companies and where only one in 125 consumer complaints resulted in any action. The FTC rarely went after any of the big companies, instead focusing on the smaller entities, such as a milliner in Massachusetts who was ordered to stop using "Milan" to describe American-made hats. They found an organization staffed by southerners, under the leadership of chairman Paul Rand Dixon of Tennessee, whose cozy culture consisted of afternoon snoozes, leisurely martini-drenched lunches, and even more leisurely investigations, including a six-year study to prove whether or not Carter's Little Liver Pills benefited livers. The final conclusion: they don't! A final report by the Raiders, together with the findings from an independent investigation by the American Bar Association, described the FTC as a failure and riddled with incompetence. Rand was forced to resign and was replaced by Casper Weinberger, who would eventually become Reagan's secretary of defense. The revitalized agency brought important charges against the likes of McDonald's and the Coca-Cola Company, further enhancing Nader's reputation.[20]

Now known simply as a consumer advocate, Nader was most concerned with the power of corporations to undercut the regulations and the agencies meant to keep them in line. He recruited more than 100 additional students to look into mine safety, water pollution, food additives, and airline service. Consumer regulation became the rage in the 1970s, with Nader leading the way, but with all his newfound celebrity, one thing never changed: his deep-seated need for privacy. A parlor game in Washington tried to determine whether he still lived in his one-room apartment or whether he had moved into a handsome suburban home that was used by the Nader siblings.[21] Ralph liked to keep them guessing. He had an aversion to handshaking and could be prickly when approached for an autograph, often telling the hapless hound, pen and pad in hand: "You should be asking what you can you do."[22]

Despite his success on Capitol Hill, Nader never really fit in with Washington's culture of favors and votes traded. To him alliances were temporary. People who were useful one day could be dropped the next. He even turned on Sen. Ribicoff when a bill to establish a consumer protection agency didn't live up to his expectations.

Calling the bill "unacceptable," he accused Ribicoff, who was guiding the bill through the Senate, of allowing "intolerable erosions." The bill passed the Senate, but because of Nader's comments did not make it through the House.[23]

Perhaps his attack on his home-state senator was simply a prelude to his next act: an all-out assault on Congress itself. In an article in *The New Republic* on August 21, 1971, he claimed that Congress was deluged by lobbyists representing special interests and that corporate cash was buying individual senators and representatives who passed legislation that sounded good but was toothless. In a speech on November 2, 1971, at the National Press Club, Nader announced the Congress Project, an investigation into all 484 members who were up for reelection the next fall. Hundreds of young volunteers were recruited. A 1,000-question form was designed for members of Congress to complete, which would be followed up with personal interviews. The end result would be 484 profiles that Grossman would publish. The project was a bust. The reports were issued in October 1972, too close to the election to have any real impact, and according to the *New York Times*, there were no great revelations. It appears that the politicians had outfoxed Nader. With little to show for all his effort, his public image was damaged as was his reputation with Congress.[24]

Resilient as ever, Nader worked to improve the Freedom of Information Act of 1974 that would make government documents available to the public and tackled the issue of nuclear energy, claiming, "This is the first time that this country has permitted the development of an industry that can wipe the country out." He was behind the successful effort to stop construction of the Cape Kiawanda Nuclear Facility in Oregon. The Palo Verde Nuclear Power Project ordered in 1973 was the last commercial plant built in the United States.[25]

As the 1976 presidential election approached, *The Nation* urged Nader to run for president. Columnist Mary McGrory thought he would be the ideal post-Watergate president. He demurred, preferring to stay above the political fray; instead, he latched on to Jimmy Carter, who sought out Nader's advice about a Carter presidency. Excited about the Georgian, he commented, "You need to watch this guy. Something's going to happen. I never met a politician quite like Carter and I know a lot of them."[26] But the four-year Carter presidency would be less productive for Nader despite the fact that the Democrats controlled Congress and the Carter administration was teeming with ex-Naderites. At times the consumer advocate-in-chief seemed more interested in investigating the transgressions of his former followers than going after real enemies. Nader endured a major defeat over legislation for the Consumer Protection Agency (CPA). He referred to the bill as "the most important piece of legislation ever to come before [C]ongress." The bill had been knocking around since the days of Ribicoff in 1970. Now, with a supposedly sympathetic president in the White House Nader tried again. He traveled to districts of recalcitrant congressmen to lobby, but the bill failed in the House by a vote of 227–189, with 101 Democrats voting no. Said Peter Barash, a legislative assistant, "He pissed off too many people. . . . [H]e just hit a critical mass. You can try to pick off a few senators or representatives here and there. When attacking members becomes a pattern—the rule rather than the exception—the whole institution turns against you."[27] Nader, however, saw things differently, claiming there were no differences between the Democrats and Republicans. The rejection of the CPA was more than just a rejection of consumerism; it represented a resurgence of corporate America, sending a message that they were sick and tired and weren't going to take it anymore! Corporate entities like the U.S. Chamber of Commerce, the Business Roundtable, and the National Association of Manufacturers joined forces to defeat the legislation.[28]

When Ronald Reagan was elected two years later in 1980, Nader commented to a friend, "I know this guy. I had dealings with him when he was governor of California. He's the worst thing we've ever seen because people are going to like him. He's unbelievably conservative and completely disengaged. It's going to be very hard to get things done in the next four years, we're up a creek." In, perhaps, an even harsher assessment, Nader said, "For all his surface charm, soft voice and angled head Reagan allowed his fervent turncoat ideology [he was once a liberal] to transform him into a cruel man with a smile." One of the ironies of Reagan's victory was that Nader had asserted that there was no difference between Carter and Reagan. The new president turned into an implacable foe who never met with him in the White House the way Carter had. Reagan called for less government, meaning less regulation of business. The so-called Reagan Revolution meant that much of what Nader fought for in the 1960s and 1970s would be reversed or not enforced. On Reagan's second day in office, January 22, 1981, he announced the formation of the Task Force on Regulatory Relief to be headed by Vice President George H.W. Bush. Enforcement budgets declined, whereas in the 1970s regulatory agency budgets had grown by 400 percent. In Reagan's first year in office the budgets stayed flat, followed by a 9 percent decline in 1982. The budget of the National Highway and Transportation Safety Agency was cut by 22 percent, and the FTC's was cut by 28 percent.[29]

The Reagan-Bush years (1981–1993) were difficult for Nader. Ignored by Washington and the national media, he returned to the grass roots, taking his message into the hinterlands. In Illinois, he helped defeat an attempt by Illinois Power and Commonwealth Edison to force consumers to pay for cost overruns on new power plants. He started a venture called Citizens Television in Buffalo that featured programs of local interest that allowed businesses to buy advertising for $10 a spot. On the lecture circuit he enjoyed visiting college campuses, especially Harvard, where he delighted in needling the students with a lecture entitled "Nabobs of Narcissism Wallowing in Complacency."[30]

Although he is most famous (or infamous) for his 2000 run at the presidency, Nader ran twice before, as a write-in candidate in 1992 and then as more serious contender of sorts in 1996. The obsessive outsider, who vowed he would never enter politics as a candidate or join a political party (his father's admonition), decided to dip his toe into the icy waters of electoral politics in 1992 because he wanted to be taken seriously again. He entered the New Hampshire Democratic primary to advocate for campaign finance reform and a "none-of-the-above" line on ballots. He urged voters to write in his name if they did not like any of the other contenders, including Tom Harkin (Iowa), Bob Kerrey (Nebraska), Paul Tsongas (Massachusetts), and Bill Clinton. He received 3,056 write-ins or 2 percent of the vote. In 1996, he was approached by the California Green Party to run for president. Although not a party member, or even in agreement with their platform, he could give them credibility as a legitimate third party. He agreed to run and ended up on the Green line in 20 additional states, but he was hesitant about making an all-out run. He took no contributions, ran no advertising, and traveled nowhere. Because of his penchant for privacy, he spent less than $5,000 of his own money to avoid federal laws that require personal financial disclosure above that amount.[31]

For his running mate he chose Winona LaDuke, a member of the Ojibway Band from the White Earth Reservation in Minnesota. Her mother was from a working-class Bronx Jewish family, making this the first Arab-Jewish ticket in American history, at least according to Judaic Law. LaDuke graduated from Harvard and became an activist on behalf of rights of women and Native Americans, an author, and a high school principal.[32] Quoted as saying, "I am interested in reframing the debate on the issues of this society: the distribution of power and wealth, the abuse of power, the rights of the natural world, the environment, and the need to consider an amendment to the U.S. Constitution in which all decisions made today will be considered in the light of their impact on the seventh generation from now."[33] LaDuke was chosen as *Ms.* magazine's Woman of the Year one year after the election.

During the summer of 1996 Nader was polling 8 percent in California, giving the Clintons a good scare. Pleased that he might tip the state in favor of Republican Robert Dole, Nader viewed the Clinton administration "as extremely sleazy[,] . . . full of cowards at the top and frustrated decent people at the bottom" who had given in to the corporate interests just like Reagan. Nader ended the election with 685,291 votes or less than 1 percent (0.71) nationally, coming in fourth behind Clinton, Dole, and Ross Perot. His best state was California, a Green Party stronghold, where he garnered 237,016 or 2.37 percent of the total.[34]

Nader's animosity to the Clinton administration continued unabated into its second term. Like Reagan in the 80s he was shut out by a Democratic administration and became resentful. He took out a lot of his frustration and anger on Vice President Gore, with whom he had had a good relationship during the Reagan years. Gore was an ally whom Nader had rated in the top 10 senators on his issues. They had worked together on tort reform (the right to sue for amounts above actual damage), broadcast licensing, biotechnology, and the environment. Now even Gore refused to see him. He was even an outcast among liberal members of Congress. To Nader, this was evidence of the Democrats morphing into big business–loving Republicans before his eyes. With the doors to the kingdom slammed shut in his face, Nader returned to the grass roots to address his issues and clarify and sharpen his anticorporate critique. His conclusion was that democracy itself was in danger because of the excessive power and influence of corporations. His answer was to break from his role as an outsider fighting the system as he had done for 35 years and to become an insider by running for elective office as a serious candidate. Only that way could he have the influence and clout of the old days.[35]

Nader announced his candidacy for president on February 21, 2000, at the Madison Hotel in Washington, D.C. He would seek the Green Party nomination because "a crash of democracy in our country convinces me to take action. . . . [O]ver the past 25 years big business has increasingly dominated our political economy[,] . . . creating a widening democratic gap between the citizens and the government. . . . Abraham Lincoln, Theodore Roosevelt, Supreme Court Justices Louis Brandeis and William O. Douglas, among others, eloquently warned about what Thomas Jefferson called the excesses of the monied interests dominating people and their governments. . . . [T]he democracy gap in our politics and elections spells a deep sense of powerlessness by people who drop out and do not vote or listlessly vote for the least worst every four years. . . . [T]he focus of our campaign is to focus on active citizenship . . . [,] to create fresh political movements that will displace control by the Democrats and Republicans . . . [:] one political duopoly, the DemRep Party."[36]

Despite the high-flown rhetoric, Nader was a realist about the chances for a third-party victory in a presidential election. What he was really after in 2000 was 5 percent of the vote, entitling him to federal matching funds that could help build a party. His next official step was to win the Green Party nomination four months later at the Denver convention, which, despite some colorful contenders, was pretty much his for the asking. In the meantime there was much to do. He had to show he was serious this time, assemble a staff, recruit volunteers, raise money, gain ballot access in all 50 states, and perhaps, most important, qualify for the crucial televised debates. He would also have to reveal his personal wealth.[37]

Nader looked to former colleagues to build a staff, but for a variety of reasons he was turned down by nearly all of them. They were a lot older now with families, other commitments, and philosophical disagreements about his candidacy. Most were Democrats well aware whom his candidacy would impact. The grueling nature of modern presidential campaigns without the hope of a victory was another reason some backed off. In the end, he chose as campaign manager Theresa Amato, a 35-year-old New York University law School graduate whose only previous political experience was running a campaign in high school. She gathered a staff around her but lacked the confidence and clout to command the campaign like James Carville for Clinton or Karl Rove for George W. Bush. Nader kept a kitchen cabinet who met with the official staff to plan strategy, but Nader called the shots, not Amato, and that was the way he liked it, anyway. Talk show host Phil Donahue, who had welcomed Nader on his show 33 times, signed on as cochair after eliciting a promise from Nader that this time he was serious. Tens of thousands of volunteers joined to get petitions signed, man the telephones, canvas for votes, and get the vote out on election day.[38]

Nader was highly successful in getting on state ballots—not to the extent of George Wallace in 1968 or Ross Perot in 1992, but he ended up on 45 state ballots and the District of Columbia. The exceptions were not exactly Green bastions: Georgia, North Carolina, Alabama, South Dakota, and Wyoming.[39]

Soon after announcing his candidacy he promised to visit all 50 states before the Green Party convention. His intent was to demonstrate his commitment and generate enough support so his poll numbers would meet the 15 percent requirement to participate in the presidential debates. The grand tour sounded like a fine idea, but without a large professional staff, the going would be tricky. He lacked the management depth and experience of the Bush and Gore campaigns. Therefore, many stops, frequent schedule changes, and delays had to be coordinated with local Green chapters' members over whom they had no control. Because of frequent uncertainties, turnout could be embarrassingly low. In North Dakota only 10 people appeared at a rally in an auditorium, and only five showed up for a press conference in New Hampshire. The 66 year old's campaign schedule was so packed with events that little time was set aside for meals, leading to total exhaustion. Local organizers might know that he would be in their town or city and want to plan a series of events, but would not know exactly when he would be arriving or departing. Commented Dan Rowland who oversaw Nader's Salt Lake City visit, "We had believed early on we would have Nader for a full day. . . . Then it became a half day. Then it was whittled down to four and a half hours. . . . We had confirmed appointments with both for editorial board meetings, one at 10 A.M. and one at 3 P.M. We ended up having to dump them both. . . . Individual local media personalities had lined up to do one-on-one interviews with Nader. We had to scrap those on the spot so we could get Nader to the airport. I'm sure he never knew and no one ever told him."[40] He kept his commitment to visit all the states even Hawaii and Alaska. His last stop was in Kansas right before the convention. While on the road his preference was for Hampton Inns because of the free breakfasts. Because he never owned a credit card, he paid his bills by check or cash.

The next step for Nader was to officially secure the Green Party nomination at the Denver convention that was held at the Renaissance Hotel on June 24–25. This was not going to be your father's convention. The hotel was chosen because it agreed to serve organic dishes. Tom-toms called the meeting to order, and applause was strictly verboten! Only "twinkling," silently wiggling one's fingers, was allowed. Perhaps because twinkling is less energy-intensive than applause, it made fewer demands on the cooling system and thus, the environment! The official title of the Denver Greens was the Association of Green Parties. There was another Green Party called the Green Party USA, which was identified with states and localities. The latter had 110,000 members in California and managed to win public office for 30 members in the state. Their convention was being held in Chicago with a platform that called for the abolition of the U.S. Senate and a 100 percent tax on all incomes greater than $100,000. They would endorse Nader, but he refused their backing. The existence of both Greens caused confusion with voters and journalists. On official state ballots Nader was simply listed on the Green Party line.[41]

Nader's opponents for the nomination in Denver were Jello Biafra (né Eric Boucher), the lead singer of the extinct rock band Dead Kennedys and a former candidate for mayor of San Francisco, whose platform called for all businessmen to wear clown suits to work; Stephen Gaskin, founder of a 1960s 1,300-member hippie commune in Tennessee; and Joel Kovel, the Green candidate for a 1998 senate seat in New York. Nader's three opponents received a combined total of 23 votes to Nader's 295. Once again he selected Winona LaDuke for his running mate. His acceptance speech attacked all the usual suspects: Democrats and Republicans, Congress, and corporate America; to this list he added the Commission on Presidential Debates. He referred to Bush and Gore as "indistinguishable—drab and dreary" and at times during the campaign as "Bore and Gush."[42]

Nader got serious about raising cash, even personally calling a list of old friends and colleagues but had little success. David Halberstam was among those who refused to make a donation but wished him good luck anyway. As an advocate of campaign finance reform he took no PAC (Political Action Committee) money or corporate donations. Most of the $8 million he raised, a decent sum for a third-party candidate, came from small donations of $100 or less. He revealed his net worth—$3.8 million—in accordance with campaign finance law, stating that most came from speaking fees and royalties; he estimated his earnings at $14 million over the years, but had given most away to his causes. He put his living expenses at $25,000 a year.[43]

In the opinion of Bill Hillsman, his media strategist who was involved with the successful runs of Jesse Ventura for governor of Minnesota and Sen. Paul Wellstone, the $8 million wasn't spent very effectively. Only $300,000 was used during the final stretch after Labor Day when he should have spent much more. He resisted television because he hated the corporate-owned stations. According to Hillsman, his stubborn streak got in the way of sound decision making.[44]

Presenting his views on the issues and organizing an infrastructure to get out the vote on election day comprised the next phase of the campaign. More than 150,000 volunteers were recruited for the election-day push. He outlined how corporate dominance of the two major parties, referred to as Tweedledee and Tweedledum, have a lock grip on the legislative and regulatory process. He described George W. Bush as a "major corporation disguised as a human being," but reserved special animus for Al Gore because "he knows so much but refuses to act on his knowledge." He thought Bush could justifiably plead ignorance but not Gore. Referring to Gore's pledge to fight big oil, big pharma, and the HMOs, he commented, "Yeah, yeah and I've got a bridge in Brooklyn to sell you."[45]

Under his anticorporate banner Nader expressed views on a whole range of topics, many of which resonated with the American people. To eliminate the power of corporations, he advocated public financing of elections. He favored universal health care, investment in mass transit, cuts in military spending, a higher minimum wage, environmental protection, greater voter participation through week-end voting or a special holiday, abortion rights, and gun control. He opposed free-trade agreements embodied in NAFTA and GATT (General Agreement on Trade and Tariff), claiming they were hastily passed with little debate, superseding domestic laws on the environment and consumer protection.[46]

He tended to stick to his own issues, but as the campaign evolved he took positions on racial profiling, the Middle East, and gay and lesbian rights. He preferred college audiences, but also spoke to other gatherings as he moved away from lengthy, legalistic, issue-ridden dirges to more crowd-pleasing sound bites. He was willing to make some compromises to modern campaigning but only so far; he eschewed celebrity endorsements and photo ops. On a trip to Boston, the town that loves the Red Sox, he argued against spending $600 million of taxpayers money to improve Fenway Park. If anything, he was consistent in his anticorporate jihad, stating, "To win a world series they don't need new sky boxes populated by gluttonous financiers freeloading on the backs of hardworking taxpayers."[47]

The polls varied by state and month, but never surged above 10 percent, with the exception of Alaska where he stood at 17 percent in September. In Ohio and Oregon his personal approval ratings were higher than for Bush and Gore, but if we assume the two states represent the nation, that did not translate into a political preference. Polls in April gave Bush 43 percent, Gore 39 percent, Nader 6 percent, and Pat Buchanan, the Reform Party candidate, 4 percent. Nader was strongest in the West; in California his preference reached 9 percent and in Oregon 7 percent.[48]

One of his frustrations early in the race was his inability to generate media attention, but this would change after a visit with Jim Roberts, the maverick political editor of the *New York Times*. The *Times* often set the agenda as the "paper of record" for the print and broadcast media, so if a story made the front page there, it would be picked up elsewhere. In their friendly meeting the subject quickly turned to California where, Roberts chuckled, "you have the potential to do the most damage," meaning he could really hurt Gore. Roberts advised him to turn his campaign "from an interesting side light, into a real factor in the race," even though it might be as a spoiler. Roberts said that if Nader started drawing big crowds, he would cover him. Roberts followed up with a Nader story the day the Green Party convened in Denver. Written by top political reporter Richard Berke, the piece was entitled "Once Seen as Odd Man Out, Nader Is Rocking Gore's Boat." Another story ran a week later, almost giving the impression that the *Times* was trying to create a spoiler and a story line, to boot![49]

At least in public the Gore campaign said little about Nader when he was on his 50-state tour. However, when bumps were noted in Nader's polls, the vice president's team devised a two-pronged strategy to stop the advance. Typically, major parties co-opt the message of threatening third parties. Gore did this by tacking left on the issues. He attacked "big oil" for their stranglehold on the economy. He advocated for more clean energy and greater efficiencies in the use of fossil fuels. Gore was credible on these topics because he was known as an environmentalist. The vice president went after pharmaceutical pricing and attacked Republicans in Congress for not enacting a prescription drug plan or a patient bill of rights. Of course, Gore never got very specific about the solutions to many problems because he did not want to alienate his corporate benefactors. Because of the presence of Nader in the race, some observers thought Gore's new-found populist rhetoric made the bloated, leaden intellectual a better candidate. Gore's line, "The question is whether you're for the people or for the powerful" may be one that even Gore may have been confused about after eight years with Clinton, at least according to Nader.[50]

Gore's other anti-Nader tactic was to attack him personally. Surrogates like Nevada Democrat Sen. Harry Reid, called Nader ". . . a very selfish person and he's on an ego trip."[51] Even the "grey lady," the *New York Times*, steadied her walker with one hand as she wacked Nader editorially with the other, calling his campaign, "a self indulgent exercise." The *Times* expressed horror with Nader's characterization of Republicans and Democrats as Tweedledee and Tweedledum, stating there were important differences, especially in relation to issues of concern to wage earning voters, and also adding that just because Nader was frustrated during the Clinton years, didn't mean he should play the spoiler role by tilting states like

California into the conservative column. Gore's offensive worked. He halved Nader's poll numbers from 6 percent to 3 percent.[52]

Nader knew he needed a boost, so he asked his friend Greg Kafoury, a lawyer and advance man, to organize an "exquisite event" for an upcoming visit to Portland, Oregon. Kafoury came up with an ambitious and risky plan to stage a rally in the 10,000-seat Portland Memorial Coliseum. As if filling all those seats wouldn't be difficult enough, they decided to charge a $7 admission fee. How would it look to the media if they couldn't fill the venue? Even their private projection was that only 3,000 would attend. They were about to find out. On the day of the rally, August 25, 6,000 tickets were sold. Granted, this was still twice as many as the estimate, but it fell short of filling the arena. In spite of this, the walkups came through; the place filled to capacity, and some even were turned away. Several local Green Party candidates appeared on the stage along with Winona LaDuke, but the star was Ralph himself, who arrived on stage to thunderous applause and enough confetti to fill a tree hugger's heart with horror. He lectured about education reform (turn kids into citizens not consumers), tax reform (tax polluters not average Americans), the political duopoly, and the corrupt political system. The Portland success led to super rallies in Minneapolis, Oakland, Seattle, Chicago, and Boston. No longer featuring a supporting cast of mere locals, the campaign recruited anticorporate fellow travelers like satirical journalist and filmmaker Michael Moore (Nader invested in his first hit *Roger and Me*), populist radio commentator Jim Hightower, the African American actor Danny Glover, the working-man's historian Studs Turkel, and 89-year-old Doris Haddock, known as Granny D, who achieved some fame by walking across America for campaign finance reform. The highlight of the rallies, and the Nader campaign, was the super-rally at New York's Madison Square Garden on October 13, just 25 days before the election: another nail biter, because only 9,000 of the 25,000 seats were sold until the day of the event; nevertheless once again the walk-ups came through to make for a sell-out crowd. The 20 and 30 year olds paid $20 for a party called Nader Rocks the Garden. Michael Moore appeared with actors Tim Robbins, Susan Sarandon, and Bill Murray, who mortified Nader when he plugged his new movie, *Charlie's Angels*. The candidate welcomed supporters to the "politics of joy and justice." In an hour-long speech he lashed out at the "corporate crime wave" and at the duopoly for "letting our country be sold to the highest bidder." Moore told the crowd not to worry about a vote for Nader meaning fewer votes for Gore and a vote for Bush. "The lesser of two evils, you still end up with evil.

You don't make a decision because of fear; you make it on your hopes, your dreams, your aspirations. Follow your conscience, do the right thing."[53]

Nader was well aware of the impact of the presidential debate on the election's outcome. He could make speeches all year long and perhaps appear before one million voters, but in the televised debates he could reach as many as 100 million Americans in just three nights. Until 1984, the League of Women voters ran the show, but beginning in 1988 the Commission on Presidential Debates took over. The word "commission" seems to conjure up an official or governmental body, but in fact, the Commission is a private organization run by Nader's so-called duopoly: the Democrats and Republicans and supported by private or corporate donations. The Commission decides who may participate in the debates. Perhaps because of Perot's strong performance in 1992 (he was not invited back in 1996), the Commission decided to raise the bar in 2000, meaning that a candidate needed an average of 15 percent or more in the five national polls taken in late September to earn a spot before the cameras. The claim by the Commission was that any lower number meant a candidate had little chance of winning. However, this self-serving justification flew in the face of certain inconvenient facts. In 1998, Jesse Ventura, the Reform Party candidate for Minnesota governor, stood at only 10 percent in the polls when he debated Republican Norm Coleman and Democrat Skip Humphrey. He went on to win the election. A similar outcome emerged in Wisconsin when Russ Feingold, who stood at 10 percent for the Democratic nomination for the U.S. Senate before the debates, defeated his Democratic rivals and proceeded to win the statewide race.[54]

Nader, noting that the federal matching funds are given to parties that generate only 5 percent of the vote, filed a lawsuit in federal court charging that corporate support for the debates violated the Federal Election Campaign Act. The lawsuit dragged on in court but got nowhere. James Raskin, a professor at American University who led Nader's challenge, advocated different criteria. Rather than a presidential preference question in the polls, he wanted to ask voters, "who would you like to see in the debates?" The professor had a point; in a Fox poll conducted in July 64 percent of respondents said they wanted Nader and Pat Buchanan, the Reform Party candidate, to be included in the debates because they would be more interesting. Nader forces organized rallies around the theme "Let Ralph Debate—Hey Hey Corporate State Let Ralph Debate." The focal point for their protests was at the Fleet Center in Boston where 12,000 supporters paid $10 each to attend a rally two days before the first debate scheduled at the Clark Athletic Center at the University of Massachusetts Boston campus. Naderites also occupied the offices of the Debate Commission in Washington. Nader announced that he would participate in the debates as a member of the audience. Even with a ticket donated by a follower, he was turned away by a Commission representative and the police, with the explanation, "it's already been decided that whether or not you have a ticket you are not invited." Following the debates and the attendant publicity over the protests, Zogby noted a rise in Nader's poll numbers. In the aftermath of the third debate at Washington University in St. Louis on October 17, polling data reported Nader at 7 percent in California; 8 percent in Minnesota, New Jersey, and Rhode Island; and 10 percent in Oregon. In a sign that voters were dissatisfied with Bush and Gore's lackluster performance in the debates, viewership declined from 46 million in the first debate to 37 million in the second and third debates. One in seven voters reported being undecided about whether to vote for one of the leading candidates.[55]

With the race between Bush and Gore tightening, attacks against Nader by Gore supporters on the left increased. Patricia Ireland of NOW (National Organization for Women), who had once threatened to support a third-party movement in the 1990s because of Clinton's rightward drift, openly pushed for Gore as did David Smith, spokesman for the Human Rights Campaign, the largest gay rights organization. Long-time feminist Gloria Steinem produced, "Top ten reasons why I'm not voting for Ralph Nader." Her reasons ranged from the obvious (he's not running for president, he's running for federal matching funds) to the relevant (the appointment of Supreme Court justices are at stake) to the historic (calling the two parties Tweedledee and Tweedledum is laughable—there are more differences between Gore and Bush than there were between Nixon and Kennedy in 1960). Even a group of former Nader Raiders went public with a request that Ralph step down.[56]

The National Abortion Rights Action League spent $1.5 million on television commercials sounding the alarm that a woman's right to choose would be endangered by a Bush victory. Nader responded that overturning *Roe v. Wade* would not end abortion rights; it would simply revert to the individual states to decide. Of course, this was the last thing pro-choice advocates wanted to hear, because in conservative states a poor woman would be deprived of her rights. His defense seemed to show that Nader had no clue about the stakes and the thinking on the abortion issue.[57]

At least objectively, Nader was not in the race to defeat Gore; all he wanted was his 5 percent of the vote and government cash. So plans emerged from onlookers and from within the Nader camp to come up with a solution to make everybody happy. Steve Cobble, an adviser to the Nader campaign, wanted people to vote their conscience (i.e., Nader) in the 35 states where Bush or Gore had a solid lead. That way Ralph could maximize his vote without tipping the election. For the 15 states that were close, columnist Molly Ivins' advice was to check out the polls right before the election, and in the close states, cast a ballot for Al Gore. Nader seemed to endorse this tactic when he said he was not bothered by "tactical voting." On the other hand, Nader seemed delighted by the fuss he was causing, because of all the publicity it generated. Ralph was relevant again! Cobble and Ivins' supporters assumed that millions of Americans would have heard of their grand plans and spent their time studying the polls, just as they had done, and then would know a "close race" when they saw one.[58]

Next, the *New York Times*, decided to wack Nader once again. In a pair of preelection editorials the *Times* called his candidacy "willful prankishness" and "ego run amok." Ridiculing his assertions that there were no differences between Bush and Gore, the editors asserted there were many on the environment, campaign finance reform, and Supreme Court nominees, who, if appointed by the Republican might give them the votes to overturn *Roe v. Wade*. The *Times* said that despite the fact that polls seemed to give Bush the edge, the race was close, and slight differences in support for Nader could make a difference.[59]

Because Gore was growing desperate, he wanted to approach Nader about dropping out of the race but was not sure whom to contact in the Nader camp. Myron Cherry, a high-ranking adviser who had worked with Nader in the 1970s, was asked to call the candidate directly about dropping out. In exchange, Gore would be receptive to Nader's recommendations for several important ranking posts such as head of the Environmental Protection Agency. Cherry reported back that Nader was totally unreceptive. Said Cherry, "It was like we were pariahs." One final attempt was made by Toby Moffett, an ex-Raider and Connecticut congressman, who agreed to approach Joan Claybrook, a former close associate of Nader's, who might still have some sway with him. She just laughed, stating, "He's one of the most stubborn people in the U.S. It would be a waste of time."[60]

Steve Cobble, Nader's most experienced strategist, sensed that his candidate was not even going to get the 5 percent. So the team had to carefully calibrate where to campaign during the final days before the election. Would they go to battleground states where media coverage was best and where Nader could generate the most publicity as a potential spoiler, or would they go to voter-rich states regardless of the stakes between Gore and Bush? In the end they split the difference between the two groups of states because that strategy maximized Nader's chance of meeting his objective. Of the 17 states he visited in the last two weeks, half were in play between the two main contenders. In terms of actual time spent, 60 percent was in safe states and 40 percent was in battleground states. If he had set out to hurt Gore, the proportion would have reversed.[61]

In the final election tally, Nader did not meet his objective of garnering 5 percent of the vote, so he did not earn federal matching funds. In a development not unusual for third parties, voters responded to Democratic scare tactics. His 2,858,843 popular votes represented only 2.7 percent of total cast. Although Gore defeated Bush by 540,519 popular votes (50,996,582 to 50,456,062), Bush carried the Electoral College 271–266. After weeks of recounts and legal wrangling, Florida's 25 electoral votes ended up in the Bush column; his total was 537 popular votes more than Gore's out of nearly six million cast in the state. Pat Buchanan came in fourth nationally with 438,760 votes.[62]

Of course, there are always many factors that play out in a presidential contest, but in the 2000 race it came down to the Sunshine State. A different outcome there would have change political history. Had Nader heeded calls to step aside, Al Gore would have become president of the United States. A poll taken after the election revealed that of Nader's 97,488 Florida votes, approximately 30 percent came from people who would not have voted at all if Nader had not run. Of the remainder, 40 percent said they would have voted for Al Gore, whereas 20 percent would have pulled the lever (or punched the hole) for George W. Bush. That 20 percent differential between the two leading candidates would have translated into 19,498 extra votes for Gore, more than offsetting Bush's 537 final advantage.[63]

Geographically, Nader showed above-average appeal in the following 10 states: Alaska (8 percent), Maine (6 percent), and Vermont (7 percent) as well as Colorado (5 percent), Washington, D.C. (5 percent), Hawaii (6 percent), Maryland (6 percent), Minnesota (5 percent), Oregon (5 percent), and Rhode Island (6 percent). He was well below average in most of the South, garnering only 1 percent in Alabama, Arkansas, Louisiana, Kentucky, Mississippi, South Carolina, and Tennessee. He obtained over half of his popular vote in just 10 states: California (418,707), New York (244,030), Texas (137,994), Minnesota (126,696), Ohio (117,799), Illinois (103,759), Pennsylvania (103,392), Washington (103,022), Florida (97,488), and Wisconsin (94,070).[64]

Demographically, his best showing was among young people under 29, especially college students. He did well in college towns like Gainesville, Florida (University of Florida), Austin, Texas (University of Texas), and Madison, Wisconsin (University of Wisconsin). Surprisingly, he did better than average among gays and, less surprisingly, among liberals. He did poorly among African Americans, Latinos, feminists, and environmentalists.[65]

From a party-building standpoint, the Greens got a boost from Nader's candidacy. It helped them take root in Nebraska, Kansas, Utah, Montana, and Mississippi and to grow in Texas, Wisconsin, Connecticut, Minnesota, Iowa, and Pennsylvania.[66]

When Nader officially conceded, he responded defiantly to reporters' questions about whether he was a spoiler, stating: "I've always said that it was Al Gore's election to lose, that only Al Gore could defeat Al Gore. In the end the Democratic Party must face the fact that it has become very good at electing very bad Republicans. Apparently it can't even win Tennessee (Gore's home state) or Arkansas (Clinton's home state)."[67]

Nader's political career didn't end in 2000; he ran four years later in 2004 as an independent against Bush and John Kerry, coming in third with 463,655 popular votes (0.38 percent), but ahead of 13 other third-party candidates. In 2008, at the age of 74, he took on Barack Obama and John McCain, boosting his independent candidacy to 739,051 popular votes (0.56 percent) and besting 20 other third-party candidates, including the Green Party's Cynthia McKinney (161,790).[68]

7

Third-Party Also-Rans

Well, back to the old drawing board.

—Peter Arno, cartoonist

Earlier chapters focused on the 11 third parties that have had a significant impact on American history based on meeting at least one of three criteria outlined in the Introduction: (1) They changed the outcome of an election. (2) Their main ideas became the law of the land or had a profound influence on the political system, or (3) they attracted mass support, defined as 10 percent or more of the popular vote. There is another group of third parties that did not make the final cut based on the three criteria but are, nonetheless, worthy of description because, taken as a whole, they demonstrate the great variety of interests and constituencies that have traveled the third-party route from the earliest days of the Republic.

The Anti-Masonic Party of 1832 was America's first third party. Although the standard two-party system did not emerge until the election of 1840, the ideas that animated the Whigs and Democrats had been around for some time. In 1832, the two ideologies, a strong central government versus states' rights, were centered on the National Republicans (who became the Whigs) and Democrats, respectively. That year the Anti-Masonic Party, the first political party to hold a national convention, ran on a platform that opposed the Freemasons, a secret elite organization that the Anti-Masons believed conspired to undermine democracy. Anti-Freemasonry swept through the northeastern United States, giving candidate William Wirt, a former attorney general and, ironically, a Mason who never renounced his membership, close to 100,000 popular votes (7.8 percent) and Vermont's seven electoral votes. The Anti-Masonic party folded into the Whig Party, but rose phoenix-like in 1876. This time, under the leadership of Jonathan Blanchard and the Christian National Association, they again attacked Freemasonry as a threat to democracy, but added three new "anti's" to their repertoire—against Catholics, Mormons, and foreigners, all based on their belief that diversity would bring secularization. They may have been correct in their assessment, but they did not exactly catch on at the polls the second time around, garnering only 2,508 votes, or less than 1 percent (0.02 percent).[1]

The longest-running third party, the Prohibition Party, has fielded a candidate in every election since 1872, but has never won a single electoral vote. Contrary to what many Americans may believe, the Prohibition Party was not responsible for passage of the alcohol-banning 18th Amendment. Credit for that feat goes to the Woman's Christian Temperance Union (WCTU) and the Anti-Saloon League (ASL). The Prohibition Party was founded in 1869 by middle-class religious activists, many of them women who transferred their militancy from abolition to prohibition, believing that drink was detrimental to family life and good regular work habits. Because neither Democrats nor Republicans cared to take up the antialcohol cause, the Prohibition Party called an organizing convention in Chicago in September 1869. Five hundred delegates, many of them women, showed up from 20 states. In 1872, they nominated Maine Quaker James Black for president and crusaded for a ban on the sale and consumption of alcoholic beverages. Because of their narrow cause and the fact that many prohibitionists supported the main parties, they only garnered 5,608 votes (0.08 percent) of 6,466,357 votes cast. By the late 1800s they broadened their platform and did significantly better, favoring protective tariffs in support of industry, religious freedom, women's rights (the vote and equal pay), restrictions on immigration and financial speculation, and government control of utilities and railroads. With a good showing in 1892 under the leadership of John Bidwell, a New York–born Mexican-American War major and congressman, the Prohibitionists won 255,841 popular votes (2.3 percent). In 1904, another good year, the party picked up 259,539 votes, perhaps because the name of their very own candidate—James Swallow—roused the righteous to the evils of drink. When the prohibition amendment was ratified in 1919, their fortunes declined but revived with the repeal of prohibition in 1933. Lately, they appear as a speck in the political heavens, winning only 140 votes in 2004, but making a modest comeback in 2008 (655 votes).[2]

Although women could not vote until passage of the 19th Amendment in 1920, this did not stop two unusual women from seeking the highest office in the land. Perhaps the founders could never imagine a woman seeking the presidency, so they did not bother to explicitly restrict the office to gentlemen only. Nonetheless, in 1872, Victoria Woodhull became the first woman to run for president. Victoria was born on September 23, 1838, in Homer, Ohio, to a small-time entrepreneur who lost much of his modest fortune in the Panic of 1837. She and her mother, Annie, never quite fit into local society. One fine day a gaggle of Homer's leading ladies paid a visit to the white cottage on Main Street to remind Annie that curtains were missing from her windows, to which Annie replied, "windows are for light and air" and sent them on their un-merry way. Like her mother, Victoria went against the grain. At 15, she married Canning Woodhull, a doctor, with whom she had two children. After learning he was an alcoholic and womanizer, she left him, married two more times, and experimented with "free love," a topic she lectured on to brimming lecture halls when she was short of cash.[3]

With the financial backing of Cornelius Vanderbilt, who was rumored to be her sister Tennessee's lover, Victoria and Tennie became Wall Street's first female stockbrokers. In 1871, Victoria addressed the House Judiciary Committee, arguing that women had the right to vote because the 14th (citizenship for former slaves) and 15th (vote for former slaves) Amendments granted the right to all citizens. Her appearance before the committee and the simplicity of her arguments catapulted her into the leadership ranks of the suffrage movement. In 1872, she became a founder of the Equal Rights Party, which would challenge the orthodoxy of her time. In New York City on May 10, 1872, Woodhull was nominated for president of the United States. Her platform advocated the vote for women, a woman's right to control her body, and better conditions for workers. In another "first" the convention selected the black abolitionist, Frederick Douglass, as her running mate. There are reports that she won about 2,000 votes, but in many precincts officials refused to count her tickets. In the 19th century, her candidacy faced cultural issues and questions about whether women were actually citizens, let alone qualified as presidential candidates. Her age was another problem. She would not have qualified even if she were a man, because she would not have been 35 at the swearing in on March 4, as the Constitution requires.[4]

Neither of the major parties would take up the cause of women's suffrage, so remnants of the Equal Rights Party approached Belva Lockwood, a 54-year-old radical from upstate New York, to be their candidate in 1884. Lockwood, a self-made professional, was one of the few female trial lawyers in the country and the first woman to argue a case before the Supreme Court. Her platform called for women's suffrage; equal rights regardless of race, sex, or nationality;

reform of marriage and divorce laws; and temperance. Lockwood won 4,149 votes in six states and ran again in 1888, but no votes were recorded for her in that election.[5]

Third parties representing aspects of racial, religious, and ethnic concerns—pro and con—have been a fixture of American political life since the middle of the 19th century. Some of the significant third parties had those concerns, but other lesser lights emerged during the 20th century as minorities pushed for their interests and others resisted those demands. The America First Party was founded in 1943 by Gerald L.K. Smith, an anti-Semitic isolationist and anti-New Dealer. With the nation in the midst of fighting a two-front war against two vicious opponents, it seemed a little late to start an isolationist political party. Nevertheless, Smith took the name from the America First Committee, which had opposed American entry into World War II. The Committee protested the use of their name by Smith, even refusing to let him join their group. Smith, an evangelical preacher was described by the writer H. L. Mencken as "the damndest orator ever heard on this or any earth." When Charles Lindbergh, a founder of the America First Committee, refused the party's presidential nomination in 1944, Smith took the nomination for himself. He called for an investigation into the war policies of FDR, whom he claimed was propping up the British Empire, and advocated a plan to create a homeland for American blacks in Africa. Smith won 1,780 votes in Michigan and Texas. In 1947, the party was renamed the Christian Nationalist Party. Aside from some positions on the economy and veterans affairs, their rabidly anti-Semitic platform called for America to be saved from "Christ-hating Jews and their communist pawns" and also called for the "deportation of all domestic supporters for the creation of a Jewish state in Palestine" and a halt to immigration by "Asiatics, including Jews, and members of the colored races." At their 1948 St. Louis convention, Smith was nominated once again to head the presidential ticket. The party tried again in 1952, this time offering the nomination to Gen. Douglas MacArthur. He declined the honor.[6]

In 1948, another racially motivated party arose when southern delegates walked out of the Democrats' Philadelphia convention because a civil rights plank was included in the party platform. Under the leadership of South Carolina senator Strom Thurmond, the bolters formed the States' Rights Party or Dixiecrats. At their Birmingham convention, Thurmond was nominated for president, and Mississippi governor Fielding Wright got the nod for vice president. The platform advocated states' rights and the continuation of racial segregation. Although the Dixiecrats won only 2.4 percent of the national vote (1,175,930), their regional strength allowed Thurmond to carry four states in the Electoral College—Louisiana, Mississippi, South Carolina, and Alabama—and rack up 39 electoral votes, second to Teddy Roosevelt's wildly popular Bull Moose Party of 1912.[7]

During the civil rights era in the 1960s, African Americans organized politically to fight for racial justice, forming the Freedom Now Party (1963–1965) and the Black Panthers (1966–1982). Neither fielded candidates for national office but focused instead on activism in states and cities with big African American populations. William Worthy, a correspondent for the Baltimore *Afro-American*, organized Freedom Now because of his deep dissatisfaction with the Democrats' and Republicans' commitment to full racial equality. He was especially angered at the Democrats' association with southern segregationists. Worthy felt that only an all-black party with the balance of power in Congress could influence the legislative process. Organized in heavily black cities such as Chicago, Cleveland, Detroit, and Los Angeles, the platform called for a commitment to "take" African American freedom, economic progress, guaranteed employment, and the end of racism in the United States, Africa, Asia, and Latin America. In 1964, the Freedom Now Party ran candidates for local office in New York, Connecticut, and California. The main effort was in Michigan under the leadership of the Reverend Albert Clevage Jr. With huge potential from more than 750,000 blacks in the state, 39 candidates stood for local and statewide office, including governor, lieutenant governor, and secretary of state. However, gubernatorial candidate Clevage won only 4,767 votes (0.2 percent) the highest of any of the candidates. In a newspaper photo, Clevage tried to suggest that Martin Luther King Jr. supported the idea of an all-black party, but King denied any involvement or support for Clevage and his cohorts. After passage of the 1964 Civil Rights Act and the 1965 Voting Rights Act, the party disbanded.[8]

With dozens of race riots as a backdrop during the summer of 1966, the Black Panther Party was organized in Oakland, California, rejecting the integrationist strategy of the more moderate civil rights organizations like the NAACP and the Southern Christian Leadership Conference. Founders Huey Newton and Bobby Seale's platform demanded black civil rights and an end to police brutality, but the party was also confrontational, calling for blacks to arm themselves and to demand their rights by "whatever means necessary." Panthers wanted a United Nations–supervised plebiscite among the "black colony" to determine the will of the black people as to their national identity. Although the party endorsed certain candidates for elective office, they were more interested in community-based action such as armed patrols to protect ghetto residents from police. Shootouts with the police resulted in the deaths of 28 members, but the Panthers also did good works such as providing free breakfasts for children, establishing medical clinics, and helping the elderly. They developed relationships with left-wing militants in the Middle East, Africa, and Europe. A 1970 Harris survey reported that 25 percent of African Americans agreed with the views of the Black Panthers. From its founding in 1966, local and national law enforcement agencies tried to undermine support for the party through court proceedings, fines, parking tickets, and bail bonds, all designed to drain the party's finances. As a result of political mistakes and financial ruin, the Black Panther movement came to an end in 1980. Perhaps its most famous legacy is their slogan, "Power to the People."[9]

Now it was the turn of Chicanos, or Americans of Mexican descent, to get organized and fight for their rights. In 1970, La Raza Unida (RUP) or United People's Party was formed to fight decades of oppression and impoverishment by the larger white society that had relegated Chicanos to second-class citizenship. RUP referred to the Democrats and Republicans as a "two-party dictatorship." Under the competing national leadership of Jose Angel Gutierrez, a Texas graduate student, and Rodolfo "Corky" Gonzales of Colorado, a professional boxer and businessman, RUP organized under state, regional, and local bosses. In 1972, RUP gained official status in Texas and became the first statewide all-ethnic third party in the nation when Ramsey Munoz, its Texas gubernatorial candidate, captured 6 percent of the vote. Munoz called for a redistribution of wealth, bilingual education, and other reforms. RUP organized chapters in California, Arizona, New Mexico, and parts of the Midwest, but in the 1978 governor's race in Texas, Mario Campean won only 2 percent of the vote, so the party was officially delisted. In some locations RUP eschewed politics altogether and organized around social services for Mexican Americans. RUP never had a cohesive structure or overall philosophy. In some places and at some times it was nationalist and at other times or places, socialist or communist. Its decline came in part from the poor showing in the 1978 election and, in part, from the belief of many Chicanos that RUP was too militant, resulting in their unwillingness to abandon the Democratic Party.[10]

Admittedly, the 10 percent cutoff established as one of the three criteria for a third party to be designated significant is somewhat arbitrary. Ten percent, however, does seem to suggest that a party has achieved a reasonable level of acceptance by voters. However, a case could be made for a 15 percent–or even 5 percent cutoff. Fifteen percent is the level of support required by the Commission on Presidential Debates to be a participant in the nationally televised Q & A.

On the other hand, the federal government is required to provide federal matching funds to any political party that garners as little as 5 percent of the vote. Political scientist Walter Dean Burnham also seems to think that 5 percent may be significant because, as he states, "at that level a party is more likely than not to be associated with a realignment or at least a period of high tension."[11] In any event, there were two parties that won between 5 and 10 percent of the vote that will be briefly profiled: The Socialist Party of the early 20th century and John B. Anderson's 1980 National Unity Party.

Socialism as a political movement had its roots in the Workingman's Party of the early 19th century. By 1877, the Socialist Labor Party (SLP) was formed, running its first presidential candidate, Simon Wing, in the election of 1892, when he won only 21,173 votes (0.02 percent). They persisted until well into the 20th century, making it the second longest-running party after the Prohibitionists. In 1901, a faction of the SLP split off and together with American Railway Union president Eugene Debs formed the Socialist Party, a much more ideologically diverse group party than its predecessor.[12]

At the turn of the 20th century most workers lived in a world of poverty and economic instability. To improve their prospects, some sought an alternative to the capitalist system, where workers would own the means of production and where wealth would be more evenly distributed. The group denounced the Democrats and Republicans for favoring the status quo and believed that the demands of the Populists and Progressives for reform of the existing system did not go far enough. Debs said, "the Democrats and Republicans are the political wings of the capitalist system and such differences that arise between them relate to spoils not principles."[13] The Socialist Party wanted to unite all workers as a class to act in concert against the power of the capitalists.

From its beginning the Socialist Party was obsessed with its independence from the two main parties and required anyone nominated for an office to be a party member for at least two years, thus ruling out any crossovers for purposes of political expediency. In 1904, the party claimed 20,000 members; by 1912, their high-water mark, membership rose to 150,000, making it a truly mass party. Although most popular among immigrants in New York City and Milwaukee, where Jewish and German newcomers brought their political ideologies with them from Europe, they also claimed thousands of members in places like Pennsylvania, Ohio, Oklahoma, California, and Washington. Three hundred twenty-three socialist newspapers were read by more than two million readers. The *Appeal to Reason*, published in Girard, Kansas, sold as many as 760,000 copies in a single issue. By 1911, more than

1,000 socialists held local political office, including 56 mayors of small towns as well as seats in 14 state legislatures. They controlled the mayor's office in Milwaukee and elected Victor Berger to Congress.[14]

Indiana-born Debs (1855–1926) worked his way up from the railway yards to become leader of the American Railway Union. When the government intervened on behalf of the owners during the Pullman Strike of 1894, Debs was arrested and imprisoned. There he spent time reading the works of Karl Marx and decided to become a Socialist. After electoral warmups in the elections of 1904 and 1908, when he won slightly less than 3 percent of the presidential vote, he reached his pinnacle in 1912, garnering 6 percent of the total and 901,873 popular votes. Debs did not expect to win these elections; his idea was to educate workers about the evils of capitalism. In the 1912 platform, the system was attacked as "corrupt and the source of unspeakable misery and suffering of the whole working class." The Democrats and Republicans were described "as the faithful servants of the oppressors." The party wanted workers to gain their rightful inheritance by seizing the powers of the government and industry. As the "political expression of the economic interest of the workers," the party platform called for a constitutional convention that would reorganize the government by abolishing the Senate, ending the presidential veto, downgrading the role of the Supreme Court (i.e., elimination of judicial review), and the curbing of a court's power to issue injunctions. Other planks demanded collective ownership of the transportation and communication networks and the banking and currency systems, a shortened workday, elimination of child labor, minimum wage scales, unemployment insurance, workman's compensation, a graduated income tax, and an inheritance tax.[15]

Although the party declined in the election of 1916 when Debs stepped aside in favor of Allan Benson, a lackluster candidate, there were other more profound reasons for its erosion. The party's opposition to American entry into World War I caused a firestorm of criticism in the jingoistic press and by politicians. Passage of the Espionage Act of 1917 allowed the Post Office to seize socialist publications sent through the mail. Some leaders, as well as the rank-and-file members, were picked up by the authorities, interrogated, indicted, and jailed. By the end of the war one-third of the local chapters closed, as membership declined by 90 percent. In 1920, the first year women could vote, Debs made his final run at the White House from an Atlanta jail. However, this didn't stop the Hoosier socialist from garnering more 900,000 votes or 3.4 percent of the total. Many who abandoned the party joined forces with the La Follette Progressives in 1924, and some joined the Communists. In 1928, ex-minister Norman Thomas retrieved the party banner and ran in every election between 1928 and 1948. In the elections of 1952 and 1956, Maryland Quaker Darlington Hoopes picked up the much tattered banner, but won only 2,000 votes. Many old socialists had simply died off or joined the New Deal's Democratic coalition.[16]

The National Unity Party's leader, John B. Anderson, was born on February 20, 1922, in Rockford, Illinois, to an intensely religious family of Scandinavian decent. After serving in a field artillery unit in Europe during World War II, he earned a law degree at the University of Illinois in 1946, followed by a graduate degree from Harvard three years later. In 1960, he embarked on a 20-year congressional career representing the 16th Congressional District as a strict conservative, voting against social welfare programs such as food stamps and Medicare. Anderson supported Barry Goldwater for president in 1964 and even sponsored a constitutional amendment recognizing "the authority and law of Jesus Christ savior and ruler of nations."[17] Later, he admitted this was a mistake, stating, "I wasn't really sensitive to the tremendous ethnic, religious and social diversity that characterized this nation."[18]

By the mid-1960s he had a change of heart about his conservative views, and although he would remain fiscally prudent, he turned liberal on the social issues, favoring the Equal Rights Amendment, choice on abortion, civil rights, and campaign finance reform, even calling for the resignation of fellow Republican Richard Nixon during the Watergate scandal. In 1978, as the third-ranking Republican in the House of Representatives, his seat was targeted by the resurgent right wing of the GOP, and after years of winning by landslide majorities, he narrowly escaped defeat. The Right smelled blood, and Anderson knew he was likely to lose in 1980, so he decided to run for the presidential nomination as the representative of his party's moderate wing. Perhaps he felt it might be better to be defeated for the presidential nomination than go down as a congressional candidate after all those years in Washington. His main opponents for the Republican nomination were the former actor and aging conservative California governor Ronald Reagan and former congressman George H. W. Bush. Anderson ran well in New England, coming in a strong second in Massachusetts and Vermont, but reached the end of the line in his home state where Reagan defeated him 49 percent to 38 percent.[19]

No longer feeling at ease in his own party and noting the weakened position of President Jimmy Carter because of the economy and Iranian hostage standoff, Anderson decided to seek the presidency as the candidate of the National Unity Party. His political calculus also took into account the high number of Americans (37 percent) who declared themselves independent, and in April 1980, he announced his decision to run. During the early stages of the campaign he appeared to be onto something, for his standing in preference polls stood at 20 percent.[20]

Anderson never expected to win the election; he wanted to be honest with the American people about the country's need for sacrifice. Unfortunately, Anderson's numbers slid steadily downhill from his spring high. The centerpiece of his program was a 50 cent per gallon gasoline tax, as a conservation measure, that would be offset by a reduction in the Social Security tax. He wanted no decreases in the personal income tax but called for a reduction in business taxes to stimulate the economy and encourage job growth. He offered to cut the defense budget by eliminating certain weapons programs and to invest in cities with money collected from new alcohol and tobacco taxes. On the social issues he opposed school prayer and favored gay rights.[21]

Like other third parties, the National Unity Party faced many obstacles. Money was short; Reagan and Carter each had three to four times more cash. Although Anderson managed to get on the ballot in all 50 states, it was at a considerable drain in money, time, and effort. He could only spend about $2 million on media, roughly 10 percent of the amount Reagan had available. By Labor Day when the real fight begins, Anderson was already $1 million in debt. However, because of his relatively good polls early in the campaign (15 percent in July) he qualified for a spot in the televised debates. However, Carter, sensing that he was being hurt more than Reagan by Anderson's presence, refused to participate in the first debate. This deprived Anderson the stature of an equal contender. By the final debate on October 28, Anderson's polls were so low that he was denied a place in the final crucial televised encounter. Meanwhile, the GOP rallied around Reagan, and Carter called Anderson just another Republican.[22]

Without the intense emotional attachment to Anderson or an issue that usually animates successful third-party candidacies, Anderson looked more and more like a conventional nominee as he headed into the final stretch. On election day he ended with 6.6 percent of the vote (5,719,850), coming in third behind Reagan and Carter. Anderson did best in the Northeast (13 percent) and worst in the South (3 percent). He did well among the young 18–24 (14 percent), students (28 percent), college graduates (12 percent), and top earners (10 percent). He performed poorly among African Americans (1 percent). Although he did relatively well for a third-party candidate, Anderson had no impact on the outcome of the race. Even if all of Anderson's votes had gone to Carter, Reagan would have maintained his popular vote majority (51 percent) and Electoral College sweep, winning 44 states and 489 electoral votes out of 538 available.[23]

Summary and Conclusions

The stability and resilience of the two main parties has been a remarkable feature of American political life. Like the mighty Mississippi that flows through the heart of America, the Democrats and Republicans just keep rolling along. This doesn't mean they haven't changed positions on the great issues or dropped and added constituencies to gain the advantage. The Grand Old Party (GOP) started life as a northern party reviled in the South because it advocated against the expansion of slavery. Now the Republicans are the voice of the white South. Originally, the Democrats found support among small farmers, many of whom lived below the Mason-Dixon Line and who believed in states' rights and supported slavery. Now the Democrats stand for big cities, minorities, and government activism at the national level. No doubt many Americans believe that the two-party system is enshrined in the Constitution. Of course, it is not. Numerous founders, including George Washington, opposed the idea of political parties.

Since the advent of the modern two-party system in 1840, there have been only three main parties. The Democrats, despite a temporary schism in 1860 over slavery, have survived for 170 years, whereas the Whigs at 14 years and the Republicans at 156 years, together have matched their rival's longevity. Although the donkey and the elephant have clearly demonstrated superior survival skills, these political animals have not always been open to new ideas advocated by outspoken political outliers. The reason is simple: they have not wanted to offend the great mass that they depend on for support. As a result, determined believers with new ideas formed their own parties. However, they too have faced constraints. Often they lacked the financial and media support enjoyed by the Democrats and Republicans. Ballot access was a problem after 1888 when official ballots replaced a freewheeling system where parties printed and distributed their own "tickets." In the new system each state made its own rules about who would be listed on the new, so-called, Australian ballot. As if the influence of two main parties hadn't made the rules difficult enough, now there would be 50 rule books to decipher and master. Third parties had to overcome the prejudices of the electorate, who were tethered to the two main parties by emotion and by the simple calculation, promoted by the Republicans and Democrats in their own interest, that a third party cannot win, so why waste a vote.

Since the early 19th century more than 100 third parties have accounted for almost 300 candidacies, but only 11 have been significant; that is, they changed history or provided important insights into what many Americans were thinking at a particular time and place in the life of the nation. Successful third parties or independent candidacies have emerged when important matters have not been adequately addressed by the two major parties. The era before the Civil War seemed a particularly fertile period. The antislavery movement gave birth to the Liberty Party and the Free Soilers, both of which were antecedents to the antislavery Republicans. The large influx of Irish and German Catholics in the 1840s and 1850s gave rise to the anti-immigrant, anti-Catholic American Party. With sectional passions near a boiling point before the election of 1860, the Constitutional Union Party tried to arrest the danger to the Union embodied in those emotions.

After the Civil War a new class of industrialists rose who were willing and able to stifle the efforts of farmers and workers to gain a fair share of the new wealth created by mass production and new technologies. The Greenback and People's (Populists) Parties emerged out of farmers' attempts to transform the government from an instrument of the rich into a benevolent representative of the people's interests. In the early decades of the 20th century, middle-class progressives sought to help the working poor. Their instruments were the Bull Moose Party and La Follette Progressives. The Great Depression of the 1930s seems to have been a period when third parties would prosper, as voters looked for solutions to high unemployment and massive foreclosures of homes and farms. In the elections of 1932 and 1936, however, third parties were not a significant factor because the people believed that Franklin Roosevelt would offer the type of radical reform that a third party might promote.

His New Deal did not end the Depression—the war did that, but daily life improved and people believed that there was some hope for the future and were willing to live with his reforms.

The 44-year period after La Follette's run as a Progressive in 1924 was a dry spell for significant third parties. In the Depression, World War II, and the postwar boom years, Americans—or perhaps it would be more accurate to say white Americans—seemed to feel the political system was in good hands. On the other hand, African Americans, many of whom fought and died in World War II to secure the freedom of others, now wanted it for themselves, and many whites resisted their demands. In the tense, racially charged atmosphere of the 1960s civil rights era, segregationist governor George Wallace of Alabama and his American Independent Party launched an anti-integration, anti-Washington movement that shook the political foundations of the country and transformed the Democratic South into a Republican stronghold.

By the early 1990s many Americans expressed frustration with "politics as usual," concerned as they were about the federal deficit, the influence of special interests, and the number of good-paying factory jobs going overseas under various trade agreements. Their savior would be a 62-year-old Texan named Ross Perot. For a while in the spring of 1992, it looked like Perot might break the statistical losing streak of third-party candidates. His poll numbers put him in first place, with nearly 40 percent of the vote, making it unrealistic for Clinton and Bush, the Democratic and Republican nominees, to use the tried-and-true tactic of portraying a vote for the third-party candidate as a wasted vote. This time people could believe that Perot would actually win the election, and the billionaire had unlimited personal funds to promote his candidacy. However, Perot's own behavior sabotaged his campaign, although, despite his kookiness, he ended with a respectable 19 percent of the vote. So potent were his issues that the Republicans incorporated them into a program called the "Contract with America," catapulting the GOP into control of Congress, in 1994, for the first time in 40 years.

Simmering personal resentments and a stubborn commitment to his issues prompted Ralph Nader to run for president in 2000. His aim was to gather 5 percent of the vote, allowing him to qualify for federal matching funds and to build a movement to take government away from corporate special interests and turn it back to the people. He did not achieve his main goal, but he had a more immediate impact by becoming the second third-party candidate ever to change the outcome of an election with less than 3 percent of the vote. (The first third party to change the outcome to an election was the Liberty party in 1844.) He accomplished this feat by taking enough votes from Al Gore in Florida to throw the election to George W. Bush.

During the 19th century, issues were the driving force behind significant third parties. Candidates for president were secondary and were usually selected at nominating conventions from a list of qualified individuals. In the 20th century, however, charismatic personalities were party founders. Issues mattered, but the entities would not have come into existence without political dynamos such as Teddy Roosevelt, George Wallace, Ross Perot, and Ralph Nader. TR, a former president, was an established political figure in his own right, but the communication and transportation revolutions made Wallace, Perot, and Nader possible. Each became a well-known media personality before his run at the White House. Ease and speed of air travel meant these candidates could efficiently traverse the nation, visiting constituencies everywhere. The media's voracious appetite for the offbeat personality and the "horse-race" aspect of modern politics made them media darlings. The candidates could reach more voters with a single national television appearance than they could in a year of personal campaigning.

If the recent past is any indication, there seems to be little doubt that third parties will persist. From 1984 to 2008, a total of 48 third parties fielded candidates in the seven presidential elections of that period. Among them were old stalwarts like the Socialists, the Socialist Workers, and the Prohibitionists as well as newer groups such as We, The People; the Greens; the Objectivists; the Constitution Party, and the Libertarians. Whether a history-making third party will emerge is less certain. There seems to be no shortage of issues on which to base a new movement. Corporate special interests still influence Congress. The deficit is bigger than ever, as is the rate of unemployment as factory jobs continue to disappear.

While the Democrats seemed fairly unified despite the dominance of the left, there appears to be a serious split in Republican ranks between the far right and the moderates. And with most Americans at the center of the political spectrum and with more identifying as independents both parties must carefully craft their appeals if they intend to capture an electoral majority. It is not inconceivable that a new party could emerge from the Republican side of the aisle. If the far right captures the Republican mantel, then the moderates could join with independents and conservative Democrats to form a new third party. The candidacy of John Anderson in 1980 offers a model for such a development. Anderson was a fiscally conservative Republican but was liberal on many of the social issues. Although his candidacy never generated the kind of enthusiasm that might have catapulted him onto a list of top-ranking third-party candidates, he managed to attract more than 6 percent of the vote. If the current Democratic administration doesn't craft solutions to the myriad of problems facing the nation and with voters wanting a change but remaining skeptical of the far right, which controls the GOP, a new centrist third-party movement may well emerge.

Appendix

Third Parties and Independent Candidacies Since 1832

Anti-Masonic	1832
Liberty	1840–1844
Free Soil	1848–1852
National Liberty	1848
Southern Rights	1852
Native American	1852
American (Know-Nothings)	1856, 1876–1880, 1888, 1920–1924
Constitutional Union	1860
Straight Out Democratic	1872
Equal Rights	1872, 1884–1888
Prohibition	1872–2008
Greenback	1876–1884
Independent Democrat	1880
Union Labor	1888
Socialist Labor	1888–1976
Peoples (Populists)	1892, 1904–1908
National Democratic	1896
National Prohibition	1896
Socialist	1900–1956, 1976–1980, 1992, 2000–2008
Continental	1904
Independence	1908
United Christian	1908
Bull Moose Progressive	1912
Progressive	1916
Farmer Labor	1920, 1928–1932
Single Tax	1920
Progressive (LaFollette)	1924

Communist	1924–1932, 1940, 1968–1984
Commonwealth Land	1924
Jacksonian	(non presidential) 1932
Jobless	1932
Liberty	1932
Union	1936
Christian	1936
Independent	1940
America First	1944
Texas Regulars	(non-presidential) 1944
States Rights (Dixiecrats)	1948, 1956
Progressive	1948–1952
Socialist Workers	1948–1908
Constitution	1952, 1964
Poor Man's Party	1952
American Third Party	1956
Christian National	1956
National States Rights	1960–1964
Constitution	1960
Conservative	1960
Tax Cut	1960
Independent Afro-American	1960
Freedom Now Party	1964
Universal	1964–1972
American Independent	1968–1980, 1988
Peace and Freedom	1968, 1988–1996, 2004
McCarthy	1968
People's Constitution	1968
Libertarian	1972–1980, 1988, 2000–2008
Peoples	1972
America First	1972, 1996
Independent	1976–1988
American	1976–1996
U.S. Labor	1976
Restoration	1976
Black Panthers	(non-presidential)
RUP	(non-presidential)
United American	1976
John Anderson (National Unity Party)	1980–1984
Citizens	1980–1984
Right to Life	1980, 1988
Workers World	1980–1996, 2004
Statesman	1980
Middle Class	1980
Down With Lawyers	1980
National Peoples	1980
Populist	1984–1988

Alliance	1984
Workers League	1984–1992
Big Deal	1984
United Sovereign Citizens	1984
New Alliance	1988–1992
Consumer	1988
National Economic Recovery	1988
Grassroots	1988–2000
Third World Assembly	1988
Ross Perot	1992
America First	1992
US Taxpayers	1992–1996
Natural Law	1992–1996
Economic Recovery	1992
Independent	1992
Take Back America	1992
Apathy	1992
Third Party	1992
Looking Back	1992–1996
Reform	1996–2000, 2008
Green	1996–2008
Social Equality	1996, 2004
Independent Grass Roots	1996
Constitution	2000–2008
World Workers	2000
Independent (Nader)	2004–2008
Christian Freedom	2004
Concerns of People	2004
Personal Choice	2004
Socialism and Liberation	2008
Boston Tea Party	2008
New	2008
New American Independent	2008
We The People	2008
Objectivist	2008
Vote Here	2008
US Pacifist	2008

Sources: Ness and Ciment, *The Encyclopedia of Third Parties in America;* Dave Leip's Atlas of U. S. Presidential Elections, http://uselectionatlas.org/RESULTS/index.html.

Notes

CHAPTER 1: ANTEBELLUM THIRD PARTIES

1. Phillips P. Moulton, ed. *The Journal and Major Essays of John Woolman* (New York: Oxford University Press, 1971), 7.

2. Merton Dillon, *The Abolitionists: The Growth of a Dissenting Minority* (DeKalb, IL: Northern Illinois University Press, 1974), 7–9; Dwight Dumond, *Antislavery: The Crusade For Freedom in America* (Ann Arbor: University of Michigan Press, 1961), 8.

3. Richard H. Sewell, *Ballots for Freedom: Antislavery Politics in the United States, 1837–1860* (New York: Oxford University Press, 1976), 4; University of Virginia Library Historical Census Browser. Available at http://fisher.lib.virginia.edu/collections/stats/histcensus/.

4. Dillon, *The Abolitionists: The Growth of a Dissenting Minority*, 10–12; Dumond, *Anti-Slavery: The Crusade for Freedom in America*, 129; Peter Kolchin, *American Slavery 1619–1877* (New York: Hill and Wand, 1993), 185.

5. University Of Virginia Library Historical Census Browser. Available at http://fisher.lib.Virginia.edu/collections/stats/histcensus/

6. Liberator Files, 1831. Available at http://www.theliberatorfiles.com/category/year/1831/.

7. Dillon, *The Abolitionists: The Growth of a Dissenting Minority*, 39, 63, 122; William B. Hesseltine, *Third Party Movements in The United States* (Princeton, NJ: Van Nostrand & Co., 1962), 32; Sewell, *Ballots For Freedom: Antislavery Politics in the United States, 1837–1860*, 6.

8. Dillon, *The Abolitionists: The Growth of a Dissenting Minority*, 126–27; Frederick Blue, *The Free Soilers* (Urbana, IL: University of Illinois, 1973), 3; Hesseltine, *Third Party Movements in the United States*, 32–33; Howard P. Nash, *Third Parties in American Politics* (Washington, D.C.: Public Affairs Press, 1959), 12, 14, 17, 20.

9. Senator Henry Clay of Kentucky, Speech, February 7, 1839, 25th Congress, 3rd Session, Appendix to the *Congressional Globe*, 355–59.

10. Sewell, *Ballots For Freedom: Antislavery Politics in the United States, 1837–1860*, 20, 48–49.

11. Ibid, 49–51.

12. Ibid, 61–63, 73; Nash, *Third Parties in American Politics*, 28.

13. Betty Fladeland, *James Gillespie Birney: From Slaveholder to Abolitionist* (Ithaca, NY: Cornell University Press, 1955), 3–4, 12, 15, 19, 24, 37, 66, 161.

14. Sewell, *Ballots For Freedom: Antislavery Politics in the United States, 1837–1860*, 94–97.

15. William A. DeGregorio, *The Complete Book of U.S. Presidents* (New York: Barnes & Noble, 2004)., 143; Scott G. Thomas, *The Pursuit of the White House* (New York: Greenwood Press, 1987), 21–23.

16. Arthur M. Schlesinger Jr. and Fred L. Israel, *History of American Presidential Elections*, Vol. II (Philadelphia: Chelsea House Publishers, 2002), 690.

17. Fladeland, *James Gillespie Birney: From Slaveholder to Abolitionist*, 188; Immanuel Ness and James Ciment, *The Encyclopedia of Third Parties in America* (Armonk, NY: M.E. Sharpe, 2000), 344–45; Steven J. Rosenstone, Roy L. Behr, and Edward H. Lazarus, *Third Parties in America* (Princeton, NJ: Princeton University Press, 1996), 49; Sewell, *Ballots For Freedom: Antislavery Politics in the United States, 1837–1860*, 74–75.

18. Blue, *The Free Soilers*, 4, 10; Nash, *Third Parties in American Politics*, 30; Arthur M. Schlesinger Jr. and Fred L. Israel, *History of American Presidential Elections*, Vol. III (Philadelphia: Chelsea House Publishers, 2002), 801–7.

19. Melba Porter Hay, ed. "Clay letter to Peters and Jackson, July 27, 1844." in *The Papers of Henry Clay: Candidate, Compromiser, Elder Statesman*, Vol. 10 (Lexington, KY: University of Kentucky Press, 1991). 89–91. Clay letter to Peters and Jackson, July 27, 1844.

20. Fladeland, *James Gillespie Birney: From Slaveholder to Abolitionist*, 236.

21. Nash, *Third Parties in American Politics*, 32; Ness and Ciment, *The Encyclopedia of Third Parties in America*, 345; Schlesinger and Israel, *History of American Presidential Elections*, Vol. II, 861.

22. Joseph G. Raybeck, *Free Soil: The Election of 1848* (Lexington, KY: University of Kentucky Press, 1970), 99; Fladeland, *James Gillespie Birney: From Slaveholder to Abolitionist*, 256, 293.

23. Blue, *The Free Soilers*, 80–83, 91–95, 123, 129; Ness and Ciment, *The Encyclopedia of Third Parties in America*, 263–64; Raybeck, *Free Soil: The Election of 1848*, 106.

24. Blue, *The Free Soilers*, 70–71; Nash, *Third Parties in American Politics*, 44; Ness and Ciment, *The Encyclopedia of Third Parties in America*, 263–64; Sewell, *Ballots For Freedom: Antislavery Politics in the United States, 1837–1860*, 156.

25. Blue, *The Free Soilers*, 76–77.

26. Ness and Ciment, *The Encyclopedia of Third Parties in America*, 265; Schlesinger and Israel, *History of American Presidential Elections*, Vol. III, 902–5.

27. Blue, *The Free Soilers*, 121–22; Ness and Ciment, *The Encyclopedia of Third Parties in America*, 263; Schlesinger and Israel, *History of American Presidential Elections*, Vol. III, 874.

28. Blue, *The Free Soilers*, 130–31; Schlesinger and Israel, *History of American Presidential Elections*, Vol. III, 872–74.

29. Charles Sumner, Letter to Salmon P. Chase. November 16, 1848. *Selected Letters of Charles Sumner*, edited by Beverly Wilson Palmer (Boston: Northeastern University Press, 1990), 253–54; Rosenstone, Behr, and Lazarus, *Third Parties in America*, 54; Schlesinger and Israel, *History of American Presidential Elections*, Vol. III, 918; Sewell, *Ballots For Freedom: Antislavery Politics in the United States, 1837–1860*, 167.

30. Schlesinger and Israel, *History of American Presidential Elections*, Vol. II, 872.

31. Sewell, *Ballots For Freedom: Antislavery Politics in the United States, 1837–1860*, 231; Raybeck, *Free Soil: The Election of 1848*, 303–10.

32. Blue, *The Free Soilers*, 241–45; Schlesinger and Israel, *History of Presidential Elections in America*, Vol. III, 1003.

33. University of Virginia Library Historical Census Browser. Available at http://fisher.lib.Virginia.edu/collections/stats/histcensus/; Ira M. Leonard and Robert D. Parmet, *American Nativism, 1830–1860* (New York: Van Nostrand and Reinhold, 1971), 11.

34. Leonard and Parmet, *American Nativism, 1830–1860*, 50–54, 60.

35. Elliot Gorn, "Good By Boys I Die a True American: Homicide, Nativism and Working Class Culture in Antebellum New York City," *Journal of American History* 74, no. 2 (Sept. 1987): 388–410.

36. Ray A. Billington, *American History after 1865* (Totowa, NJ: Littlefield, Adams & Co., 1979), 380–81; Nash, *Third Parties in American Politics*, 14; Schlesinger and Israel, *History of American Presidential Elections*, Vol. III, 1013.

37. Jon Preimesberger, ed. *National Party Conventions 1831–1992* (Washington, D.C.: Congressional Quarterly, 1995), 37; Schlesinger and Israel, *History of American Presidential Elections*, Vol. III, 1041–43.

38. DeGregorio, *The Complete Book of U.S. Presidents*, 217; Thomas, *The Pursuit of the White House*, 42.

39. DeGregorio, *The Complete Book of U.S. Presidents*, 217.

40. Schlesinger and Israel, *History of American Presidential Elections*, Vol. III, 1094.

41. Albert D. Kirwan, *John J. Crittenden: The Struggle For The Union* (Lexington, KY: University of Kentucky Press, 1962), 125–26.

42. "Mr. Crittenden in New York." *New York Times*, December 2, 1858, 1–2. Available at http://query.nytimes.com/mem/archive-free/pdf?_r=1&res=9902E2DF1E31EE34BC4A53DFB4678383649FDE. *New York Times*, December 2, 1858, 2.

43. John J. Crittenden, Speech to U.S. Congress, *Congressional Globe*, Special Session, 35th Congress, 2nd Session, Washington, D.C., February 15, 1859, 1274.

44. *National Intelligencer*, Washington, D.C., February 25, 1860, 1.

45. Donald Walter Curl, "The Baltimore Convention of the Constitutional Union Party," *Maryland Historical Magazine* 67, no. 3 (Fall 1972): 258.

46. Murat Halstead, *Three against Lincoln: Murat Halstead Reports the Caucuses of 1860*, edited by William B. Hesseltine (Baton Rouge, LA: Louisiana State University Press, 1960), 122–29.

47. Schlesinger and Israel, *History of American Presidential Elections*, Vol. III, 1127.

48. Halstead, *Three Against Lincoln: Murat Halstead Reports the Caucuses of 1860*, William Hesseltine, Editor, 132–135.

49. Joseph H. Parks, *John Bell of Tennessee* (Baton Rouge, LA: Louisiana State University Press, 1950), 13, 56, 114–15.

50. *New York Times*, Able Speech of Hon. J.J. Crittenden–His Opinion of the Candidates August 8, 1860, 2. Available at http://query.nytimes.com/search/query?query=August+8%2C+1860&srchst=p&d=&o=&v=&c=&sort=closest&n=10&dp=0&daterange=period&year1=1851&mon1=09&day1=18&year2=1980&mon2=12&day2=31&frow=0.; *National Intelligencer*, Speech of Mr. Crittenden Washington, D.C., August 18, 1860, 2.

51. David Potter, *The Impending Crisis* (New York: Harper and Row, 1976), 430–32.

52. John Bell, July 2–30, 1860 letter to Alexander Boteler, Alexander Robinson Boteler MSS, Duke University Library Mss.

53. Schlesinger and Israel, *History of American Presidential Elections*, Vol. III, 1152.

54. Alan Nevins, *The Emergence of Lincoln*, Vol. 2 (New York: Charles Scribner & Sons, 1950), 281.

CHAPTER 2: THE REVOLT OF THE FARMERS

1. Encyclopedia of World Biography. Available at http://www.bookrags.com/biography/oliver-hudson-kelley.

2. Rosenstone, Behr, and Lazarus, *Third Parties in America*, 63.

3. Lawrence Goodwyn, *The Populist Movement* (Oxford: Oxford University Press, 1978), 10; Ness and Ciment, *The Encyclopedia of Third Parties in America*, 271.

4. David J. Gillespie, *Politics at the Periphery* (Columbia, SC: University of South Carolina Press, 1993), 64–65; Frederick Haynes, *Third Party Movements after the Civil War* (New York: Russell and Russell, 1966), 64; Jennifer Lee, "New York and the Panic of 1873," *New York Times*, October 14, 2008. Available at http://www.nytimes.com/ref/topnews/blog-index.htm.

5. Hesseltine, *Third Party Movements in the United States*, 52; Ness and Ciment, *The Encyclopedia of Third Parties in America*, 272; Arthur M. Schlesinger Jr. and Fred L. Israel, *History of American Presidential Elections*, Vol. IV (Philadelphia: Chelsea House Publishers, 2002), 1395.

6. Schlesinger and Israel, *History of American Presidential Elections*, Vol. IV, 1394–95.

7. Ibid., Vol. IV, 1487.

8. Ness and Ciment, *The Encyclopedia of Third Parties in America*, 273.

9. Ness and Ciment, *The Encyclopedia of Third Parties in America*, 273–74; Schlesinger and Israel, *History of American Presidential Elections*, Vol. IV, 1521.

10. Schlesinger and Israel, *History of American Presidential Elections*, Vol. IV, 1558.

11. Ibid., 1611.

12. Goodwyn, *The Populist Movement*, 20–25.

13. Ibid., 26, 33.

14. Billington, *American History after 1865*, 89.

15. Arthur M. Schlesinger Jr. and Fred L. Israel, *History of American Presidential Elections*, Vol. V (Philadelphia: Chelsea House Publishers, 2002), 1741–1744.

16. Ibid., 1784; James Turner, "Understanding the Populists," *Journal of American History*, 67, no. 2 (Sept 1980): 354–73.

17. Gary B. Nash, Julie Roy Jeffrey, Allen F. Davis, Peter J. Frederick, John R. Howe, and Allan M. Winkler. *The Americans People: Creating a Nation and a Society* (New York: Harper and Row, 1986), 636.

18. Thomas, *The Pursuit of the White House*, 58, 59.

19. Gillespie, *Politics at the Periphery*, 75.

20. Schlesinger and Israel, *History of American Presidential Elections*, Vol. V, 1840–1844.

21. Thomas, *The Pursuit of the White House*, 59.

22. Schlesinger and Israel, *History of American Presidential Elections*, Vol. V, 1896.

CHAPTER 3: THE PROGRESSIVES

1. George E. Mowry, *Theodore Roosevelt and the Progressive Movement* (New York: Hill and Wang, 1946), 114.

2. DeGregorio, *The Complete Book of U.S. Presidents*, 374.

3. Ibid., 389.

4. Nash et al., *The American People: Creating a Nation and a Society*, 711.

5. Schlesinger and Israel, *History of American Presidential Elections*, Vol. V, 2046.

6. Theodore Roosevelt's New Nationalism Speech. Available at http://www.theodore-roosevelt.com/trnationalismspeech.html/.

7. Arthur M. Schlesinger Jr. and Fred L. Israel, *History of American Presidential Elections*, Vol. VI (Philadelphia: Chelsea House Publishers, 2002), 2144.

8. Rosenstone, Behr, and Lazarus, *Third Parties in America*, 85; Schlesinger and Israel, *History of American Presidential Elections*, Vol. VI, 2151–53.

9. Schlesinger and Israel, *History of American Presidential Elections*, Vol. VI, 2151–153.

10. Ibid., 2151–53.

11. Ibid., 2242.

12. Ibid., 2242.

13. Kenneth Mackay, *The Progressive Movement of 1924* (New York: Octagon Publishers, 1947), 39–42.

14. Ibid., 23–26.

15. Rosenstone, Behr, and Lazarus, *Third Parties in America*, 94.

16. Ness and Ciment, *The Encyclopedia of Third Parties in America*, 456–57.

17. Ibid., 457.

18. Ibid., 457.

19. Rosenstone, Behr, and Lazarus, *Third Parties in America*, 94.

20. Mackay, *The Progressive Movement of 1924*, 110–16; David P. Thelen, *Robert M. La Follette and the Insurgent Spirit* (Boston: Little, Brown and Company, 1976), 183.

21. Ness and Ciment, *The Encyclopedia of Third Parties in America*, 458; Thelen, *Robert M. La Follette and the Insurgent Spirit*, 183.

22. MacKay, *The Progressive Movement of 1924*, 143; Thelen, *Robert M. La Follette and the Insurgent Spirit*, 182–83;

23. Mackay, *The Progressive Movement of 1924*, 143; Ness and Ciment, *The Encyclopedia of Third Parties in America*, 456;

24. MacKay, *The Progressive Movement of 1924*, 125–34.

25. Ness and Ciment, *The Encyclopedia of Third Parties in America*, 461; *Robert M. La Follette and the Insurgent Spirit*, 188–89.

26. Ness and Ciment, *The Encyclopedia of Third Parties in America*, 460; *Robert M. La Follette and the Insurgent Spirit*, 189.

27. Gillespie, *Politics at the Periphery*, 89; MacKay, *The Progressive Movement of 1924*, 175, 193–96; Ness and Ciment, *The Encyclopedia of Third Parties in America*, 459–65; Rosenstone, Behr and Lazarus, *Third Parties in America*, 96.

28. *Robert M. La Follette and the Insurgent Spirit*, 190–91; Schlesinger and Israel, *History of American Presidential Elections*, Vol. VI, 2581.

29. Thelen, *Robert M. La Follette and the Insurgent Spirit*, 191.

CHAPTER 4: GEORGE C. WALLACE

1. Stephan Lesher, *George Wallace: American Populist* (New York: Addison Wesley Publishing, 1994), 2–3.

2. Ibid., 2–4.

3. Dan T. Carter, *The Politics of Rage* (New York: Simon & Schuster, 1995), 17, 22; Lesher, *George Wallace: American Populist*, 17–20.

4. Lesher, *George Wallace: American Populist*, 21–23.

5. Ibid., 26–27.

6. Carter, *The Politics of Rage*, 23; Lesher, *George Wallace: American Populist*, 26.

7. Lesher, *George Wallace: American Populist*, 162.

8. Carter, *The Politics of Rage*, 62.

9. Ibid., 46.

10. Ibid., 27.

11. Lesher, *George Wallace: American Populist*, 23.

12. Carter, *The Politics of Rage*, 30–31.

13. Lesher, *George Wallace: American Populist*, 37–39.

14. Ibid., 44–46, 54.

15. Ibid., 63–64.

16. Ibid., 66.

17. Carter, *The Politics of Rage*, 75.

18. Ibid., 76.

19. Ibid., 78–79.

20. Lesher, *George Wallace: American Populist*, 95.

21. Carter, *The Politics of Rage*, 90.

22. Lesher, *George Wallace: American Populist*, 115.

23. Carter, *The Politics of Rage*, 95.

24. Ibid., 96.

25. Ibid., 97–98, 107.

26. Ibid., 105.

27. Lesher, *George Wallace: American Populist*, 156.

28. Carter, *The Politics of Rage*, 109.

29. Ibid., 113.

30. Ibid., 149.

31. Lesher, *George Wallace: American Populist*, 261–62.

32. Ibid., 263.

33. Ibid., 264–65.

34. Ibid., 270.

35. Ibid., 275.

36. Carter, *The Politics of Rage*, 203.

37. Lesher, *George Wallace: American Populist*, 276–79.

38. Ibid., 284.

39. Ibid., 285.

40. Ibid., 287–97.

41. Ibid. 297.

42. Ibid., 297.

43. Ibid., 298.

44. Ibid., 304

45. Ibid., 305.

46. Ibid., 358.

47. Ibid., 366.

48. Carter, *The Politics of Rage*, 307, 312; Lewis Chester, Godfrey Hodgson, and Bruce Page, *An American Melodrama: The Presidential Campaign of 1968* (New York: The Viking Press, 1969), 284; Gillespie, *Politics at the Periphery*, 107; Lesher, *George Wallace: American Populist*, 397; Ness and Ciment, *The Encyclopedia of Third Parties in America*, 126.

49. Carter, *The Politics of Rage*, 299.

50. Ibid., 341–43.

51. Jody Carlson, *George C. Wallace and the Politics of Powerlessness* (New Brunswick, NJ: Transaction Books, 1981), 77; Chester, Hodgson, and Page, *An American Melodrama: The Presidential Campaign of 1968*, 273.

52. Chester, Hodgson and Page, *An American Melodrama: The Presidential Campaign of 1968*, 274.

53. Carter, *The Politics of Rage*, 335.

54. Ibid., 335.

55. Ibid., 336–38.

56. Ibid., 337–38.

57. Ibid., 338.

58. Ibid., 352–54.

59. Ness and Ciment, *The Encyclopedia of Third Parties in America*, 125.

60. Ibid., 128.

61. Ibid., 128.

62. Carlson, *George C. Wallace and the Politics of Powerlessness*, 81–82.
Rosenstone, Behr and Lazarus, *Third Parties in America*, 111–12.

63. Carlson, *George C. Wallace and the Politics of Powerlessness*, 83; Carter,
The Politics of Rage, 355; Lesher, *George Wallace: American Populist*, 403.

64. Carter, *The Politics of Rage*, 354–56; Carlson, *George C. Wallace and the
Politics of Powerlessness*, 82–83; Lesher, *George Wallace: American Populist*, 424.

65. Carter, *The Politics of Rage*, 357–58; Chester, Hodgson, and Page, *An
American Melodrama: The Presidential Campaign of 1968*, 695.

66. Carter, *The Politics of Rage*, 359–60; Chester, Hodgson, and Page, *An
American Melodrama: The Presidential Campaign of 1968*, 695, 699–700.

67. Carlson, *George C. Wallace and the Politics of Powerlessness*, 83; Chester,
Hodgson, and Page, *An American Melodrama: The Presidential Campaign of
1968*, 703–10.

68. Arthur M. Schlesinger Jr. and Fred L. Israel, *History of American Presidential Elections*, Vol. IX (Philadelphia: Chelsea House Publishers, 2002), 3865.

69. Ibid., Vol. IX, 3869.

70. Carter, *The Politics of Rage*, 386.

71. Carter, *The Politics of Rage*, 391–93; Lesher, *George Wallace: American
Populist*, 451.

72. Carter, *The Politics of Rage*, 412.
Lesher, *George Wallace: American Populist*, 461.

73. Carter, *The Politics of Rage*, 435–37; Lesher, *George Wallace: American
Populist*, 479–81.

74. Ness and Ciment, *The Encyclopedia of Third Parties in America*, 129; Dave
Leip's Atlas of U.S. Presidential Elections. Available at http://uselectionatlas.
org/RESULTS/index.html/.

75. Carter, *The Politics of Rage*, 400; Lesher, *George Wallace: American Populist*,
461.

76. Lesher, *George Wallace: American Populist*, 479.

77. Ibid., 480.

78. Ibid., 480.

79. Ibid., 481.

80. Ness and Ciment, *The Encyclopedia of Third Parties in America*, 129; Dave
Leip's Atlas of U.S. Presidential Elections. Available at http://uselectionatlas.
org/RESULTS/index.html/.

CHAPTER 5: ROSS PEROT

1. Gerald Posner, *Citizen Perot* (New York: Random House, 1996), 3;
Rosenstone, Behr, and Lazarus, *Third Parties in America*, 236.

2. Todd Mason, *Perot* (Homewood, IL: Richard D. Irwin Co., 1990), 16–18.

3. Posner, *Citizen Perot*, 12.

4. Ibid., 12.

5. Ibid., 13.

6. Ibid., 15.

7. Mason, *Perot*, 29; Posner, *Citizen Perot*, 16.

8. Posner, *Citizen Perot*, 17–19.

9. Ibid., 19–23.

10. Ibid., 23–24.

11. Ibid., 25–28.

12. Ibid., 48.

13. Ibid., 60–64.

14. Ibid., 89.

15. Ibid., 100–2.

16. Ibid., 107–9.

17. Posner, *Citizen Perot*, 109–13; Ronald B. Rappaport, and Walter J. Stone, *Three's a Crowd* (Ann Arbor, MI: The University of Michigan Press, 2005), 53.

18. Posner, *Citizen Perot*, 115–19.

19. Ibid., 160–63, 169, 186.

20. Ibid., 191, 194–95, 199–200, 215–17.

21. Rappaport and Stone, *Three's a Crowd*, 53–55.

22. Posner, *Citizen Perot*, 6.

23. Ibid., 7.

24. Ted G. Jelen, *Ross for Boss* (Albany, NY: State University of New York Press, 2001), 66–68; Rosenstone, Behr, and Lazarus, *Third Parties in America*, 233.

25. Posner, *Citizen Perot*, 253.

26. Rappaport and Stone, *Three's a Crowd*, 61–62.

27. Posner, *Citizen Perot*, 249–50.

28. Rappaport and Stone, *Three's a Crowd*, 60–61.

29. Posner, *Citizen Perot*, 254–55.

30. Ibid., 255–56.

31. Ibid., 259.

32. Posner, *Citizen Perot*, 262; Rappaport and Stone, *Three's a Crowd*, 62.

33. Posner, *Citizen Perot*, 264.

34. Ibid., 275, 280–81.

35. Ibid., 279.

36. Ibid., 280, 283.

37. Posner, *Citizen Perot*, 284–85; Rappaport and Stone, *Three's a Crowd*, 57.

38. Jelen, *Ross for Boss*, 20.

39. Posner, *Citizen Perot*, 289.

40. Ibid., 289–91.

41. Perot, *United We Stand*. Available at http://uwsa.com/books/Uwsabook.html/.

42. Ibid.

43. Posner, *Citizen Perot*, 291–92; Rappaport and Stone, *Three's a Crowd*, 68.

44. Posner, *Citizen Perot*, 292–94.

45. Ibid., 294.

46. Ibid., 295–96.

47. Rosenstone, Behr, and Lazarus, *Third Parties in America*, 243; Arthur M. Schlesinger Jr. and Fred L. Israel, *History of American Presidential Elections*, Vol. XI (Philadelphia: Chelsea House Publishers, 2002), 4466.

48. Schlesinger and Israel, *History of American Presidential Elections*, Vol. XI, 4466.

49. Gillespie, *Politics at the Periphery*, 136; Rosenstone, Behr, and Lazarus, *Third Parties in America*, 242; Steven Holmes, "The 1992 Elections: Disappointment—News Analysis," *New York Times* November 5, 1992, New York Edition, Section A. Available at http://www.nytimes.com/1992/11/05/us/1992-elections-disappointment-analysis-eccentric-but-no-joke-perot-s-strong.html?scp=1&sq=&st=nyt.

50. Posner, *Citizen Perot*, 328–29.

51. Ibid., 331–32.

52. Ibid., 334.

53. Ibid., 336.

54. Ibid., 337–38.

55. Ness and Ciment, *The Encyclopedia of Third Parties in America*, 487.

56. Ibid., 487.

57. Ibid., 488.

58. Ibid., 488.

59. Ibid., 488, 490.

60. Rappaport and Stone, *Three's a Crowd*, 74; Schlesinger and Israel, *History of American Presidential Elections*, Vol. XI, 4567.

61. Dave Leip's Atlas of U.S. Presidential Elections. Available at http://uselectionatlas.org/RESULTS/index.html/.

CHAPTER 6: RALPH NADER

1. Justin Martin, *Nader: Crusader, Spoiler, Icon* (Cambridge MA: Perseus Publishers, 2002), 7.

2. Patricia Cronin Marcello, *Ralph Nader: A Biography* (Westport, CT: Greenwood Press, 2004), 3. Martin, *Nader: Crusader, Spoiler, Icon*, 1, 6.

3. Marcello, *Ralph Nader: A Biography*, 4; Martin, *Nader: Crusader, Spoiler, Icon*, 9.

4. Marcello, *Ralph Nader: A Biography*, 6; Martin, *Nader: Crusader, Spoiler, Icon*, 11, 13.

5. Martin, *Nader: Crusader, Spoiler, Icon*, 15–17.

6. Ibid., 18, 20.

7. Ibid., 5, 25, 28–29.

8. Marcello, *Ralph Nader: A Biography*, 7; Martin, *Nader: Crusader, Spoiler, Icon*, 29–30.

9. Marcello, *Ralph Nader: A Biography*, 13; Martin, *Nader: Crusader, Spoiler, Icon*, 33.

10. Martin, *Nader: Crusader, Spoiler, Icon*, 33–34.

11. Ibid., 39.

12. Marcello, *Ralph Nader: A Biography*, 17; Martin, *Nader: Crusader, Spoiler, Icon*, 41–42.

13. Martin, *Nader: Crusader, Spoiler, Icon*, 44.

14. Ibid., 44–45.

15. Ibid., 47, 50, 112.

16. Marcello, *Ralph Nader: A Biography*, 27; Martin, *Nader: Crusader, Spoiler, Icon*, 59, 62.

17. Martin, *Nader: Crusader, Spoiler, Icon*, 65–69.

18. Ibid., 69.

19. Ibid., 70.

20. Ibid., 71, 76–81.

21. Ibid., 81–82, 46–147.

22. Marcello, *Ralph Nader: A Biography*, 53; Martin, *Nader: Crusader, Spoiler, Icon*, 145.

23. Martin, *Nader: Crusader, Spoiler, Icon*, 117.

24. Marcello, *Ralph Nader: A Biography*, 73–76; Martin, *Nader: Crusader, Spoiler, Icon*, 152–53.

25. Martin, *Nader: Crusader, Spoiler, Icon*, 174, 179.

26. Ibid., 179–80.

27. Ibid., 192.

28. Ibid., 193.

29. Martin, *Nader: Crusader, Spoiler, Icon*, 201, 204–5, 207; Ralph Nader, *Crashing The Party: Taking on the Corporate Government in the Age of Surrender* (New York: Thomas Dunne Books/St. Martins Press, 2002), 25.

30. Martin, *Nader: Crusader, Spoiler, Icon*, 209–10, 213.

31. Marcello, *Ralph Nader: A Biography*, 126.

32. Marcello, *Ralph Nader: A Biography*, 128; Martin, *Nader: Crusader, Spoiler, Icon*, 238, 253.

33. Marcello, *Ralph Nader: A Biography*, 128.

34. Marcello, *Ralph Nader: A Biography*, 118; Dave Leip's Atlas of U.S. Presidential Elections. Available at http://uselectionatlas.org/RESULTS/index.html/.

35. Martin, *Nader: Crusader, Spoiler, Icon*, 226.

36. Nader, *The Ralph Nader Reader*, 2–5.

37. James Dao, "The 2000 Campaign: The Third Parties; Nader Runs Again, This Time with Feeling." *New York Times*, April 15, 2000. Available at http://www.nytimes.com/2000/04/15/us/the-2000-campaign-the-third-parties-nader-runs-again-this-time-with-feeling.html?scp=1&sq=The+2000+Campaign%3A+The+Third+Parties&st=nyt.

38. Martin, *Nader: Crusader, Spoiler, Icon*, 231–32; Micah L. Sifry, *Spoiling for a Fight* (New York: Routledge, 2003), 178, 186–87, 189.

39. Martin, *Nader: Crusader, Spoiler, Icon*, 232–33.

40. Sifry, *Spoiling for a Fight*, 188.

41. Martin, *Nader: Crusader, Spoiler, Icon*, 234–36.

42. Michael Janofsky, "The 2000 Campaign: The Green Party; Nader Nominated by Greens, Attacks Politics as Usual," *New York Times*, June 26,

2000. Available at http://www.nytimes.com/2000/06/26/us/2000-campaign-green-party-nader-nominated-greens-attacks-politics-usual.html?scp=1&sq=Nader+nominated+by+Greens&st=nyt.

43. Martin, *Nader: Crusader, Spoiler, Icon*, 260; "Nader Reports Big Portfolio in Technology," *New York Times*, June 19, 2000. Available at http://www.nytimes.com/2000/06/19/us/nader-reports-big-portfolio-in-technology.html.

44. Martin, *Nader: Crusader, Spoiler, Icon*, 260.

45. Martin, *Nader: Crusader, Spoiler, Icon*, 230–54; Sifry, *Spoiling for a Fight*, 178.

46. James Dao, "The 2000 Campaign: The Green Party; 10,000 Turn out to Hear Nader Urge 'Shift in Power,'" *New York Times*, November 6, 2000. Available at http://www.nytimes.com/2000/11/06/us/2000-campaign-green-party-10000-turn-hear-nader-urge-shift-power.html?scp=1&sq=10%2C000+Turn+Out+To+Hear+Nader&st=nyt; Martin, *Nader: Crusader, Spoiler, Icon*, 251.

47. Janet Elder, "The 2000 Campaign: The Polls; 4 New Polls Show Bush with Advantage, and Nader as a Factor," *New York Times*, November 2, 2000. Available at http://www.nytimes.com/2000/11/02/us/2000-campaign-polls-4-new-polls-show-bush-with-advantage-nader-factor.html?scp=1&sq=4+New+Polls+Show+Bush&st=nyt; Martin, *Nader: Crusader, Spoiler, Icon*, 253.

48. Sifry, *Spoiling for a Fight*, 192, 204.

49. Ibid., 193–94.

50. Dao, "The 2000 Campaign: The Third Parties; Nader Runs Again, This Time with Feeling." *New York Times*. Available at http://www.nytimes.com/2000/04/15/us/the-2000-campaign-the-third-parties-nader-runs-again-this-time-with-feeling.html?scp=1&sq=The+2000+Campaign%3A+The+Third+Parties&st=nyt; Sifry, *Spoiling for a Fight*, 199.

51. Sifry, *Spoiling for a Fight*, 200.

52. "Mr. Nader's Misguided Crusade," Opinion, *New York Times*, June 30, 2000. Available at http://www.nytimes.com/2000/06/30/opinion/mr-nader-s-misguided-crusade.html?scp=1&sq=Editorial&st=nyt; Sifry, *Spoiling for a Fight*, 201.

53. Martin, *Nader: Crusader, Spoiler, Icon*, 247–50; "The 2000 Campaign: The Green Party; Nader Supporters Fill Madison Square Garden," *New York Times*, October 14, 2000. Available at http://www.nytimes.com/2000/10/14/business/the-2000-campaign-the-green-party-nader-supporters-fill-madison-square-garden.html?scp=1&sq=Nader+Supporters+Fill+Garden&st=nyt.

54. Martin, *Nader: Crusader, Spoiler, Icon*, 233–34; Sifry, *Spoiling for a Fight*, 201–2.

55. Martin, *Nader: Crusader, Spoiler, Icon*, 254; Sifry, *Spoiling for a Fight*, 201–4.

56. Sifry, *Spoiling for a Fight*, 204; Gloria Steinem, "Top Ten Reasons Why I'm Not Voting for Nader." Available at http://www.Hartford-hwp.com/archives/45c/072.html/.

57. Sifry, *Spoiling for a Fight*, 205.

58. Martin, *Nader: Crusader, Spoiler, Icon*, 241; Sifry, *Spoiling for a Fight*, 207.

59. "Al Gore in the Home Stretch," *New York Times*, November 3, 2000. Available at http://www.nytimes.com/2000/11/03/opinion/al-gore-in the-home-stretch.html/; "Mr. Nader's Electoral Mischief." Editorial, *New York Times*, October 26, 2000. Available at http://www.nytimes.com/2000/10/26/opinion/mr-nader-s-electoral-mischief.html?scp=1&sq=Editorial&st=nyt.

60. Martin, *Nader: Crusader, Spoiler, Icon*, 264.

61. Sifry, *Spoiling for a Fight*, 209–10.

62. Schlesinger and Israel, *History of American Presidential Elections*, Vol. XI, 4784.

63. Martin, *Nader: Crusader, Spoiler, Icon*, 272.

Schlesinger and Israel, *History of American Presidential Elections*, Vol. XI, 4784.

64. Schlesinger and Israel, *History of American Presidential Elections*, Vol. XI, 4784.

65. Sifry, *Spoiling for a Fight*, 210.

66. Ibid., 211.

67. Martin, *Nader: Crusader, Spoiler, Icon*, 267–68.

68. Dave Leip's Atlas of U.S. Presidential Elections. Available at http://uselectionatlas.org/RESULTS/index.html/.

CHAPTER 7: THIRD-PARTY ALSO-RANS

1. Dave Leip's Atlas of U.S. Presidential Elections. Available at http://uselectionatlas.org/RESULTS/index.html/; Earl R. Kruschke, *Encyclopedia of Third Parties in The United States* (Santa Barbara, CA: ABC-CLIO, 1991), 35.

2. Dave Leip's Atlas of U.S. Presidential Elections. Available at http://uselectionatlas.org/RESULTS/index.html/; Schlesinger and Israel, *History of American Presidential Elections*, Vols. IV–V, 1375, 1784, 2046.

3. Lois Beachy Underhill, *The Woman Who Ran for President* (Bridgehampton, NY: Bridge Works Publishing Co., 1995), 11–12, 16, 24.

4. Ibid., 62–63, 102–6, 164, 208, 211.

5. Gillespie, *Politics at the Periphery*, 145–47; Jill Norgren, *Belva Lockwood: The Woman Who Would Be President* (New York: New York University Press, 2007), 86–87.

6. Ness and Ciment, *The Encyclopedia of Third Parties in America*, 116–18, 198–200.

7. Ness and Ciment, *The Encyclopedia of Third Parties in America*, 595; Arthur M. Schlesinger Jr. and Fred L. Israel, *History of American Presidential Elections*, Vol. VIII (Philadelphia: Chelsea House Publishers, 2002), 3211.

8. Ness and Ciment, *The Encyclopedia of Third Parties in America*, 268–70.

9. Ibid., 190–97.

10. Ibid., 323–25.

11. Walter Dean Burnham, *Critical Elections and the Mainstream of American Politics* (New York: W.W. Norton & Co., 1970), 28.

12. Rosenstone, Behr, and Lazarus, *Third Parties in America*, 89.

13. Eric Thomas Chester, *Socialists and the Ballot Box* (New York: Praeger Publishers, 1985), 33.

14. Chester, *Socialists at the Ballot Box*, 32–34; Rosenstone, Behr, and Lazarus, *Third Parties In America*, 90.

15. Ness and Ciment, *The Encyclopedia of Third Parties in America*, 641–43; Schlesinger and Israel, *History of American Presidential Elections*, Vol. VI, 2242.

16. Chester, *Socialists at the Ballot Box*, 32–33; Dave Leip's Atlas of U.S. Presidential elections. Available at http://uselectionatlas.org/RESULTS/index.html/; Schlesinger and Israel, *History of American Presidential Elections*, Vol. VI, 2456.

17. Ness and Ciment, *The Encyclopedia of Third Parties in America*, 383.

18. Frank Smallwood, *The Other Candidates: Third Parties in Presidential Elections* (Hanover, NH: University Press of New England, 1983), 229.

19. Gillespie, *Politics at the Periphery*, 123.

20. Ness and Ciment, *The Encyclopedia of Third Parties in America*, 383–84; Rosenstone, Behr, and Lazarus, *Third Parties in America*, 117.

21. Smallwood, *The Other Candidates*, 231; Rosenstone, Behr, and Lazarus, *Third Parties in America*, 117.

22. Gillespie, *Politics at the Periphery*, 127; Ness and Ciment, *The Encyclopedia of Third Parties in America*, 386; Rosenstone, Behr, and Lazarus, *Third Parties in America*, 118.

23. Rosenstone, Behr, and Lazarus, *Third Parties in America*, 117; Arthur M. Schlesinger Jr. and Fred L. Israel, *History of American Presidential Elections*, Vol. X (Philadelphia: Chelsea House Publishers, 2002), 4135.

Bibliography

Bell, John, July 2–30, 1860, letter to Alexander Boteler, Alexander Robinson Boteler MSS, Duke University Library Mss. http://library.duke.edu.

Billington, Ray A. *American History after 1865*. Totowa, NJ: Littlefield, Adams & Co., 1979.

Billington, Ray Allen. *The Protestant Crusade 1800–1860*. Chicago: Quadrangle Books, 1964.

Blue, Frederick. *The Free Soilers*. Urbana, IL: University of Illinois, 1973.

Burnham, Walter Dean. *Critical Elections and the Mainstream of American Politics*. New York: W.W. Norton & Co., 1970.

Carlson, Jody. *George C. Wallace and the Politics of Powerlessness*. New Brunswick, NJ: Transaction Books, 1981.

Chester, Eric Thomas. *Socialists and the Ballot Box*. New York: Praeger Publishers, 1985.

Chester, Lewis, Godfrey Hodgson, and Bruce Page. *An American Melodrama: The Presidential Campaign of 1968*. New York: The Viking Press, 1969.

Carter, Dan T. *The Politics of Rage*. New York: Simon & Schuster, 1995.

Clay, Henry. Speech to Congress, February 7, 1939, 25th Congress, 3rd Session, Appendix to the *Congressional Globe*, Washington, D.C.

Crittenden, John J. Speech to Congress, February 1859, Special Session, 35th Congress, 2nd Session. *Congressional Globe*, Washington, D.C.

Curl, Donald Walter. "The Baltimore Convention of the Constitutional Union Party." *Maryland Historical Magazine* 67, no. 3 (Fall 1972).

Dao, James. "The 2000 Campaign: The Third Parties: Nader Runs Again, This Time with Feeling." *The New York Times*, April 15, 2000. http://www.nytimes.com/2000/04/15/us/the-2000-campaign-the-third-parties-nader-runs-again-this-time-with-feeling.html?scp=1&sq=The+2000+Campaign%3A+The+Third+Parties&st=nyt.

Dao, James. "The 2000 Campaign: The Green Party; 10,000 Turn out to Hear Nader Urge 'Shift in Power,'" *The New York Times*, November 6, 2000. http://www.nytimes.com/2000/11/06/us/2000-campaign-green-party-10000-turn-hear-nader-urge-shift-power.html?scp=1&sq=10%2C000+Turn+Out+To+Hear+Nader&st=nyt.

DeGregorio, William A. *The Complete Book of U.S. Presidents*, New York: Barnes & Noble, 2004.

Dillon, Merton. *The Abolitionists: The Growth of a Dissenting Minority*. DeKalb, IL: Northern Illinois University Press, 1974.

Dumond, Dwight. *Antislavery: The Crusade For Freedom in America*. Ann Arbor: University of Michigan Press, 1961.

Elder, Janet. "The 2000 Campaign: The Polls; 4 New Polls Show Bush with Advantage, and Nader as a Factor," *The New York Times*, November 2, 2000. http://www.nytimes.com/2000/11/02/us/2000-campaign-polls-4-new-polls-show-bush-with-advantage-nader-factor.html?scp=1&sq=4+New+Polls+Show+Bush&st=nyt.

Encyclopedia of World Biography. http://www.bookrags.com/biography/oliver-hudson-kelley/.

Fladeland, Betty. *James Gillespie Birney: From Slaveholder to Abolitionist*. Ithaca, NY: Cornell University Press, 1955.

Gillespie, David J. *Politics at the Periphery*. Columbia, SC: University of South Carolina Press, 1993.

Goodwyn, Lawrence. *The Populist Movement*. Oxford: Oxford University Press, 1978.

Gorn, Elliot. "Good Bye Boys, I Die a True American: Homicide, Nativism and Working Class Culture in Antebellum New York City." *Journal of American History* 74, no. 2 (Sept.1987).

Halstead, Murat. *Three Against Lincoln: Murat Halstead Reports the Caucuses of 1860*, edited by William B. Hesseltine. Baton Rouge, LA: Louisiana State University Press, 1960.

Hay, Melba Porter, ed. "Clay Letter to Peters and Jackson, July 27, 1844." In:, *The Papers of Henry Clay: Candidate, Compromiser, Elder Statesman*, Vol. 10, edited by Melba Porter Hay. Lexington, KY: University of Kentucky Press, 1991.

Haynes, Frederick. *Third Party Movements after the Civil War*. New York: Russell and Russell, 1966.

Hesseltine, William B. *Third Party Movements in the United States*. Princeton, NJ: Van Nostrand & Co., 1962.

Holmes, Steven. "The 1992 Elections: Disappointment—News Analysis," *The New York Times* November 5, 1992, New York Edition, Section A. http://www.nytimes.com/1992/11/05/us/1992-elections-disappointment-analysis-eccentric-but-no-joke-perot-s-strong.html?scp=1&sq=&st=nyt.

Janofsky, Michael. "The 2000 Campaign: The Green Party; Nader Nominated by Greens, Attacks Politics as Usual," *The New York Times*, June 26, 2000. http://www.nytimes.com/2000/06/26/us/2000-campaign-green-party-nader-nominated-greens-attacks-politics-usual.html?scp=1&sq=Nader+nominated+by+Greens&st=nyt.

Jelen, Ted G. *Ross for Boss*. Albany, NY: State University of New York Press, 2001.

Kirwan, Albert D. *John J. Crittenden: The Struggle For The Union*. Lexington, KY: University of Kentucky Press, 1962.

Kolchin, Peter. *American Slavery 1619–1877*. New York: Hill and Wand, 1993.

Kruschke, Earl R. *Encyclopedia of Third Parties in The United States*. Santa Barbara, CA: ABC-CLIO, 1991.

Lee, Jennifer. "New York and the Panic of 1873," *The New York Times*, October 14, 2008. http://www.blogs.nytimes.com/2008/10/14/learning-lessons-from-the-panic-of-1873.

Leip, Dave. Atlas of U.S. Presidential Elections. http://uselectionatlas.org/RESULTS/index.html/.

Leonard, Ira M., and Robert D. Parmet. *American Nativism, 1830–1860*. New York: Van Nostrand and Reinhold, 1971.

Lesher, Stephan. *George Wallace: American Populist*. New York: Addison Wesley Publishing, 1994.

Liberator Files, 1831. http://www.the liberatorfiles.com/category/year/1831/.

Mackay, Kenneth. *The Progressive Movement of 1924*. New York: Octagon Publishers, 1947.

Marcello, Patricia Cronin. *Ralph Nader: A Biography*. Westport, CT: Greenwood Press, 2004.

Martin, Justin. *Nader: Crusader, Spoiler, Icon*. Cambridge MA: Perseus Publishers, 2002.

Mason, Todd. *Perot*. Homewood, IL: Richard D. Irwin Co., 1990.

Moulton, Phillips P., ed. *The Journal and Major Essays of John Woolman*. New York: Oxford University Press, 1971.

Mowry, George E. *Theodore Roosevelt and the Progressive Movement*, New York: Hill and Wang, 1946.

Nader, Ralph. *Crashing The Party: Taking on the Corporate Government in the Age of Surrender*. New York: Thomas Dunne Books/St. Martins Press, 2002.

Nader, Ralph. *The Ralph Nader Reader*. New York: Seven Seas Press, 2000.

Nash, Gary B., Julie Roy Jeffrey, Allen F. Davis, Peter J. Frederick, John R. Howe, and Allan M. Winkler. *The American People: Creating a Nation and a Society*, New York: Harper and Row, 1986.

Nash, Howard P. *Third Parties in American Politics*. Washington, D.C.: Public Affairs Press, 1959.

National Intelligencer, To The People of the United States Washington D.C.: February 25, 1860.

National Intelligencer, Speech of Mr. Crittenden Washington D.C. August 18, 1860.

Ness, Emmanuel and James Ciment. *The Encyclopedia of Third Parties in America*. Armonk, New York: M.E.Sharp, 2000.

Ness, Immanuel, and Ciment, James, eds. *The Encyclopedia of Third Parties in America*, Vol. 1. Armonk, NY: M.E. Sharpe, 2000.

Nevins, Alan. *The Emergence of Lincoln*, Vol. 2. New York: Charles Scribner & Sons, 1950.

The New York Times. "Mr. Crittenden in New York." December 2, 1858, 2. http://query.nytimes.com/search/query?query=The+New+York+Times.+December+12%2C+1858%2C+2&n=10&dp=0&sort=closest&daterange=period&srcht=a&year1=1851&mon1=09&day1=18&year2=1980&mon2=12&day2=31&srchst=g.

The New York Times. "Able Speech of Hon. J.J.Crittenden—His Opinion of the Candidates." August 8, 1860, 2. http://query.nytimes.com/search/query?frow=0&n=10&srcht=s&query=The+New+York+Times%2C+August+8%2C+1860&srchst=p&hdlquery=&bylquery=&daterange=full&mon1=01&day1=01&year1=1981&mon2=02&day2=25&year2=2010&submit.x=20&submit.y=11

The New York Times. "Nader Reports Big Portfolio in Technology." June 19, 2000. http://www.nytimes.com/2000/06/19/us/nader-reports-big-portfolio-in-technology.html/.

The New York Times. "Mr. Nader's Misguided Crusade." Editorial, June 30, 2000. http://www.nytimes.com/2000/06/30/opinion/mr-nader-s-misguided-crusade.html.

The New York Times. "The 2000 Campaign: The Green Party; Nader Supporters Fill Madison Square Garden." *The* October 14, 2000. http://www.nytimes.com/2000/10/14/business/the-2000-campaign-the-green-party-nader-supporters-fill-madison-square-garden.html?scp=1&sq=Nader+Supporters+Fill+Garden&st=nyt.

The New York Times. "Mr. Nader's Electoral Mischief." Editorial, October 26, 2000. http://www.nytimes.com/2000/10/26/opinion/mr-nader-s-electoral-mischief.html.

The New York Times. "Al Gore in the Home Stretch." November 3, 2000. http://www.nytimes.com/2000/11/03/opinion/al-gore-in-the-home-stretch.html.

Norgren, Jill. *Belva Lockwood: The Woman Who Would Be President*. New York: New York University Press, 2007.

Parks, Joseph H. *John Bell of Tennessee*. Baton Rouge, LA: Louisiana State University Press, 1950.

Perot, Ross. *United We Stand*. http://uwsa.com/books/Uwsabook.html.

Posner, Gerald. *Citizen Perot*. New York: Random House, 1996.

Potter, David. *The Impending Crisis*. New York: Harper and Row, 1976.

Preimesberger, Jon, ed. *National Party Conventions 1831–1992*, Washington D.C.: Congressional Quarterly, 1995.

Rappaport, Ronald B., and Walter J. Stone. *Three's a Crowd*. Ann Arbor, MI: The University of Michigan Press, 2005.

Raybeck, Joseph G. *Free Soil: The Election of 1848*. Lexington, KY: University of Kentucky Press, 1970.

Roosevelt, Theodore. *New Nationalism Speech*. http://www.theodore-roosevelt.com/trnationalismspeech.html.

Rosenstone, Steven J., Roy L. Behr, and Edward H. Lazarus. *Third Parties in America*. Princeton, NJ: Princeton University Press, 1996.

Schlesinger, Arthur M., Jr., and Fred L. Israel. *History of American Presidential Elections*, Volumes II, III, IV, V, VI, VIII, IX, X, and XI. Philadelphia: Chelsea House Publishers, 2002.

Sewell, Richard H. *Ballots for Freedom: Antislavery Politics in the United States, 1837–1860*. New York: Oxford University Press, 1976.

Sifry, Micah L. *Spoiling for a Fight*. New York: Routledge, 2003.

Smallwood, Frank. *The Other Candidates: Third Parties in Presidential Elections*. Hanover, NH: University Press of New England, 1983.

Steinem, Gloria. *Top Ten Reasons Why I'm Not Voting for Nader*. http://www.Hartford-hwp.com/archives/45c/072.html.

Sumner, Charles. Letter to Salmon P. Chase. November 16, 1848. *Selected Letters of Charles Sumner*, edited by Beverly Wilson Palmer. Boston: Northeastern University Press, 1990.

Thelen, David P. *Robert M. La Follette and the Insurgent Spirit*. Boston: Little, Brown and Company, 1976.

Thomas, Scott G. *The Pursuit of the White House*. New York: Greenwood Press, 1987.

Turner, James. "Understanding the Populists." *Journal of American History* 67, no. 2 (1980): 354–73.

Underhill, Lois Beachy. *The Woman Who Ran for President*. Bridgehampton, NY: Bridge Works Publishing Co., 1995.

University of Virginia Historical Census Browser. http://fisher.lib.Virginia.edu/collections/stats/histcensus.

Index

About the Author

DONALD J. GREEN is an adjunct lecturer in American history at Hillsborough Community College in Tampa, Florida. His previously published work is a history of the Constitutional Union Party of 1860 in *The Historian*.